Transformative learning support models in higher education

educating the whole student

Edited by
Margaret Weaver

facet publishing

Published by Facet Publishing,
7 Ridgmount Street, London WC1E 7AE
www.facetpublishing.co.uk

Facet Publishing is wholly owned by CILIP: the
Chartered Institute of Library and Information
Professionals.

British Library Cataloguing in Publication Data
A catalogue record for this book is available from
the British Library.

ISBN 978-1-85604-644-2

First published 2008

PEFC
PEFC/16-33-111
CATG-PEFC-052
www.pefc.org

Typeset from author/editors' disks by Facet
Publishing in 10.5/14pt Bembo and Nimbus Sans.
Printed and made in Great Britain by
MPG Books Ltd, Bodmin, Cornwall.

Contents

Contributors

Pat Atkins has been the Director of the Personalised Integrated Learning Support (PILS) Centre for Excellence in Teaching and Learning (CETL) at the Open University (UK) since February 2005. She has a wide experience of supporting higher education students, particularly those studying at a distance. Her previous roles include working as an academic tutor, designing and delivering induction and study skills programmes, researching student retention and improving practice in the design and delivery of student information, advice and guidance. More recently she has focused on working with and developing colleagues who deliver student support in all its forms, to look for ways to enhance, capture and disseminate good practice in a large institution with several thousand teaching staff. She has a particular interest in helping colleagues develop and acquire expertise in online support of students, built on an early career in software development. Pat's experience of working with systems has also influenced her holistic view of learning support, looking at ways to improve the integration of student's developing skills, interests, motivations and confidence within their chosen academic discipline.

Professor Peter Brophy was Professor of Information Management at Manchester Metropolitan University (MMU) from April 1998 until August 2008. He founded the Centre for Research in Library & Information Management (CERLIM) at the University of Central Lancashire (UCLAN) in 1993, moving with the Centre to MMU in 1998. At UCLAN he had, as well as directing CERLIM, been responsible for the University's library and IT services. Previously, he had held posts at Bristol and Teesside Polytechnics and Strathclyde and Lancaster Universities. Peter has extensive management, research, development and consultancy experience. He has directed a series of large European Commission funded research projects as well as a variety of studies in the UK. In 1998–99 he was the elected President of the UK Institute of Information Scientists. He is a Fellow and Honorary Fellow of the

Chartered Institute of Library & Information Professionals, a Fellow of the Royal Society of Arts and a Fellow of the Higher Education Academy. He has published widely in the field, including numerous journal papers and four recent monographs, the first three for Facet Publishing: *The Academic Library* (2nd edition, 2005), *Measuring Library Performance* (2006), *The Library in the Twenty-first Century* (2nd edition, 2007) and *Narrative-based Practice* (2008). Currently Peter is Principal Consultant with LIMC Ltd. He can be contacted at office@limc.co.uk.

Dr Scott C. Brown has been active in higher education through leadership involvement in state associations and national conventions, publications and presentations on a wide range of topics such as creating powerful learning environments, understanding complex issues of identity, and examining student affairs as a profession. He has served as the Convention Chair of the 2005 American College Personnel Association (ACPA) National Convention, editorial member of the *Journal of College Student Development*, and recipient of the Fulbright Seminar Grant (Germany), ACPA Annuit Coeptis and the ACPA Emerging Scholar awards. His research on student learning includes 'Learning Across the Campus: how college facilitates the development of wisdom', a theory detailing the process of how students integrate and what they learn in and out of class and on and off campus. He is currently developing the Wisdom Development Scale (WDS) with Jeffrey A. Greene. He played a significant role in the creation of 'Powerful Partnerships: a shared responsibility for learning', a collaborative project between ACPA, American Association for Higher Education (AAHE) and National Association of Student Personnel Administrators (NASPA), to create synergy among all members of the academic community concerned with undergraduate education. Scott currently serves as Associate Vice President and Dean of Students at Colgate University.

Dr Philip Cohen was appointed Head of Library Services at Dublin Institute of Technology in 2004. Before that, he worked for more than 20 years in a variety of posts in various university libraries in the UK: Manchester Metropolitan (twice), Northumbria, Bournemouth and Liverpool. Philip has been involved with library design projects throughout his career. He is particularly interested in finding solutions to reconcile the competing space demands of different groups of library users.

Dr Jen Harvey is currently the Head of the Learning, Teaching and Technology Centre (LTTC) of the Dublin Institute of Technology (DIT). The LTTC provides a range of academic development and support for staff involved in third level teaching including a suite of postgraduate programmes. Jen has been in this role from

2003; prior to this she was the DIT Head of Distance Education. Before moving to Dublin she worked as an Implementation Consultant for the Learning Technology Dissemination Initiative (LTDI), a Scottish Higher Education Funding Council (SHEFC)-funded project based in ICBL (the Institute for Computer Based Learning), Heriot Watt University, Edinburgh. She is actively involved in both the Learning Spaces and Grangegorman Project Planning groups, working towards the relocation of the Institute to a single-site campus. Her current research interests relate to the use of technology to support learning, student assessment strategies, practitioner-based evaluations and communities of practice.

Hannah Hough is the Head of Academic Services at the University of Cumbria, managing the resource collections of the Library and leading the information fluency skills agenda across the institution. Hannah has oversight of the Learning Gateway at the Fusehill Street Campus in Carlisle, a large technology-rich, flexible, learning environment with a specialist facilitation team for the development of user skills and experience. Hannah has a professional interest in embedding key skills into the curriculum, bridging the skills gaps that can emerge between all levels of study and the application of interactive online learning for the effective support of information skills. She also sits on the CILIP Information Literacy Group Committee as International Liaison Co-ordinator and Training Officer, co-ordinating national continuing professional development workshops for information professionals and maintaining links with international contacts.

Professor Philippa Levy is Academic Director of CILASS, the Centre for Inquiry-based Learning in the Arts and Social Sciences, and a member of the Department of Information Studies at the University of Sheffield. She is also currently leading an institutional development project on the theme 'strengthening research–learning–teaching linkages'. Her research interests are in the areas of higher education pedagogy and learning support/development, including the educational roles of information professionals, and in the scholarship of learning and teaching. She has a special interest in the use of digital technologies in learning and teaching, including in design for learning. She recently led an evaluation project that focused on the role of the learning activity management system in design for inquiry-based learning; this project, entitled DeSILA, was funded by the Joint Information Systems Committee (JISC) of the Higher Education Funding Council for England. Through her role with CILASS she is taking forward a number of research projects exploring aspects of the student and staff experience of inquiry-based learning, and she has also become involved in the design of new learning spaces, including an 'inquiry collaboratory' that was selected by JISC in early 2007 as an exemplar of good practice. Philippa was awarded a University Senate Award for Excellence in Teaching in 2002, and jointly won a Fédération Internationale de Documentation 'paper of the year' award in 1995 on the subject of networked learner support.

Sara Marsh took up the post of Director of Learner Support Services at the University of Bradford in Summer 2007, assuming responsibility for a wide range of support services including library, IT, careers, disability, counselling, staff and student development, the Graduate School, and a range of educational development and teaching quality enhancement initiatives. Previously she was Deputy Director of Library and Information Services at Swansea University where she had worked since 1996. She was involved in a range of externally funded projects including the ongoing development of the University's South Wales Coalfield Collection and the establishment of the regional library collaboration group ATLIS. Sara has been an active contributor to the profession through CILIP and more recently in SCONUL through UK Libraries Plus and SCONUL Research Extra. Sara was a key member of the group that worked to unify these two external access schemes to create SCONUL Access. She was on the steering group for the HAERVI project looking at visitor access to e-resources in HE institutions, and also member of the INSPIRE steering group.

Lindsey Martin is the eLearning Strategy and Development Manager at Edge Hill University. She has an institution-wide remit to assist and support staff in faculties and services to implement flexible and distributed learning and e-learning. This role includes responsibility for managing the Learning Technology Unit within Learning Services and SOLSTICE, the Higher Education Funding Council for England (HEFCE)-funded Centre of Excellence for Teaching and Learning, which has a focus on supported online learning. She was awarded an Edge Hill Learning and Teaching Fellowship in 2004. She won the Society of College National and University Libraries Staff Development Award in 2001 for an innovative approach to new staff induction and training using a virtual learning environment. In 2005, she led a 'New Academic Team' that achieved runner-up status in the Times Higher Education/Learning and Teaching Support Network's eTutor of the Year Award for an online information skills module. Lindsey has researched and published in the fields of changing learner support roles, e-learning and cultural change, and information and digital literacies; she is currently interested in researching academic literacies and tutor and student experiences of online learning.

Glynis Platt began her career in academic libraries at the University of Hull where Philip Larkin was Librarian. She spent 13 years working in further education libraries as College Librarian before moving to the South West Manchester College of Nursing as Division Leader for Learning Resources. In 1996 the nursing college merged with the University of Manchester. Glynis became a subject specialist in modern languages at the John Rylands University Library but was also appointed as Widening Participation Co-ordinator, the first and only such post in a UK university library, co-ordinating outreach work with local schools and colleges including the access scheme for young people working closely with the University's Widening Participation Team on activities like research projects and summer schools. She has given presentations and papers at several conferences on the subject of widening participation in university libraries. Professionally, she became a Chartered Librarian in 1977 and was President of the North Western Branch of The Library Association in 1999. She has served as Chair of the CoFHE (Colleges of Further and Higher Education) North West Circle for many years.

Dr Kent Porterfield has worked in higher education, specifically in the field of student affairs administration, for nearly 20 years. He has been actively involved in professional associations, having held various leadership positions at the state and national level. He has presented on a range of topics at state and national conferences, including student affairs leadership and administration, student learning/development, academic and student affairs partnerships, multiple identities and issues of inclusion, and professional development competencies. He has served as Professional Development Chair for the American College Personnel Association, President of the Missouri College Personnel Association and Co-Chair of the American College Personnel Task Force on Professional Certification. He has received state and national awards and recognition for his outstanding contributions to professional associations and the college student personnel field. Since 2006, he has served as Vice President for Student Development at Saint Louis University. Prior to this, he held four different positions at Northwest Missouri State University, including serving as Vice President for Student Affairs for more than eight years. He has degrees from the University of Missouri (EdD) and Northwest Missouri State University. With his wife and two daughters, he resides in St Louis, Missouri.

Frank Rennie is Professor of Sustainable Rural Development at the UHI Millennium Institute in the Highlands and Islands of Scotland and is the Head of Research and Post Graduate Development at Lews Castle College, UHI. He is the course leader for the MSc in Managing Sustainable Rural Development at the

UHI. His research interests lie in the general areas of rural and community development, especially in community-based approaches to integrated sustainable development. Recent work has been on new approaches to online education and distributed learning with rural communities and individuals, particularly open access and open content resources. He is an adviser to several government programmes and committees and is a Fellow of a number of learned societies. Frank has been involved in developing and delivering various combinations of distributed learning solutions (with a particular emphasis on networked solutions for rural areas) with colleges and university partners in Europe, Asia, Amazonia, Africa and New Zealand. He has published a wide range of materials related to rural issues, including over 20 books, and is a regular keynote speaker at international conferences. For further details see www.lews.uhi.ac.uk/frennie.

Sue Roberts is University Librarian at Victoria University of Wellington. Prior to coming to New Zealand in early 2007, Sue was Dean of Learning Services at Edge Hill University in Lancashire (UK) and the Director of SOLSTICE, a Centre for Excellence in Learning and Teaching with a focus on supported online learning. Sue has also researched and published in the fields of learner support roles and teams, leadership and management, continuing professional development, digital library development and e-learning, and is the co-author with Jennifer Rowley of *Leadership: the challenge for the information profession* (Facet Publishing, 2008).

Dr Craig D. Stephenson is Head of Student Development and Advisory Services at the University of Cumbria. Working across two continents, in seven higher education institutions, Craig has operated in both the academic and service arenas of higher education institutions, most recently at the University of Cumbria (UK). Awarded a PhD in the Social History of Medicine (University of Warwick, 1993), Craig went onto research and publish in his academic field before developing a professional interest in working with students beyond the classroom and embracing the 'seamless learning' agenda pioneered in the USA. Consequently, he read for a Masters in Student Personnel at the University of South Carolina (USA) and then moved to the University of California, San Diego, where he directed the International House and oversaw a range of programming initiatives that strengthened a students' leadership, cultural competency and employability skills. Returning to the North of England in 2002, Craig assumed his current position at St Martin's College (now the University of Cumbria). His University awarded him a Teaching Fellowship in 2008 for his leadership of complex change in student development services. He has presented widely on the topic of seamless learning and has served as a guest lecturer for the Student Services Masters' Course at the University of Huddersfield.

Jan Stewart is manager of Student Learning Support Services at Victoria University of Wellington, New Zealand. She has 17 years' experience in tertiary teaching and learning, particularly of retention and transition issues, and is currently looking to develop more collaborative models across the university to improve best practice in teaching and learning and student outcomes.

Les Watson runs his own educational consultancy providing advice to universities and colleges on aspects of student support, learning space and library development, and the strategic deployment of information technology. He worked recently as interim Director of Information Services at Royal Holloway University of London, developing new learning spaces, and is also currently an expert consultant to the Joint Information Systems Committee e-learning programme on Technology Enhanced Learning Environments. Prior to this consulting career he worked as a teacher, senior lecturer, Dean and Pro-Vice Chancellor in a number of UK higher education institutions. He has a reputation as an inspirational speaker and has undertaken many presentations and workshops for a wide range of organizations including a lecture tour on 'Places and Spaces for Learning' organized by the Carrick Institute for Learning and Teaching in Higher Education in Australia. Les has authored papers on many subjects, including aspects of higher education for the European Parliament, contributed to a number of books on the use of IT in education, and was the author of *Multimedia in Schools: the transition from primary to secondary schools* for the Scientific and Technological Options Assessment Office of the European Parliament. He is particularly well known for his development of the Learning Café Real@Caledonian in 2001 and the Saltire Centre at Glasgow Caledonian University. He can be contacted at www.leswatson.com.

Margaret Weaver is Head of Learning and Information Services at the University of Cumbria (formerly St Martin's College). She is a Fellow of the Higher Education Academy and a Teaching Fellow of the University. At her current institution she is the strategic lead for the Learning Gateway, the University's new flexible learning and teaching space, which is a Joint Information Systems Committee (JISC) Infokit case study exemplar. In 2005–6 she led the Change Academy team, a national programme for change managers sponsored by the UK Higher Education Academy and the Leadership Foundation, working with others on an action plan to further implement flexible and distributed learning. At Huddersfield University, she was the Project Director of the JISC INHALE (Information for Nursing and Health in a Learning Environment) Project, funded as part of the Distributed National Electronic Resource programme, and Academic Librarian for the Faculty of Human and Health Sciences. Her research interests are concerned with understanding staff perceptions of learning in higher education, and she has written various articles on enhancing practice to better support learning and teaching within a changing higher education setting. Margaret was nominated by her institution for a National Teaching Fellowship in 2008.

Preface

This book is about learners (students), their supporters (professional service staff) and our expectations of each other in conceiving the true value of a higher education experience. It attempts to show how they are each being remodelled and utterly transformed through purposeful delivery of increasingly integrated learning support services.

It is a timely text – there is increasing recognition that the total learning environment impacts on educating and supporting individual attainment in HE. As such, it takes the student view – inside and outside the classroom, on and off campus, physically and virtually and across professional boundaries. With the realization that all staff and the students themselves have a role to play in supporting and enhancing learning comes a lessening of the traditional gap between students, academics and service staff. In this new world, silo working is a thing of the past as institutional responses become more strategic in relation to learning support.

This book confirms that students no longer take a linear approach to education; they dip in and out as their circumstances dictate, and technology is enabling new ways to support them as they blend home, work and education. Increasingly their expectations are that there will be flexibility and support embedded in their course and that it will be pervasive – seamless, in fact. Consequently institutions need to take a holistic approach to supporting student learning – and many have, as evidenced by the rich case studies presented herein.

While researching my PhD on learning support professionals' beliefs about student learning, I became aware that in contrast to other educational research areas (e.g. learning styles or academic conceptions of learning), there has been little study of the impact of learning environments on student learning behaviours, and on support for learners. This was borne out by the fact that the literature is largely clustered around the 'professions' rather than on the holistic academic support needs of the student. However, on the ground, staff are working innovatively in complex multiprofessional contexts for, and with, students – and this is a global phenomenon.

This book brings those perspectives together for the first time, allowing personal stories from several countries to surface through narrative and through a sharing of the intimate experiences of leaders and practitioners in the field. Their voices transcend the interfaces between structure and context, providing a new frame of reference for our work in higher education. What is striking about the varied contributions, from the UK and abroad, is their unequivocal passion for students and how the transferability of the concepts, seemingly in diverse organizations, indicates a coherence between the professions previously undocumented.

These 'conversations' are not unique in themselves. I believe that they are happening in a great many universities, colleges, schools, workplaces and homes, in some cases virtually, at various stages of the student journey. Consequently the chapters in this book have been carefully developed to illustrate key dimensions required for supporting students today and in the future, and also present a fresh approach to learning support. Further, it is hoped that these contributions will inspire, inform and raise the profile of learning support in higher education with informed practice at its heart.

In considering the situated nature of learning support, the work is firmly located at grass-roots level, at the nexus between the professions, to illustrate the synergies between cases. Hence the chapters are deliberately varied and eclectic, revealing the insights that are gained by coverage of a wide spectrum of experience among librarians, student affairs professionals, IT and learning technologists, educators and researchers. The cases are distinctive in their own right but each has elements of a new community of professional practice in a global context. The latter is concerned with integration, with extended dialogue with peers and students and with close alignment of pedagogy across the spectrum of learning support. The interplay of these perspectives means that the language and terminology used are challenging at times. It is hoped that you will persevere and consider the implications of the chapters and their applicability to your own situation as a way to see a different future, to build on your own repertoire of reflections on practice supporting student learning.

The book is divided into three parts, each providing a thematic framework concerned with a contemporary perspective on modern learning support practice. Every author is a leader and thinker in their own institution and in their field. The chapters can be read in any order, but there is a logic to their organization.

Part 1 discusses high-level government strategy and policy, with England and New Zealand as a backdrop for the book. Initial chapters consider the changing characteristics of our students and what shapes their experience, and include a case study of a holistic university – one that employs pan-university collaborative approaches. This is followed by practical demonstrations of the opportunities and challenges involved in bringing about organizational redesign and redirection of resources while maximizing strategic investment to better support the 21st-century student. An Anglo–American perspective is contrasted with a British university approach. In all cases, alignment with academic practice and mission is considered and the advantages for students, academic staff and learner support professionals in working together are explained. Outcomes have certainly influenced new services at these institutions and affected complex cultural change informed by the changing profile of learners.

Part 2 is concerned with the design and practice of learning support services in shaping the learning environment. First, two exemplars of learning space design are presented, which have influenced institutional views of learning support and changed how services are being delivered, with positive effects on learners (in England and Ireland). The role of learners and their supporters in the planning and implementation of space yields unique insights into the pedagogy of the built environment, leading to the creation of a toolkit that can be used for planning new age campuses; a profile of active facilitative practice and possible future enhancements to an existing flexible learning space are also disclosed. Next are two contributions on learner support practices across distributed institutions and networks, focusing on online media and their relation to physical environments, using examples in Scotland and a pan-European summary of projects that are influencing libraries in Europe. The latter reveals that to enhance the connectedness between the UK and Europe requires some exposure to a wider range of practitioner groups. How much greater then would the join-up be across academic and public sectors at the policy and strategy level? Professor Brophy's insightful exposition begins this process, successfully highlighting the massive shift that is taking place across Europe and offering a glimpse of the future for our increasingly digital libraries and learning resources services. In this context student learning support has yet to be fully understood – suggesting a potentially rich area for future research. A case study on the widening participation initiatives of a British research-intensive university completes the broad perspective on learning support, and the way that the library has hugely developed its role in assisting student progression is revealed and is perhaps unexpected.

Part 3 is about truly integrative practice examined through the lens of multi-professional teams and through a reflective review of the composition of their skills portfolio and how they work together. The voices of the various professions are strong here, and linked to the view of the modern student is a case study on a staff development initiative that united staff in their support of online learning (in England). There is a powerful essay taking the American perspective on personal effectiveness, with practical suggestions about how to maximize your influence – working strategically and intentionally – to increase your standing and gain personal agency. This is a difficult subject expertly presented – in effect a toolkit that is transferable to any academic institution. Finally, the book concludes with two chapters on research-informed practice and how relationships between the affective and cognitive are becoming better understood and acknowledged and are transforming our thinking about the orality of learning and its diffusion. The work of three Centres of Excellence in Learning and Teaching (CETLs) provides a focus for this part of the book, which outlines a range of problem-based learning approaches taken by practitioners and students.

Throughout the book connections are made between the literature, professional practice and ongoing research to inform future developments and draw out the implications for services, institutions and individuals wishing to remain at the forefront of the student development agenda.

A number of core concepts emerge:

- The global learning support culture in the Western world is becoming established and increasingly homogenous as students take more control of their learning.
- Learning is complex, and our thinking on support must be sophisticated yet sufficiently simple in practice for maximum engagement.
- Partnership and collaboration is being extended across professional boundaries for the good of students and ourselves.
- The 'experience' matters more than it used to, and emotion in learning will transform higher education significantly in the future, with implications for the support of learning.
- We need to shift our thinking further to empathize more deeply with students; further research is needed into the conceptions of learning that staff hold in order to enhance learning support
- Technology is important and accepted.
- Personal skills are an intangible yet very significant area: the behaviours we exhibit through our professional judgement and commitment are more important than ever.
- We need to strategize learning support even further so that the full range of professional expertise is focused on what learners need (not what we think they need).

- We need new ways to measure the impact of learning support services and student expectations, beyond the mechanistic, focusing on the experience and using rigorous qualitative methods.

Gathering such expert opinion together has indeed been a positive experience for me as editor, and an opportunity to engage with a wide variety of new thinking. I have learned a great deal about consensus in our support professions, their similarities and their differences (but more about their similarities), and I am full of admiration for the vitality that is present in each and every case study. Diversity is of course also present in our students, so it is only appropriate that we utilize this in our work to transform our own potential for growth and to understand more fully the complex and rewarding nature of learning support.

Finally, we should listen to the voices in this book, through the case study presenters, their thoughts, feelings and actions, and reflect on the soft skills that underpin them – in fact, the new skills needed that we all possess, sharing the traditions of our respective expertise. I have no doubt that new roles will emerge and become the next generation of learning support. Strategic and pragmatic approaches to learning support are required in this increasingly distributed, cross-cultural educational environment. This book cannot cover all elements, but I hope you will enjoy reading it and take what you need from it to develop your thinking and your practice – once read, there's no going back!

Acknowledgements

Grateful thanks to all the chapter writers for their contribution, patience and constructive comments on my editorial feedback to them. Thanks also to the Gateway facilitators for use of their personal quotes: Heather Benson, Claire Foster and Linda Moses-Allison of the University of Cumbria. And, last but not least, thanks to my family for their support and patience during the writing of this book.

Margaret Weaver

Part 1

Transformation through strategy, policy and organization: the changing profile of learners and the redesign of learning support

1

It's not about us: it's about them

Overview

This chapter reviews some of the changes that the UK higher education system has seen over the last 15 years or so. Policies increasing access to higher education and introducing tuition fees, in particular, have combined with the impact of new technology and a society that is increasingly consumer-orientated to demand that universities and colleges pay attention to greater student diversity, learning that is independent of time and place, and the need to provide a student experience that goes beyond service and exceeds expectations. While there is a great deal still to be done before institutions become real players in the emerging 'experience economy', progress has been made on integrated models of service delivery, the provision of inspirational venues in which students can interact with the institution and its staff, and attempts to use technology to enhance the student experience. This chapter explores some of the background to such initiatives, thus providing a context for the examples covered in the rest of the book, and suggests some themes for future development.

Introduction

It really is not about us. It is about them – our students. Many of us employed by universities have been so for most of our working lives – and we are also products of the higher education system in which we work. We have no problem getting to grips with what a university is, how it works, what schools, faculties and departments it might have, how they inter-relate and where we go to get done what we want done. We know what a university should be like. For students, and this applies to myself when I think back to my undergraduate days, this is often not the case. Many students, particularly but not exclusively the large numbers of 18-year-olds now entering our universities, find the university bewildering and the vocabulary alien. For the mature student, who may have delayed interaction with the university until later in life and who often engages with us on a part-time basis, there is a similar lack of familiarity. It can take some new university entrants a year or more to understand the university and its service offering. In the modern world, many of these students are the first in their family to attend university; there is no family knowledge of university structures, vocabulary and processes. In addition, many of these students are attempting to study full-time while engaging in full-time employment.

Simplifying the availability of, and access to, our support services is therefore more important now than ever before. The suggestion in this chapter, and throughout this book, is that by taking a student view we can not only improve and simplify but also transform the experience of students as learners and members of our institutions. This is not always easy for us, as comments from teachers who participated in the Higher Education Academy ESCalate project (Campbell et al., 2007, 32, 97) on the differences in perceptions about learning and teaching between staff and students indicate:

> Our discourse of teaching and learning is not one that students necessarily have. . . . Most staff are the successful product of a traditional learning approach and find it hard to put themselves in the shoes of the students who learn in different ways to themselves and in the case of direct or recent school leavers who have grown up with a different technological and education culture.

It is clear that transforming the student experience needs leaders in institutions, and in information services, who can see beyond operational effectiveness and who have a vision for new staff structures and service configurations driven by the needs of students rather than the needs of the institution, or their chosen profession.

Government policies increasing access to higher education and introducing tuition fees have affected the demand for, and the competitiveness of, higher education and are partly behind the need to take a fresh look at the student experience. The improvements described in other chapters of this book show a range of responses to government policies and societal and technological trends, with the common aim of improving the quality of the student experience. Government intentions, independent of which political party is in power, have been clear for almost two decades. In a 1991 white paper (Bekhradnia, 2001) stated:

> The Government's policies for schools, and in particular examination reforms, are encouraging more young people to stay on in school or college after 16 and

then to apply for a place in higher education – by the year 2000 the Government expects that approaching one in three of all 18–19 year olds will enter higher education.

Growth in higher education numbers has been with us for some time.

From elite to mass higher education

We have seen significant sector growth over a long period, both in the number of universities and in the numbers of students that attend them. There are now more universities, each with more students, than ever before.

The removal of the binary divide in 1992, when existing polytechnic institutions in the UK became universities overnight, and the subsequent granting of university and university college status to a greater number of institutions over the past ten years has seen the number of UK universities roughly double since 1992. The key effect here is a larger and hence more competitive sector.

The growth in student numbers has been significant, producing a dramatic shift from an elite to a mass system of higher education (HE). This growth in student numbers has been a feature of HE for many years now: for example, between the academic years 1988–9 and 1993–4 there was a 67% increase in full-time undergraduate students (Higher Education Funding Council for England, 2001). Student numbers have continued to increase in more recent years: for example, between 2005–6 and 2006–7 the number of students in UK HE institutions increased by 6%. This recent growth was accompanied by a growth of only 3.1% in academic staff numbers and 1.9% in non-academic (or professional) staff (Higher Education Statistics Agency, n.d.). The slower rate of growth in academic and support staff numbers is a factor causing universities to devise innovative ways to improve the student experience. Innovations that invest in technology and systems, which are usually one-off capital costs, such as self-service access to information, services and resources, rather than people with their accompanying continued financial burden, not only improve the student experience but also improve access and can be cost-effective.

Growth in student numbers is not limited to UK students. Recent growth in overseas student numbers is even more remarkable than domestic growth, as evidenced by this recent answer to a parliamentary question (*Daily Hansard*, 2007):

Over the last five years, the number of UK based students at English higher education institutions increased by 200,000 (14 per cent) to 1.67 million and the number of overseas students at such institutions increased by 80,000 (40 per cent) to 275,000.

Bill Rammell

This statement goes on to confirm that further growth is to be expected:

Against that background, we expect many more students from both the UK and abroad to participate in higher education over the next five years.

Bill Rammell

It should also be noted that HE growth is strategically important to the government, both economically and socially: an educated workforce enables UK plc to be more competitive in the global marketplace, and widening participation in higher education and developing a more inclusive society means greater numbers participating in and hence contributing to national competitiveness (Department for Innovation, Universities and Skills, 2008). However, there is evidence that the strategy of widening participation has been only partially successful and that many of the additional students in universities are more of the same middle-class entrants. Widening participation does, however, in its own right provide a rationale for rethinking student support.

Higher education is clearly a booming industry but, as in all periods of expansion in all businesses, high rates of growth have consequences. Greater student numbers of all types have clear consequences for the range of support services to be provided, and for the methods deployed to provide these services effectively and efficiently. At the very least, more students put additional pressure on current learning support services, but there are also more subtle effects such as increasing pressure on service providers to innovate, to address not just increased numbers but the resulting greater diversity of student needs. The key effect here is that more students and greater diversity drive innovative service delivery and greater personalization of services.

The introduction of fees

The funding of the developing mass higher education system in the UK has been a major battleground between university vice chancellors and the government for many years. The Blair government 'solved' this problem with the highly contentious introduction of tuition fees. For the first time in the history of UK higher education, students were expected to make a financial contribution to the costs of their tuition. Many involved in higher education were opposed to this development. However, despite initial opposition tuition fees have now become part of the accepted higher education landscape. It is unlikely that England will reverse this development (as happened in Scotland).

The argument is now moving to focus on fee levels. It is expected that, following review in 2009, the fee system will be further developed to allow universities to levy fees at a rate of their choosing within a limit set by legislation. Interestingly, the current system was established with a cap of £3000 per student per year, and did have an option for universities to set a lower fee. Only a few universities differentiated themselves by setting lower fees. If the introduction of fees was an attempt to establish a 'market' for higher education, as many would argue, it clearly failed. However, fees have moved the sector closer to the idea of a market in HE, and a variable fees regime that does result in significant variations across the sector, if introduced, will complete that move. Despite the limited market that has resulted thus far, the reality is that the introduction of fees has produced more market-like behaviour with students being more critical than ever before of the 'services' that they receive at university and clearly regarding themselves as 'paying customers' – as evidenced by recent litigation from dissatisfied students. The outcome is that while HE may not be a true market just yet, students are more likely to view themselves as consumers than ever before and there is no doubt that the introduction of tuition fees has contributed to rising student expectations. This attitudinal change has been driven partly by tuition fees but also by a more sweeping change to consumer society in the UK, which will be discussed later in this chapter.

Forget analysis: think about synthesis

The massification of the sector and the introduction of tuition fees clearly have strategic implications for universities (Scott, 2005). It is worth considering here how institutions might respond strategically. Proving a direct link between a cause, such as the introduction of tuition fees, and an effect, such as greater student expectations, is not attempted here, but it is clear that the causes discussed have been highly influential in creating a changed environment around students and their HE experience. It is also clear that this will inevitably influence strategy and policy in our institutions. However, direct attribution of a single cause to a consequence is, in the author's view, often pursued with unreasonable vigour in our institutions, as we tend to rely predominantly on analysis to provide clear 'scientific' rationales for action. If only things were this simple.

Attempts to identify single causes and manage situations by taking specific actions can often, due to the interconnectedness of our activities, make the situation worse. The point here is that the system is inherently complex, and the student experience is also highly complex, involving all of the interactions and events that make up a student's life experience while at university. Many factors interrelate and interact. It is this interconnectedness that requires an integrated holistic approach to improvement, rather than a piecemeal atomistic approach. Rather than using analysis as our main tool, we need to make use of synthesis.

Taking a holistic approach to student experience issues does inevitably mean that we have to work across several structural silos. The structures that we have historically created ensure that fragmentation of thinking and action is built in to the system, and while we might attempt to deal with this through the formation of student experience committees, real 'joined-up' non-partisan working is doomed when the co-operating parties know that they will be competing for resources in the annual budget round. Taking a holistic, joined-up view does not come naturally to us, partly because of our structures but also because of our tendency to seek refuge in analysis as our default approach, which has been driven by a managerialist culture of facts and accountability. Indeed, as Taylor (2003) points out:

> The fact that professional academics, trained to deconstruct and reflect upon the ways in which power is exercised, have failed to call managerialism's bluff is particularly worrying and again cause for concern.

The student experience is of such a complexity that analytical approaches are unlikely to produce the transformational thinking that we need. Rather, an approach based on synthesis, that looks for connections and synergies between activities, and that unites resources (and resource holders) in the common interest of transforming the student experience, is what is needed.

In the area of student support there are three factors that, in my view, benefit from taking an approach based on synthesis. These are:

- the staff that work in the services
- the technologies that are deployed
- the physical and virtual environments that we create.

These three factors benefit from being considered together, rather than separately as they are in many organizations: see Figure 1.1 (from Watson, 2005). The skills, attitudes and behaviours of our staff are deeply affected by the technologies that

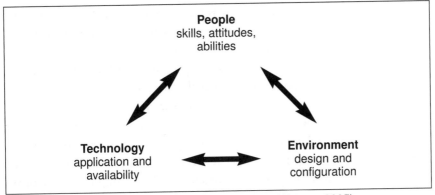

Figure 1.1 Synergy – a strategy of synthesis (from Watson, 2005)

we deploy and how we make them available, and also by the design and configuration of the environments in which they work. An approach based on synthesis, which considers people, technology and the environment, brings out synergies between these areas of investment. For example a strategy of self-service can use the best technology available but is unlikely to succeed without staff that embrace it and physical space that enables easily understood access to, and use of, the facilities.

Looking forward

We know that of the many factors affecting the experience of students in our institutions, only some are within our control while others are to do with personal circumstances and relationships. We must therefore capitalize on those things that we can control, and improve and use them thoughtfully – not as short-term fixes but as long-term strategies to achieve our high-level hopes and aspirations. The issues of complexity, synthesis and synergy, in my view, mean that we must take a forward-looking rather than a data-focused, backward-looking view. While the data sets we have might point to some general lessons for us, more often they tell us what not to do rather than what to do. To find out what we should do, we need to concentrate on what we wish to create. Transforming the student support offering in our universities is a creative activity requiring imagination and risk-taking. We need to adopt a creative world view, as expressed well by Land and Jarman (1992, 166):

> . . .the reference point is the future, not the past. We don't need to fall back on the past for our decisions. Choices are based on alignment with our purpose and our vision for a different world.

At the heart of this creative worldview is the thought that we 'don't need to fall back on the past for our decisions'. In other words, what we think the student experience should be like, in our richest picture of it, should be what we use to make decisions – and not mere data about past events. Taking such a forward-looking, integrated, holistic view not only acknowledges the complexity of factors affecting the student experience but also suggests that we need to look across the departmental silos of library, IT and student services. Taking this broad view, as many examples in this book illustrate, enables us to find solutions that arise not just within but also at the interfaces of these separate services, increasing the chance of finding simplicity within our complex structures and helping us deal with the unexpected.

Indeed, dealing with the unexpected may be the biggest challenge that we face. Taleb (2007), in his book *The Black Swan*, highlights the increasing frequency of unexpected world events in these early years of the 21st century. These events, such as 9/11, might not initially be perceived to have direct effects on higher education UK but, over time, they do – for example via the tightened visa regulations which are a reaction to the growing threat from terrorism. A creative worldview is a form of preparation for the consequences of such events – when faced with the unexpected, knowing where you wish to go is the best planning you can have.

Do structures matter?

An obvious response to the call for a holistic approach to the student experience is to converge, merge or integrate the departments that contribute to the student experience. Integration does make sense and can take different forms. An initial look at the issues in this chapter might suggest that structural integration is an obvious answer. However, the structural silos that we have in our institutions have, in many cases, long histories and are steeped in institutional politics. Often the energy and human effort required to combine these silos operationally, and more important culturally, exceeds the gain and should only be attempted by the brave or, some would say, foolhardy.

A focus on students clearly provides the imperative for an integration strategy: integration has to be about simpler, more easily understood services that are more widely available. The focus of integration, therefore, should be at the point of delivery. For students it does not matter how complex the organization is in the back office, provided that services are integrated at the point of delivery. Students should not have to understand how the university is structured in order to access its services.

So how can integration at the point of delivery be achieved? There are examples throughout the HE sector that illustrate what is possible. One route is through a service integration strategy driven by a single (physical and virtual) point of contact with the students, whereby a single desk, and web enquiry service, provides top-level access to all services for students – a strategy attempted, partially successfully, at Glasgow Caledonian University.

Integration of systems can be as important as physical service point integration. Technology is an important force for integration, in terms of sharing data and combining access to various services online. The holy grail of at least an integrated virtual learning environment, student record system, library collection management system and finance system has been vigorously pursued by many institutions and, when done well, can help unite the services offered. However, as with services, systems have a range of different 'owners' in institutions – and how should library systems relate to student record systems and HR and finance systems, and what happens when there is a new system development such as the MLE (managed learning environment) vying for a position in the systems hierarchy? Developments with portals did help to move the debate from systems to services, by integrating offerings on a common presentation screen, and Web 2.0 architectures can take this further. However, as with departmental structures, system structures and their ownership can become the issue and prevent progress with the real problem – what the student sees and interacts with.

The development of space in libraries and learning centres (see Chapters 5 and 6) can also aid an integration strategy. Open-plan, technology-rich spaces attract students, and where students are is where most student services want (and need) to be. A strategy that does not coerce departments such as IT and student services to merge with the library but makes space available in the modern library building for service delivery enables integrated access to services.

The service expectations of a diverse student body, the impact of new technologies and the importance of the emerging experience economy (Pine and Gilmore, 1999) are all factors that affect the way staff and students view facilities and services within the institution.

The student experience

What happens to students during their time at university clearly has an impact that shapes their lives. We used to take pride in the fact that students were treated as individuals, but in the 21st century mass system of education, this can no longer be the case. However, paradoxically, the student experience is now more important to the success of not only individual students but also to the universities they attend than ever before (Shepherd, 2008):

> The national student survey – which asks students to rate their university and then publishes the results – has created a certain pressure. This [higher education] is now a very competitive environment.

Setting aside for now the issue of whether post-experience surveys such as the national student survey (NSS) have any real value, it is clear that their very existence is a key driver for universities in improving the student experience. An institution's position in the resulting league tables from this and other surveys lies behind much current university investment. Indeed, those that can ill-afford to invest continue to do so in response to this new-found competitiveness, as Shepherd (2008) highlights in respect of investment in buildings:

> And some, despite being millions of pounds in the red, still plan to spend millions more on buildings and refurbishments. This at a time when recession is thought to be around the corner, and borrowing money is getting more expensive.

The key effect is that we now have a larger and more competitive higher education sector than ever before, and the bulk of competition between institutions is focused on the support of students and their overall student experience.

Society in transition

Earlier in this chapter I discussed the increased consumer stance taken by students as a result of the introduction of fees, but also hinted that there was something else affecting increased consumerism. Pine and Gilmore (1999) in *The Experience Economy* identify a progression over time from a society focused on the sale of commodities to one selling goods and then services. This change is clearly evident in the UK, where shopping has become a predominant form of leisure-time activity and the 'rights' of the consumer are a dominant force for improved quality of goods and services. Students are members of this culture. However the progression, according to Pine and Gilmore, does not stop here – beyond services lie experiences. There is a view that experiences transcend the need for goods and services, which is supported by Richard Florida (2000) in his work *The Rise of the Creative Class*. Working with focus groups of creative class people such as IT professionals, health specialists, teachers and others (that is, the people who graduate from our universities), Florida notes:

> Experiences are replacing goods and services because they stimulate our creative faculties and enhance our creative capacities. This active, experiential lifestyle is spreading and becoming more prevalent in society.

I cannot help but be struck by how fortuitous this is. Creative class people – those students who populate our universities – value experience more than anything else. This suggests that it may be more important than we ever imagined that we take seriously the quality of the experience that we provide. Adding this general societal shift towards a need for experiences to the pseudo-market produced by tuition fees suggests that the student experience may not only be more important than ever before but that those universities providing an excellent student experience are most likely to succeed in the competition for students. Could it be that students are more likely to choose their university on the basis of the support it offers outside the teaching that it delivers?

The technology effect

Universities have spent enormous sums of money on technology over the past 20 years or so, but exactly how beneficial this expenditure has been is unclear (Watson, 2008). One thing, however, is certain – today's students, the Google-eyed Facebook generation, are much more familiar with technology than students ever were before – they have technology-based lifestyles. And technology-based lifestyles are not the sole preserve of the young – on average, 57% of homes in the UK now have broadband access, indicating a broader spectrum of users in the general population (Allen, 2008). Students' expectations of the technology to be made available by institutions are very high. Importantly, these expectations are generally related to technologies that are personal and service-oriented rather than those, based on control and corporate systems approaches, that we currently provide. In relation to both learning and service the expectations of technology-capable students – which, it is acknowledged, does not include all students but does include many of them, and is also an increasing proportion of students – is for technology that enables them to contribute (through self-service and self-controlled pace of learning) and participate (through interaction and membership), and enables self-promotion and engagement through social software. Web 2.0 and social software services such as Facebook and MySpace give these digital natives (Prensky, 2001) a completely different view of technology than the (largely) digital immigrants that currently run our IT services in universities. The challenge for universities is to find ways of providing technologies that students can relate to and want to use as they do the current public domain offerings. The Joint Information Systems Committee student expectations study (2007) tells us that (future) students do not want universities to invade their Facebook space, but this does not and should not prevent us from developing new technological approaches that engage students in new ways. One example might be a move from corporate virtual learning environments to modular Web 2.0-based personal learning environments that provide a greater choice of tools, content and services for individuals as learners.

Scrutiny: a new environment for improvement?

For many years universities have been driven to improve by quality watchdogs such as the Quality Assurance Agency (QAA), which regularly inspects institutions to ensure that they meet expected standards. The QAA is part of what Lord Broers (2005) calls the:

> Faustian compact between universities and state [that] requires in exchange for state funding an elaborate process of scrutiny, evaluation, measurement and quality assurance, to persuade those who pay the piper that the tune is at least worth listening to even if not wholly understood.

While this quality drive continues, there is now a new kid on the block – student expectations. One outcome of students' extensive use of Web 2.0 software is their involvement in the 'recommendation revolution'. Websites that enable students to rate their university or rate their tutor are now ubiquitous and, when combined with the Facebook/MySpace opportunities for praise and criticism, represent a powerful new version of 'quality'. It remains to be seen what will damage the health of the university more – a poor report from the QAA or a flaming on Facebook. What's certain is that:

> It just doesn't do to have grotty student halls, peeling lecture theatre walls, or unsightly leisure areas. Students are paying fees and can choose to go elsewhere.
>
> (Shepherd, 2008)

And if you do, then thanks to the rapid spread of opinion on the web it won't be just your current students that know about it. Scrutiny based on the student experience, expressed through opinions on the web, accompanied by the current 'surveyitis' in HE, brings a whole new perspective to university quality.

How have universities responded to the challenges of transforming the student experience?

There are many examples of responses to the forces described in this chapter, in all three of the categories of service, systems and space. The quest for excellent learning support services and a remarkable student experience is a continuing one – it is a journey, and not a destination. Some of the emerging issues on that journey that we will need to address are:

- how to make effective use of IT
- how to unite real and virtual worlds
- how to capitalize on emerging technologies
- how to improve how we evaluate the student experience.

How do we harness the real power of IT for support and service delivery? Carr (2004) talks of IT no longer being strategic. We all have it, tons of it, and for most of us it does the same things. IT is now plumbing. For excellent support and service delivery we need plumbing that works – fantastically. So far we have systems that merely work. They don't exceed expectations and delight our students. As we struggle to cope with greater diversity of students and greater numbers than ever before, then, we really do need to harness the power of IT, and we do need to ensure that it is deeply embedded in what we do. From a service perspective this means concentrating on excellent service and not getting hung up on the IT aspects of delivery, and from a learning perspective it means having IT as plumbing that works and supports innovative pedagogy. Excellent plumbing facilitates excellent service by providing us with self-service opportunities that are always on and infallible.

Excellent plumbing also facilitates the personalization agenda. For example, it helps us move our thinking from one-size-fits-all virtual learning environments to personal learning environments that enable students to use modular Web 2.0 tools to build a learning environment that suits their life and learning styles.

Richard Florida's work on the rise of the creative class shows us that our students will not live solely online. They will continue to value place – especially those 'third places' that enable learning conversations and community engagement. A key issue for universities is what they can do to work across the real and the virtual so that these worlds are united and complementary and not divided. What emerging technologies might there be that bring together the real and the virtual? One example is the shotcode – a variation on the barcodes used on retail packaging – which is used increasingly in museums. When a shotcode is 'photographed' by a mobile phone it takes the user to a website with further information. This clearly provides an opportunity to link the real and virtual worlds.

There are technologies that we know are almost there and will continue to be developed – airborne networks, radio frequency identification and immersive environments, to mention just a few. The key questions here are what to adopt, when to adopt it and, returning to the technology arm of the synergy strategy, how to apply it. Emerging technologies will provide, at least for a short period of time, a possible competitive advantage from IT that goes beyond plumbing – but it won't last for long.

And lastly, what of evaluation? This is becoming extremely important both as a tool for student choice and as a driver of university strategy. How good is our current evaluation of the student experience (e.g. the NSS)? In general it is post-event and suffers from the negative effects of all other post-event evaluations: poor memory, grudges, lack of relevance to those completing the survey (outcomes usually only affect the next cohort) and formats that reflect more what the questioner thinks than what students might feel. There are two points here. First, we should be interested in how students feel about their experience – it is emotional and it is an experience. Second, we should be interested in sampling it as it happens. A system that samples the student experience in real time is not impossible. The experience sampling method (Hektner, Schmidt and Csikszentmihalyi, 2006) is one way of doing this that has been used extensively and successfully in psychological research, particularly in studies of happiness. There are clear benefits to such an approach, which gives students an opportunity to tell us not just what they think but what they feel about the experience as they experience it.

Conclusion

While we have made enormous progress in improving our support for students and consequently providing them with the best experience that we can, this is a continuing journey. One of the key points as we continue on this journey is that we should get the focus right, as described in this quote from Charles Dunstone CEO of carphone Warehouse:

> When we fail, and we do fail, often you can trace that failure back to the fact
> that we became too focused on internal priorities. We've been thinking too

much about what's good for Carphone Warehouse and forgetting what it's like to be a customer.

Similarly for higher education:

> When we fail, and we do fail, very often you can trace that failure back to the fact that we became too focused on internal priorities. We've been thinking too much about what's good for the university and forgetting what it's like to be a student.

After all, it's not about us. It's about them.

References

Allen, K. (2008) Fears of Digital Divide Groundless as Online Access Soars in Rural Areas, *Guardian Technology*, (22 May), www.guardian.co.uk/technology/2008/may/22/internet.digitalmedia.

Bekhradnia, B. (2001) *20 Years of Higher Education Policy: looking back 10 years and forward to the next decade*, www.hepi.ac.uk/pubdetail.asp?ID=97&DOC=Lectures.

Broers, A. (2005) *University Courses for Tomorrow: annual Higher Education Policy Institute lecture*, www.hepi.ac.uk/pubdetail.asp?ID=188&DOC=Lectures.

Campbell, F. et al. (2007) *ESCalate Project – Hearing the Student Voice: promoting and encouraging the effective use of the student voice to enhance professional development in learning, teaching and assessment within higher education*. Final Report, Napier University, http://escalate.ac.uk/2222.

Carr, N. (2004) *Does IT Matter? Information technology and the corrosion of competitive advantage*, Harvard Business Press.

Daily Hansard Written Answers (2007) Bill Rammell, www.publications.parliament.uk/pa/cm200607/cmhansrd/cm070502/text/70502w0029.htm.

Department for Innovation, Universities and Skills (2008) *High Skills High Value*, www.dius.gov.uk/consultations/con_0408_hlss.html.

Florida, R. (2000) *The Rise of the Creative Class: and how it's transforming work, leisure, community and everyday life*, Basic Books.

Hektner, J. M., Schmidt, J. A. and Csikszentmihalyi, M. (2006) *Experience Sampling Method: measuring the quality of everyday life*, Sage.

Higher Education Funding Council for England (2001) *Expansion of Student Numbers Depends on Raising Aspirations*, www.hefce.ac.uk/News/HEFCE/2001/supply.htm.

Higher Education Statistics Agency (n.d.) *Data Tables*, www.hesa.ac.uk/index.php/component/option,com_datatables/itemid,121/.

Joint Information Systems Committee (2007) *Student Expectations Study*, www.jisc.ac.uk/search.aspx?keywords=student%20expectations%20study&filter=s.

Land, G. and Jarman, B. (1992) *Breakpoint and Beyond Mastering the Future: today*, Harper Business.

Pine, II, B. J. and Gilmore J. H. (1999) *The Experience Economy*, Harvard Business Press.

Prensky, M. (2001) *Digital Natives Digital Immigrants*, http://marcprensky.com/writing/.

Scott, P. (2005) *Mass Higher Education: ten years on*, AUA conference, Coventry, March, www.aua.ac.uk/publications/conferenceproceedings/2005warwick.

Shepherd, J. (2008) Who Will Weather the Financial Storm? *Guardian Education*, 19 February, http://education.guardian.co.uk/egweekly/story/0,,2257797,00.html.

Taleb, N. N. (2007) *The Black Swan*, Random House.

Taylor, P. (2003) The Project Meets the Office: managerialism in UK plc, *Variant*, www.variant.randomstate.org/16texts/Project_Office.html.

Watson, L. (2005) Synergy: considering technology in the context of strategies for people and the campus environment. In Clark, M. J. (ed.), *EUNIS 2005: Conference Proceedings*, University of Manchester.

Watson, L. (2008) Where Are We Now? In Boys, J. and Ford, P. (eds), *The e-Revolution and Post-Compulsory Education: using e-business models to deliver quality education*, Routledge in association with the Joint Information Systems Committee.

2

Towards the holistic university: working collaboratively for student learning

SUE ROBERTS AND JAN STEWART

Introduction

The global tertiary educational environment is increasingly taking an inclusive approach. The holistic model for student learning support and engagement is often viewed as an answer to the demands that this generates. This chapter acknowledges the value of the holistic model while recognizing the challenges and pressures it creates for universities – especially their programmes, policy and people. It is argued here that the pivotal ingredient for success is effective pan-university collaboration. This chapter explores the barriers to and enablers of such collaboration in the university setting, using a case study of collaboration between student learning support services, library services and academics at Victoria University of Wellington, New Zealand.

The global tertiary environment

An analysis of trends in the global tertiary education sector in the late 20th and early 21st centuries points to a rise in the profile of the inclusion agenda. This, it can be argued, is informed by the need for institutions to think differently about the student population, in terms of both recruitment and retention. This shift in thinking can be attributed to demographic changes, government imperatives and policy and – more altruistically – growing awareness that an inclusive approach benefits the university community and wider society. Government agendas with regard to widening participation and lifelong learning have helped to shape the tertiary education sector and as such are crucial drivers. Government influence is therefore not simply reserved to expanding or limiting the size of the sector, but can determine the very nature of its institutions and their strategies for learning, teaching and research. One example in the UK was *The Future of Higher Education* (Department for Education and Skills, 2003), a policy document which reflected a sector undergoing considerable change and an increasingly interventionist central government. *The Future of Higher Education* saw all higher education institutions as providing excellent teaching and learning and supporting widening participation, but diverging considerably beyond this. Taylor (2003) usefully terms this 'diversity within commonality', and many authors have argued that there is no single model of a higher education institution.

Similarly, there is an interventionist policy approach in New Zealand. The government agenda is to 'provide education for the development of skills and knowledge that supports New Zealand and New Zealanders to compete internationally' (Tertiary Education Commission, 2008). Widening access to under-represented groups such as the Maori is a core obligation under the Treaty of Waitangi. All NZ universities under the Education Act 1989 have to have this obligation enshrined in their charters. More recent government policy continues to emphasize widening access, and also quality and performance and the importance of teaching and research to New Zealand's economy, but there have been two new unique shifts. The Tertiary Education Commission (n.d., 10) highlights these key shifts:

- enhanced differentiation and complementarity among universities (and with other sub-sectors) to ensure an effective, high quality network of university provision
- increasing collaboration and building critical mass in teaching and research, particularly in postgraduate research degree provision, and in more specialised areas of undergraduate teaching.

This policy shift towards collaboration and complementary approaches for universities is a relatively recent requirement, and not one easily achieved.

With the imperative to widen access, particularly to traditionally under-represented groups, tertiary education institutions have taken a variety of approaches to ensure inclusion and to enable student success. As Florian (2007, 8) states, '. . . when access to education is widened, it puts pressure on education to accommodate increasingly diverse student populations.' This has created challenges for universities.

The holistic approach encourages a collaborative view of student support, whereby all members of the university take responsibility for students' learning and well-being (Kennedy, 2007, 14). In practice, the holistic approach applies on a number of levels. We can speak of a holistic approach to student needs, to student services structures and to university-wide student support. The holistic approach stands in contrast to the deficit model of student services, and to the silo approach that often characterizes the structure and delivery of a wide range of services including library and information services and student learning support, which are the focus of this chapter's case study. This perception that academic services are disjointed from the academic units of an institution is explored throughout the literature. Consequently, the widening participation agenda questions traditional forms of delivery.

Viewing students holistically

A holistic view of student needs is one that recognizes that students are, in Chickering's words, 'not just degree seekers and test takers' (Chickering and Reisser, 1993, 41).' Students have a number of competing pressures: part-time (or even full-time) employment, family responsibilities and social commitments. All come to university with different aspirations for university study, and different approaches to learning (Gosling, 2003, 163). The holistic approach aims to support the student as a 'whole' person: socially, physically and academically. An institution with strongly academic goals for student support will gain from viewing students holistically, since personal and emotional issues have direct consequences for successful study (e.g. McInnis et al., 2000)

Holistic student services

At a wider level, dedicated student support services can also be structured holistically. This follows directly from the view of student support presented above: if students are viewed as complete individuals, then collaborative links among student services staff will be required to respond effectively to students' needs.

Consolvo (2002) describes a number of benefits of a coordinated student services group at a US university. These include:

- enhanced contact with staff and students: 'Faculty and staff refer students to one location and we determine the most appropriate way to meet students' needs'
- more knowledgeable student services staff: 'The organisational structure fosters collaboration . . . all staff learn about service provision in each area'
- better service uptake: 'Students come in for one service and become aware of others'
- reduced stigma: physically grouping personal, social and academic services reduces any stigma attached to visiting individual units, for example for personal counselling.

While reaping some of these benefits involves considerable financial investment – for example, creating a central reception desk for student services – others involve simply a change in outlook for staff. Learning about other support areas encourages staff to consider how all contribute to individual students' outcomes. In addition, regular collaboration among staff can reduce students' perception of being 'passed around' between services (Consolvo, 2002, 286).

Many discussions of student services make a distinction between services which support learners (students) and services which support the learning process (Gosling, 2003; Prebble et al., 2004). It appears, however, that this division is conceptual rather than intended as an organizational structure. Prebble et al. (2004), for example, separate social/emotional support and academic support to emphasize the range of needs affecting student outcomes.

University-wide holistic student support

At its widest level, the holistic approach refers to a collaborative approach to student support involving all staff at an institution. The theoretical basis for this approach derives from the argument that if support mechanisms are to address the 'whole' student, institutions need to build contacts between staff with the relevant expertise to provide this support.

There are many arguments for teaching staff to take an active role in providing holistic support for students. Kelly (2006, 20) makes the point that the one experience 'common to all students . . . is their participation in academic courses'. Teaching staff are at the centre of this unifying context, and therefore in a crucial position to promote the university's goals for supporting students. According to Kelly:

> Providing orientation programmes, mentoring schemes and a range of student support systems, while important, will only lead to student success and retention if the educational setting in which students learn also promotes engagement and connectedness.

The effect of the teaching and learning context on student support outcomes has empirical support. Abbott-Chapman (1998, cited in McInnis et al., 2000, 53) found that students who say they enjoy their courses are less likely to use dedicated support services, and more likely to say they have no need to do so. McInnis et al. (2000) present this finding as an incentive for student services staff to collaborate more closely with teaching staff, especially in environments where one-on-one services are becoming stretched financially.

Researchers disagree as to who in the university should have ultimate responsibility for supporting students. It is possible to imagine a scenario where staff who begin working collaboratively with a student assume that another has followed the student's progress, when this has not taken place. Kinzie and Kuh (2004) studied 20 US college campuses with high engagement and graduation rates, observing that student affairs staff took 'primary responsibility' for supporting students, but that they worked 'in partnership with faculty members . . . to discharge these duties' (Kinzie and Kuh, 2004, 4). In contrast, Barwuah, Green and Lawson (1997, cited in McInnis et al., 2000, 52) argue that in order 'to meet additional student needs, a shift of responsibility is needed from specialist to mainstream staff'. Of course, this statement does not argue for teaching staff to become entirely accountable for supporting students. Articulating and encouraging a balance of responsibility – across all staff groups – is one of the challenges of student support policy within the holistic model. This requires long-term cultural change, to shift attitudes and behaviours.

The entire issue of responsibility is further complicated in that one of the goals often put forward for university study is for students to become independent learners, responsible for their own outcomes. Kinzie and Kuh report that the successful colleges they surveyed support this goal: 'DEEP [Documenting Effective Educational Practice] Schools create structures for shifting responsibility for the student experience to the students themselves' (Kinzie and Kuh, 2004, 6). The researchers present this as one component of the 'widely shared sense of responsibility' they observed at the institutions.

The holistic model and the convergence of services and roles

This chapter has focused so far on the literature concerning student support in general and student services. We see this as directly relevant to the library and information services literature. The forces influencing the shift towards holistic student support strategies have led to what is often termed the 'convergence' of services and roles in many tertiary education institutions. The notion of convergence is particularly prevalent in the literature on library and information services, with an emphasis on convergence between libraries and technology services. This is most notable in the UK literature but is also evident in the US and Australia. Specific drivers identified in the literature include:

- rapid technological changes bringing roles within library and computing services closer together

- new affinities between groups of staff
- acknowledgement that services had to break away from rigid hierarchies and traditional modes of practice
- a new focus on the learner and services based on their needs and not structural and organizational concerns.

Convergence can be defined relatively narrowly as 'the bringing together of the library and computing services, possibly with other separate support services, under the management of an executive director' (Pugh, 1997, 50). Or, more loosely, it can be defined as the bringing together, either organizationally or operationally, of different elements of academic support services (Higher Education Funding Council for England, 1993). Fielden (John Fielden Consultancy, 1993) cautions, 'It would be a mistake to focus just on computing and libraries coming together,' and points to different convergence models between library and information services and other services with responsibilities for IT, staff development, media, reprographics, student welfare and educational development. The concept of convergence can be interpreted in various ways, from the bringing together of structures and operations to an organic approach to developing student support.

Some authors see the concept of convergence physically embodied in the development of learning centres, describing the learning centre as 'a distinctive, learner-centred, response to supporting and improving the quality of student learning' (Oysten, 2003, ix). The real value of this model, according to its supporters, lies in its holistic approach to student learning; consequently, learning centre facilities encompass an extensive range of facilities, support, advice and staff. While each permutation of the learning centre model varies, examples in the UK include the Saltire Centre at Glasgow Caledonia University and in New Zealand the Information Services Building at Otago University.

Whether or not universities invest in a physical learning centre to bring together services for students, we see convergence as a valuable philosophical concept to define the bringing together of different perspectives and practices across a university with the aim of creating a more holistic model of student support.

Case study: Victoria University of Wellington, New Zealand

This chapter now turns to a case study of one New Zealand university in order to illustrate challenges and approaches to developing the holistic student support model. Victoria University of Wellington is based in New Zealand's capital city and is the country's second largest university. In 2007 21,889 students were enrolled, equating to 17,085 equivalent full-time students. These figures exclude students enrolled with the New Zealand School of Music, a centre of musical excellence established by Victoria and Massey universities. The make-up of the student population can be summarized thus:

- 57% women
- 43% men
- 1769 Mâori students
- 1008 Pacific students
- 18,923 domestic students
- 2966 international students.

As previously discussed, the New Zealand government has taken an increasingly interventionist approach to the tertiary sector. Victoria University strategy reflects these government priorities; in particular in its *Investment Plan* (2007a), *Research Strategy* (2007b) and *Pathways to Success* (2007c). The *Investment Plan* sets out the commitments of the university in the use of government funding over the next three to six years, and focuses on several key themes.

Both the *Investment Plan* and the *Research Strategy* highlight the strategic importance of developing research excellence particularly (but not exclusively) in the context of the NZ-wide Performance-Based Research Fund (PBRF): 'Victoria will develop its research capability by focusing on increasing [the] proportion of postgraduate students; raising the individual research performance of academic staff' (Victoria University of Wellington, 2007b, 15).

The *Investment Plan* also emphasizes 'highly effective student support' and Victoria's aim to prepare students 'for citizenship and leadership in an increasingly diverse, technologically sophisticated and complex global society' (Victoria University of Wellington, 2007a, 11). Excellence in learning and teaching, and the development of graduate attributes, are therefore key strategic drivers. *Pathways to Success* provides the framework for this, within the disciplinary context, highlighting the importance of skills development embedded within student learning and the need to consider and enhance the wider student learning experience and environment. An example of a Victoria University policy initiative that focuses on student input and acts as an impetus to academic curriculum and academic services development is a student engagement survey (AUSSE) used to monitor and identify areas of student engagement in teaching learning. Benchmarks can be established through comparison with other Australasian universities using the same survey.

It can be argued that striving for excellence in learning and teaching and also in research in the PBRF context creates tensions. The PBRF rewards academic staff for demonstrated research output, partially replacing funding based on enrolment numbers. Victoria University researchers Morris Matthews and Hall (2006) surveyed staff views and found that 27.8% of academic staff reported a decreased emphasis on teaching since the PBRF was implemented (12). Changes to teaching activities included decreased time spent on 'student advice, fewer assignments and less marking, less quality feedback to students, and greater encouragement of student responsibility for their own learning'.

Victoria University has also embarked upon a capital management plan which sees the university addressing its campus at Kelburn. A master planning approach has been taken that considers the learning, teaching, research and student support needs for the future. The redevelopment incorporates new student accommodation, increased research and teaching space and the concept of a 'Campus Hub'. The Campus Hub aims to maximize new build and reorganize and redevelop existing spaces to revitalize the campus heart. At the centre of this redevelopment is a reconceptualized and renovated academic library that will reflect the world's best practice. The library will interlink and integrate with social learning spaces, student support, student union activities and retail opportunities, providing a one-stop-shop approach for the staff, student and researcher experience. The Campus Hub project therefore has significant strategic potential and could represent a major step change in the conceptualization and delivery of holistic student support.

This case study will now focus on how two specific academic service areas have responded together to this environment: library services and student learning support services (SLSS). Both areas are extremely cognisant of the strategic drivers affecting the university and of the need to respond proactively to university strategy. Both areas have developed strategic plans which reflect this and highlight the importance of collaboration and partnership with academic colleagues and other academic services. Both areas aim to be a true partner in learning and teaching, and see student success as a primary concern. Both areas have a strong joint philosophical approach built on the principle of holistic practice. While the two service areas vary significantly in terms of size, culture and priorities, the similarities emphasized here have provided a strong basis for collaboration. SLSS and library collaboration is still in its infancy (beginning in 2007 with a change in library management and strategy), with joint action planning being developed for a longer-term partnership. The collaboration has been characterized to date by the following initiatives:

- a philosophy of holistic student support shared by the manager of SLSS and the university librarian, which translates into role modelling of collaboration and a commitment to joint projects and goals
- regular meetings between the two senior managers to share ideas, discuss issues and generate new approaches
- meetings of staff from across SLSS and the library to facilitate shared understanding of each area's work, with a focus on supporting the student experience and facilitating student success; this has also facilitated shared problem-solving and peer support
- collaborative work on specific projects, beginning with small steps such as joint approaches to orientation, more joined-up strategies for specific student groups and promotion of each other's services
- an SLSS help desk positioned in the Kelburn Library next to the library information desk, which has had an impact on several levels – there have been referrals between staff and services, increased student awareness and use of SLSS and informal peer observation of student support practices
- planned joint staff development for supporting effective learning
- a joint information channel for student information.

As highlighted above, both services view partnership working with academic colleagues as pivotal to their success in supporting students and view this as a key priority. Examples of collaborative working with academics include:

- new student orientation practices where student services staff and academic faculty work alongside each other
- customized academic skills workshops in course and tutorial programmes
- customized information literacy workshops in course and tutorial programmes.

One planned initiative is to set up a joint assignment planning project that links stages of writing an essay at first-year level with an actual essay topic in a first-year course and with the relevant library resources. This illustrates how the two services will work collaboratively, both together and with academic departments, for direct student benefit.

What we learned and future directions: policy, programmes and people

From our initial experiences on these joint projects, the focal points are around policy (and strategic direction), active programmes and the right people. The vital ingredient for all three is undoubtedly effective collaboration. So what is collaboration? Some would see collaboration as any situation where people work together, but in a university context perhaps Engstrom and Tinto's (2000, cited in Cook and Lewis, 2007) model better demonstrates the degree of involvement required. Although their model was defined mainly with student services in mind, it is a useful framework for any cross-university collaboration.

They model three stages:

- the information clearing-house, where information is disseminated or provided
- co-operation, where groups interact and work together but traditional roles remain
- collaboration, where there is equal respect and a sharing of roles and experiences.

This model shows that collaboration is more than just working together. Successful collaboration (as in the third stage of the model) requires that roles and experiences are shared. Many barriers can stand in the way of good collaborative efforts of this kind in the university setting. Cook and Lewis (2007) have identified the following:

1   Staff attitudes are by far the biggest barrier, whether about students (and whether they 'should even be at university') or about workload ('I don't have time to do this' or 'I have to commit to research'). Changes of attitude present a major challenge that requires a shift from individualistic to holistic approaches across the university as a whole.

2   History can dictate that often the way things have been determines what is expected, and this can become the habit that is hard to break. Simply because we haven't perhaps had a history of collaboration does not mean it is not worth a try.

3   Different cultures can exist in the university setting, between academic staff in different subject areas or between student or administrative staff and their academic colleagues. Crossing the border of these cultures can be daunting but enriching at the same time.

4   Communication is the key, but as universities get larger and workloads increase the opportunities to communicate across the usual barriers can become less frequent.

5   The autonomy of individual groups, schools, disciplines or units can also act as a barrier to improving cross collaboration.

Working to counter these barriers is not necessarily easy, but our experiences of working together have provided us with some insight into what constitutes key enablers. We recognize the importance of sharing a philosophy and goals and valuing each other's professional practice in order to learn from each other. You can break down silos and lack of trust through pan-university projects, and encourage and engage staff in these. We also recognize the value of investing in training and enriching development and project opportunities for staff that will help to change attitudes; collaboration can be supportive and fun. Team-building exercises and collaborative approaches can provide the synergy to overcome huge barriers. We also argue that you don't need to wait for a new building to bring about a change in how you work together.

We have identified numerous possibilities for the future direction of such collaboration, including: integrated publicity materials, integrated workshops, staff development for working in partnership with academics and encompassing other academic services in our approach and the holistic student support model. We would like this philosophy and approach to become a formally acknowledged strategy for Victoria, viewed as a distinctive characteristic of the university and its student experience.

Conclusion

This chapter discusses the holistic model of student support and asks 'How realized is this in practice?' The strategic drivers outlined above and current policy for student support at Victoria University indicate considerable potential for a collaborative, holistic approach to student support provision. The trick will be to gather momentum and cultivate this collaborative approach in order to maximize holistic student support. Policy, facilities and strategy don't necessarily ensure collaboration: there needs to be an emphasis on building staff capacity and skills and a culture of collaboration with support for student learning at its heart. Engstrom and Tinto's third level of collaboration is the ideal, which requires personal and professional commitment. At Victoria we are still working towards this. Moving towards a holistic university is not necessarily a new approach but this case study highlights a different emphasis and angle, being not simply about shared spaces, facilities and services but also about shared understanding, behaviours and beliefs.

References

Chickering, A. and Reisser, L. (1993) *Education and Identity*, 2nd edn, Jossey-Bass.

Consolvo, C. (2002) Building Student Success through Enhanced, Coordinated Student Services, *Journal of College Student Development*, **43** (2), 284–7.

Cook, J. H. and Lewis, C. A. (2007) *Student and Academic Affairs Collaboration: the divine comity*, National Association of Student Personnel Administrators (NASPA).

Department for Education and Skills (2003) *The Future of Higher Education*, HMSO, www.dfes.gov.uk/hegateway/uploads/white%20pape.pdf.

Florian, L. (2007) Reimaging Special Education. In Florian, L. (ed.), *The Sage Handbook of Special Education*, Sage.

Gosling, D. (2003) Supporting Student Learning. In Fry, H., Ketteridge, S. and Marshall, S. (eds), *A Handbook for Teaching and Learning in Higher Education*, Kogan Page.

Higher Education Funding Council for England (HEFCE) (1993) *Joint Funding Council's Libraries Review Group: report* (Follett Report), HEFCE.

John Fielden Consultancy (1993) *Supporting Expansion: a report on human resource management in academic libraries, for the Joint Funding Council's Libraries Review Group* (Fielden Report), HEFCE.

Kennedy, M. (2007) Supporting Staff to Support Students: a literature review with particular reference to Victoria University of Wellington (unpublished).

Kelly, L. (2006) *Pathways to Success: report of the 2006 working group on undergraduate and honours degrees at Victoria University*, Victoria University of Wellington.

Kinzie, J. and Kuh, G. D. (2004) Going DEEP: learning from campuses that share responsibility for student success, *About Campus*, **9** (5), 2–8.

McInnis, C., Hartley, R., Polesel, J. and Teese, R. (2000) *Non-completion in Vocational Education and Training and Higher Education*, Centre for the Study of Higher Education, University of Melbourne.

Morris Matthews, K. and Hall, C. (2006) *The Impact of the Performance-Based Research Fund on Teaching and Learning and the Research–Teaching Balance: survey of a New Zealand university*, report presented at the Symposium on the Evaluation of the PBRF.

Oysten, E. (ed.) (2003) *Centred on Learning: academic case studies on learning centre development*, Ashgate.

Prebble, T., Hargraves, H., Leach, L., Naidoo, K., Suddaby, G. and Zepke, N. (2004) *Impact of Student Support Services and Academic Development Programmes on Student Outcomes in Undergraduate Tertiary Study: a synthesis of the research*, Ministry of Education.

Pugh, L. (1997) *The Convergence of Academic Support Services*, BLRIC Report 54, British Library.

Taylor, J. (2003) Institutional Diversity in UK Higher Education: policy and outcomes since the end of the binary divide, *Higher Education Quarterly*, **57** (3), 266–93.

Tertiary Education Commission (n.d.) *Investment Guidance 2008–2010*, TEC, www.tec.govt.nz/upload/downloads/investment-guidance.pdf.

Tertiary Education Commission (2008) *About the TEC*, www.tec.govt.nz/templates/standard.aspx?id=448.

Victoria University of Wellington (2007a) *Investment Plan*, www.victoria.ac.nz/home/about/newspubs/publications/investment_plan.pdf.

Victoria University of Wellington (2007c) *Pathways to Success*, https://intranet.victoria.ac.nz/academic/documentation/ab16novdocs/0652.pdf.

Victoria University of Wellington (2007b) *Research Strategy*, https://intranet.victoria.ac.nz/research-office/research-strategy/docs/research-strategy.pdf.

3

Widening horizons, dissolving boundaries: organizational change and the seamless learning environment

CRAIG D. STEPHENSON

> The change process, especially transformational change, is a difficult one. Managers and staff members must have not only vision and creativity but also endurance, allies, clear goals, and a well-laid plan. Yet nothing is as rewarding as successfully building scaffolding and helping people use it to reach their goals.
>
> (Woodard, Love and Komives, 2000, 70)

Introduction

Within the UK higher education sector, student services have been, and still are, in an exciting state of flux. The Universities UK and Standing Conference of Principals and Colleges of Higher Education report *Student Services* concluded that student services 'have much to contribute' to student retention and the student life-cycle model, and as a result could constitute 'an important dimension of institutions' strategic planning' (2002, 4). Simultaneously, in the USA, the 'seamless learning'/'learning reconsidered' agenda (National Association of Student Personnel Administrators or NASPA, 2004) has been gathering momentum, emphasizing the notion of shared responsibility for student learning and calling upon student services to play a key partnership role in the student learning experience.

At the University of Cumbria in the UK, both these transformational opportunities have been seized upon in an Anglo-American fusion of holistic approaches to student learning and partnership working. This fusion, and its cause, history and effect, is the focal point of this chapter. The chapter identifies the themes that influenced the transformation, examines the nature of the redesign process and assesses the impact upon the institution, the staff and, most significantly, the students themselves.

The focus of this case study is the recently inaugurated University of Cumbria (UoC) and one of its three legacy institutions, St Martin's College (SMC). SMC was a national provider of teacher education and training, medical professional qualifications (e.g. in nursing, midwifery, occupational therapy and radiography) and courses in the arts, outdoor studies, youth and community and sport science, operating over three campuses (Ambleside, Carlisle and Lancaster) and several sites. The institution had a pre-merger enrolment of about 11,500 students, part-time and full-time, more than two-thirds of whom were adult returners (21 years plus) juggling jobs, family commitments and long commutes. SMC secured taught degree awarding powers in 2006 and university status in 2007. Following the merger in August 2007 with the University of Central Lancashire campuses in Cumbria (Penrith and Carlisle) and the Cumbria Institute of the Arts (Carlisle), the newly formed University of Cumbria was launched into diverse realms of teaching and research. This included forestry, media and design, policing, criminal justice, transport, logistics and further education provision. The University delivers undergraduate and postgraduate courses to over 15,000 students. It is against this rich backdrop of rapid change and expansion that Student Services was re-invented.

Why the change? UK and institutional context

Following the appointment of a new Head of Student Services at SMC in 2002, Student Services was reassessed. It is true to say that at that time Student Services was in its infancy; it was reactionary, pastoral-focused and peripheral to the learning experience – 'the Cinderella of University Services' (unpublished staff feedback, SMC, 2004). It had a strong student focus, but its activities on the whole could be related to that of a hospital emergency unit, dealing almost exclusively with students suffering from specific, often serious, problems requiring immediate redress. This is borne out by student evaluations. Respondents who hadn't used the Service had not done so because: 'I have not needed to at this point of my course', 'I am satisfied with my college experience, I have no problems', and ' [Student Services] do not apply . . . I find support through friends' (unpublished student feedback, SMC, 2004). 'Many HEIs have recognised this is a slippery slope and have moved to more preventative care through more proactive student support models' (Layer, 2002).

The shift in emphasis 'from a reactive, welfare orientated service . . . to a proactive, developmental service that is fundamental to the work of the HEI as a whole, in particular with regard to recruitment, retention and completion, the employability of students and the overall quality of the student experience' required a significant change in the way the service conducted business (quoted in Thomas et al., 2002, 17). The SMC Corporate Plan 2004–9, further emphasized the point when it called on services and faculties to 'provide a truly flexible, student-centred approach to learner support, with central support services working in partnership with individual academic staff and course teams to provide a comprehensive, high quality support framework facilitating student progression, retention and achievement' (SMC, 2004, 5). These cultural shifts in the way we view the student experience required investment by the institution and a broad interpretation of the student journey with all its diversity and stages, as advocated by Layer, Srivastava and Stuart (2002).

This holistic approach was not simply about Student Services' involvement in core activities but about collaborative working practices and dissolving boundaries. 'Effective student support', as one Head of Student Services at a post-1992 university noted, 'is not the province of one particular group of staff or department . . . it is a shared commitment which relies on good working relationships and effective communication' (Aynsley-Smith, 2002). However, the partnership approach goes beyond shared responsibilities and collaborative practices with other key services and the Students' Union. It goes into the heart of academia itself: 'Integration into teaching and learning and the embedding of inclusive practice into academic departments is clearly seen by many as the way forward for student services' (Thomas et al., 2002, 18). Only when Student Services is regarded as a partner in the academic enterprise, rather than as a support service per se, can the holistic approach to the student lifecycle be adopted and seamless learning provision for students assured.

Seamless learning provision, however, is not just about working alongside faculties to support individual student needs, admirable and important as that is. It is also about the role Student Services can play in the personal and academic development of the whole student, 'facilitating and affecting learning outcomes for students' (Fuller and Haugabrook, 2001, 75) and creating 'a seamless learning environment between in- and out-of-class experiences for students' (Kellogg, 1999, 1; Kuh, 1996, 136). A fellow Head of UK Student Services, Kenneth Hopkins (2001, 51), captured it most succinctly;

Like poor children, with our noses pressed against the outside of the window of the candy shop, most of us return to the United Kingdom from our visits to the States wondering how to get at the sweets, how to demonstrate that student support, the whole infrastructure that enables student enrichment and development, is as important as teaching and research – perhaps in the long term more important, both to individual human beings and to society.

Seamless learning: an American perspective

The 'candy shop' analogy is accurate: review the 'Student Affairs' web pages of any mid to large US university and you cannot but be in awe of the range of services and programmes dedicated to student enrichment and development. The University of South Carolina, the author's *alma mater* and host to the National Resource Center for the First Year Experience in Transition, is a case in point. The Student Affairs Division there consists of four key areas: the Office of the Vice President of Student Affairs and Academic Support, Student Development and University Housing, Academic Support and Student Life (www.sa.sc.edu/departments.htm). Within Student Life alone there are 13 service departments focusing on mind, body and soul, ranging from Campus Ministries, Parent Programmes and Alcohol and Drug Programmes through to the Offices of Multi-Cultural Student Affairs, Student Leadership, Community Service, Campus Recreation and Student Government and Organisations. Within Academic Support there is Enrolment Management (where, interestingly, Careers and Student Finance sits), Residential Learning Communities and Student Engagement, each comprising several departments in their own right. Thus, for example, Student Engagement consists of a Student Success Centre, Academic Centres for Excellence, Initiatives for Special Populations, the Creating Academic Responsibility Initiative, Supplemental Instruction and Tutoring and University 101 – and all of this constituting just one strand of one specialist area within a Student Affairs Division.

The candy shop has recently got bigger. Defining learning as 'a comprehensive, holistic, transformative activity' integrating academic learning and student development, 'learning reconsidered' (the latest iteration of seamless learning) is prompting American student affairs units to aspire to become partners in the broader campus curriculum and to co-producing intentional learners who 'can adapt to new environments, integrate knowledge from different sources and continue learning throughout their lives' (NASPA, 2004, 1, 2, 9). 'Such an approach to teaching and learning', the learning reconsidered protagonists argue, 'must include the full scope of a student's life' and 'cannot be accomplished in the classroom alone' (NASPA, 2004, 10).

Consequently, American HE institutions are being called on to bring to bear all of their resources on the student learning process and create 'a new configuration of learning processes and outcomes' (NASPA, 2004, 10). Already regarded as educators with the skill set 'necessary to design, implement and carry out learner-centred approaches', US student affairs professionals are well placed 'conceptually and practically' to work in partnership with academic staff in implementing a transformative, integrated education (NASPA, 2004, 24, 29) – especially when you consider the opportunities they provide to students 'to learn through action, contemplation, reflection and emotional engagement as well as information acquisition', via, for example, student participation in student governance, honour code and integrity systems, leadership and residence life activities, diversity and cross-cultural programming, living-learning communities, community service and peer mentoring (NASPA, 2004, 11). Some student affairs professionals would add that in areas such as classroom dynamics, experiential education and student development processes, they can act as 'accessible and flexible consultants, advisors and resources for faculty members' seeking to reconfigure their pedagogical approaches to academic learning (NASPA, 2004, 13, 18; Fuller and Haugabrook, 2001).

This takes us a long way from the current UK student services' staff experience of, at best, supporting curriculum delivery via the skills and employability route, and, at worst, having little to no role in academic activity. It is arguable, given the two different contexts (many US four-year institutions still largely target traditional-age college students) and student services histories, whether or not the UK is ready or suited for this. However, having worked in student affairs (at the Universities of South Carolina and California, San Diego, 1995–2002) and become familiar with the range of learning opportunities offered to students beyond the formal curriculum (e.g. in areas of leadership, engaged citizenship, cultural competence, cross-cultural understanding, informed decision-making and emotional intelligence) and the value-added impact this has on student learning, I believe there is merit in encouraging student services professionals to engage with the seamless learning/learning reconsidered agenda. Indeed, this point was not lost at a recent annual conference of the UK's Association of Managers of Student Services in Higher Education (AMOSSHE), where the focus was on the student learning experience and a keynote presentation, delivered by a senior US student affairs professional, was on putting 'learning reconsidered' into practice (AMOSSHE, 2007).

Scanning the horizon: pre-restructure considerations

Inspired by this partnership approach to learning and caught in the current of transformative change characterizing higher education delivery, I was able to redefine Student Services at St Martin's College and the University of Cumbria. Reflecting back on the restructure period (2004–5), and considering organizational change theory related to the field, the variables required to secure organizational change and the integration of curriculum and extra curriculum were largely in place (Guskin, 1996; Kezar, 2001; Kuh, 1996; Taylor and Matney, 2007). According to Kuh, with an emphasis on human relations and environmental change theories, the variables necessary for initiating change to achieve a seamless learning environment include:

- an enthusiasm for institutional renewal
- a shared vision of learning
- the development of a common language
- the fostering of collaboration
- a focus on systematic change

(Kuh, 1996, 137–43).

The first of these, an enthusiasm for institutional renewal, was very apparent at appointment, for along with an influx of new senior managers full of 'confidence, enthusiasm and commitment' (Kuh, 1996, 138) and the emergence of 'change agents' among existing staff, I was appointed with a change management remit. This was part of an institution–wide recognition that change across the board was necessary in order to sustain growth, ensure agility in a competitive market and gain taught degree awarding powers and university status.

This enthusiasm for renewal was paralleled by a drive for more learning and less teaching, supported by a corporate plan and a learning and teaching strategy that not only created a common language and shared vision of learning (the second and third variables), but, more significantly, recognized the role services had to play in realizing that vision. The plan's vision for the new student experience was partnership-based and learner focused; 'In partnership, faculties and services will offer a "seamless learning" experience, recognising the need for developmental and educational opportunities beyond the classroom' (SMC, 2004, 5). The learning, teaching and assessment (LTA) strategy, via 'the faculties and partner central services', sought to deliver that vision and embed those values by developing and nurturing 'in our students the key skills, cultural and intellectual capital necessary to maximise achievement, employability, delight in lifelong learning and the ability to make a meaningful contribution to society' (the LTA strategy's core aim).

The inclusion of such language and service references was by no means accidental, and was undoubtedly influenced by the Head of Student Services' role on the Academic Board and other key committees. The strategic positioning, the drip feeding of new language and the nurturing of a collaborative culture created the foundations upon which the restructure could take place (the fourth variable). Moreover, without working alongside faculty staff in drafting support plans for at-risk students, for example, or helping them to facilitate their widening participation and retention strategies or to handle student complaints and well-being issues quickly and effectively, there would have been neither the credibility nor the support there to launch a new structure – one that arguably drew monies away from the faculties and gave the service a much more central role in the life of the institution.

Integrating the shared language and thinking required a systematic approach to change (the fifth variable). Kezar (2001) argues that this approach needs to be under-pinned by planned change and intentional leadership if processes, and not just values, are to be altered and deep organizational change achieved. Establishing leadership, developing strategy, creating objectives and goals, setting expectations, demanding accountability, using external consultants, planning and promoting change and offering incentives and staff development opportunities are the key strategies of planned change (Kezar, 2001, 66). At SMC and, more recently, the University of Cumbria, these are the letters running through the proverbial stick of rock. The Student Services restructure was part of a systematic and planned series of pre-merger restructures which have continued post-merger. These restructures have been co-ordinated centrally and supported heavily by Human Resource input, procedures and guidelines, to achieve success.

Widening the horizon: the restructure

Underpinned by a clear strategy and long-term goals which reflected current think-ing, national agendas and institutional aspirations, the intention was to create a Student Services structure that was student-focused, responsive, pro-active and developmental – something far more substantial than a hospital emergency unit. It had to achieve a balance between support, advisory and operational work on the one hand and preventative, strategic and developmental work on the other. While supporting students with a range of quality-assured, responsive and regularly mon-itored information, advice and guidance services, the structure had to be robust enough to step into the learning arena and take a holistic approach to the devel-opment of students as confident, independent learners. All of this had to be integrated, systematic and partnership-based: no more silo working. The new structure also had to be staff-sensitive, providing professional growth and progression and oper-ating an appropriate reward strategy and pay structure for all Student Services staff. Additionally, it had to meet a need particular to the institution and provide a com-prehensive, multisite approach, assuring equivalence of provision across all campuses and sites. Most significantly, if the structure was to gain approval from the University Directorate and senior colleagues, it had to be cost-effective, affordable and repre-sent value for money. The result? The Student Development and Advisory Service; SDAS for short.

Student Development and Advisory Services

The new SDAS structure replaced service sections (e.g. Money Advice, Disability, Counselling, Learning Support) with integrated services. It focused initially on three key elements: Advisory and Community Support, Academic Skills and Employability and Career Development. At the core of each specialism was a team of advisers and co-ordinators who were specialist practitioners in their field, responsible for ensuring their particular area was embedded into mainstream activity, pro-active and learner focused. Within the Advisory and Community Support specialism, besides the usual suspects (International Student Support, Student Finance, Disability), new roles were created that addressed specific needs such as mental health and student policy implementation and focused on building community and developing living-learning communities. After the University was formed, a fourth specialism, Student Health and Wellbeing, was added, partly to accommodate further education students, not previously supported at SMC, and also to focus this important area more closely for all students across the University's campuses (see Figure 3.1).

Another new and significant dimension of SDAS is the Academic Skills Centre (ASC). The ASC provides academic support for all students wishing to improve their academic achievements, not just those needing learning support. Indeed, the ASC seeks to de-stigmatize learning support and to provide opportunities for students to take control of their own learning and approach ASC staff to enhance their academic performance and build on their existing skills, regardless of ability level. The ASC has also been charged with working closely with faculties and Learning and Information Services (LIS), to complement and strengthen the range of academic skills modules and skills audit tools available and to be a point for informed referral to other experts such as librarians, helpdesk professionals and learning technologists (for discussion of the seamless learning approach between library and student services, see Schmidt and Kaufman, 2007, 242–56).

Similarly, the newly re-aligned careers service, the Centre for Employability and Career Development (CECD), was also directed and resourced to engage more systematically with academics to 'provide a curriculum and learning experience that engages students and prepares them for employment and life-long learning' (SMC, 2004, 15). It was intended that the CECD would further strengthen the institution's corporate employability goals via the provision of impartial guidance and advice, work experience opportunities, exit management and employer liaison. In partnership with the Business Enterprise Unit and the Students' Union, the Centre seeks to enhance a student's life and employability skills and opportunities at every stage of the student life-cycle.

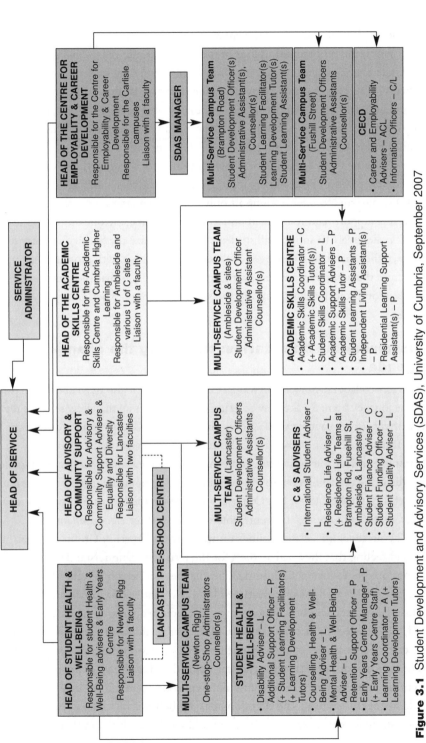

Figure 3.1 Student Development and Advisory Services (SDAS), University of Cumbria, September 2007

The heads of all four services were each assigned a faculty with which to liaise and (significantly for a multicampus institution) a campus one-stop-shop team.

These teams, replicated on each campus and staffed by student development officers (SDOs) and administrative assistants, serve as the first port of call for students and deal with all initial service enquiries, process applications and forms, book appointments and signpost to specialists when required. Whatever the requirement, a student sees a generalist (SDO) in the first instance, trained in money advice skills, disability awareness and the processing of the relevant DSA (Disability Support Allowance) applications, procedures and policies, etc. The SDO is expected to refer or signpost only when the matter is complex and more specialist support required. The intention is twofold: first, the one-stop-shop team work collectively to support all students and normalize the Service's use by students, rather than being perceived as a last resort for those with problems; second, this frees the advisers from the 'work on the ground', so that they have time to focus upon their specialist area and the student learning experience.

Dissolving the boundaries: delivering the change agenda

If greater collaborative working was an end destination, it also needed to form part of the journey. Hence, a Review Steering Group was set up that drew selected representatives from each of the faculties, the Centre for Development of Learning and Teaching (CDLT), Learning and Information Services (LIS), Hospitality and Campus Services, the Students' Union and Human Resources, 'thereby taking the restructuring process deep into the institution and bringing many new people into the effort' (Guskin, 1996, 17). Other key people on the Steering Group were an elected Student Services staff representative and an external consultant.

The presence of a staff member on the Review Steering Group was critical to staff feeling that they had a voice, for the restructure, understandably, was not a comfortable experience for some. The change process can be very challenging at a personal as well as an institutional level. No matter how much staff consultation takes place and how much the new structure addresses the weaknesses of old, the change process may not be without its casualties, for inevitably working practices and 'comfort zones' are challenged, office locations are reviewed, current roles and associated salaries are questioned and, above all, staff are expected to make 'an uncertain leap into an unknown future' (Guskin, 1996, 4). Stark and cold as this may sound, the decision-making behind the changes has to focus upon student need, corporate objectives and service goals rather than individual personalities. The restructuring decisions, as Mielke and Schuh argue (1995, 80), need to be 'consistent with the mission of the institution . . . not what might be most satisfactory to staff or those defending the status quo'.

However, the 'human dynamic' also has to be paramount in the change methodology, for the enthusiasm, dedication, professionalism and commitment of staff is our most valuable asset (Taylor and Matney, 2007). Change managers 'are in a better position psychologically if they can accept that some degree of unhappiness is natural during this phase and [do] not appear overly defensive', and can actually 'create an environment where people are comfortable to speak freely' and their ideas and opinions are valued and considered (Mielke and Schuh, 1995, 82; Woodard, Love and Komives, 2000, 68). The importance of regular staff updates, individual consultations and open forums, to test the thinking and offer critical feedback, can never be overestimated.

This human engagement, dealing 'honestly with people's fears and anxieties' (Guskin, 1996, 12), was part of a managed approach to the change agenda, as was the work of the Review Steering Group. The Group's objectives were to consider the internal stakeholder feedback, current research and sector best practice, and to shape and agree the Head of Student Service's restructure proposals. This was very much an iterative process, conducted over a nine-month period; '. . . revolutionary changes require evolutionary processes' (Guskin, 1996, 13).

The Head of Student Services was responsible for bringing evidence together for the Group to consider, engaging with stakeholders, drafting the initial proposals and maintaining the focus and momentum of the change process. The Head also took responsibility (with student/staff input) for drafting the Service's mission statement, values and objectives – the 'conceptual building blocks' that help form the overall vision and restructure proposal (Taylor and Matney, 2007, 167). The Service Mission – to enable full student participation and progression; empower students to become confident, independent learners; exceed student and staff expectations; and embrace an integrated approach to widening participation, transition and progression – provided a framework on which to hang the new structure (www.cumbria.ac.uk/Services/SDAS/Mission.aspx).

Staff roles, culture and practice

None of this, however, would have been deliverable had the change strategy not included reference to changes in staff roles, culture and practice. In a service area which can so easily disintegrate into an umbrella organization for several silo operations, the content of job descriptions can be significant in drawing staff into teams, ensuring the various specialists have shared goals and cross-service tasks and that they work collaboratively with other areas of the university. The drafting of a new job description for every Service role, and the subsequent selection and training for these roles, was a key element of the re-orientation process. Even those 'slotted in' to roles received a new job description. Consequently, all specialist advisers and co-ordinators had to work within a collaborative framework, and actively partici-pate in widening participation, seek innovative solutions to reviewing hidden demand and develop and deliver peer mentor support and educational programmes for students. Drafting, implementing and evaluating policies/procedures; provid-ing input into strategic and annual operating plans; engaging with equality and diversity issues; and ensuring compliance and application of best practice, these were all key elements of each adviser job description, regardless of role. ASC and CECD co-ordinators also had to operate within a flexible distributed learning con-text and to keep abreast of new developments and initiatives in relation to research, assessment, learning and teaching – and to take a lead accordingly. Overseeing Student Services' engagement with faculty activities, learning and teaching objec-tives and the institution's Skills and Employability Strategy was the collective remit of the SDAS Head and Deputy Heads, but all to what effect?

To what effect? Two years on
External audit

Ofsted inspections for both primary and secondary teacher training were con-ducted independently of each other during the 2007–8 academic year, two years after the last round of inspections; both received 'outstanding' grades. One of the significant differences identified in both inspections that contributed to an 'out-standing' grade was the 'strong partnership' link with university services, namely SDAS and LIS. SDAS, in the primary Ofsted inspection, was selected for special mention, as it enables 'the University to make bespoke arrangements to support school placements and to meet individual needs' (Ofsted, 2008, 6).

Academic practice

Student Development and Advisory Services' mission is to embrace an integrated approach to a student's transition and progression through the University. One example of this focuses acutely on the student learning experience: 'new academic teams' (NATs) were developed within a skills and employability framework, to ensure that academic programmes address 'the skills elements of relevant subject benchmark statements and/or professional body requirements' and meet 'the aspirations of current HE students concerning their employability and further study options'. SDAS partners with LIS, CDLT and the faculties to form NATs and deliver this new agenda. Acting on the premise that 'teaching is no longer the preserve of academics', the Information Fluency and Skills Support Teams within LIS and the Careers and Academic Skills Teams within SDAS pool resources, skills and effort with CDLT and faculty lecturers, 'to more effectively contribute their resources and support to underpin the design and delivery of programmes and modules across the University' (SMC, 2006–8).

Example: case study

The following case study illustrates what this actually means for students. An SDAS (ASC) co-ordinator sets the scene; 'I recently set up a discussion board via Blackboard (the University's virtual learning environment) with distance learning students. . . . the topic was "writing at level 3" and followed a series of materials posted on the site.' The co-ordinator went on to share the content of that Blackboard discussion. 'The most valuable piece of advice I was given from [the ASC coordinator]', one student commented, 'was to turn each learning outcome into a question and proceed to answer that question within the essay.' Another added that they had created 'a file with all the information in, in order . . . to advance onto the next stage of critical thinking'. Indeed, the co-ordinator's focus on the critical thinking stage prompted one of the lecturers to contribute to the discussion and reflect on his own nurse training. He suspected that 'a good number of students (and staff!) cringe at the "critical thinking" stage', adding that 'it is not a way of thinking that the [nursing] profession has historically promoted' (e-mail correspondence with ASC co-ordinator, January 2008).

The SDAS mission

The four elements of the SDAS mission (to enable, to embrace, to empower and to exceed) are beginning to be met. However, progress regarding seamless learning is not consistent across the Service, or necessarily among the faculties themselves. Thus while the notion of new academic teams may be warmly embraced by one faculty, it may not have been as fully considered or even understood by another, and while SDAS may have strong, productive partnership links with one faculty the links with another may be far more casual and less productive. Progress has inevitably been interrupted by the institutional mergers and the launch of the university, which have absorbed time, resources and focus and meant that the momentum to embed seamless learning practice, across all courses and campuses, was temporarily thwarted. In addition, the pace of embedding seamless learning and integrating SDAS into academic practice is somewhat dictated by the number and influence of 'change agents' and 'champions' within the faculties, who recognize the importance of the changes to the teaching–learning agendas and respond to them collaboratively.

Within the Advisory and Community and Student Health and Well-Being units, progress in empowering and enabling students has been much slower than within the ASC and the CECD. Clearly, when a student is working as a residential co-ordinator in the halls of residence, grappling with personal issues during a well-being session, discussing their behaviour under the Code of Conduct or attending a 'Money Doctors' session, then they are enriching their personal skills. All these activities, devised and delivered by SDAS, have the potential to encourage curiousity, challenge ideas and inspire new ways of thinking, and in so doing strengthen a student's learning experience – a critical theme of seamless learning. However, within the more traditional administrative areas, where teaching and learning is not as pronounced or as obvious, more needs to be done to empower staff to see themselves as educators, with the ability 'to engage students in active learning' and 'forge education partnerships that advance student learning' (Kellogg, 1999, 2).

Student residential spaces

University owned and run student residences offer particularly fertile ground for planting the 'seamless learning seed' and linking to more formal learning outcomes and personal development planning. Residential focus groups carried out at UoC during the academic year 2007–8, began to highlight the learning opportunities available outside the formal curriculum. Within the focus groups, for example, when asked if 'their residential experience had enhanced their academic experience, a number of students said they felt it had, and that as a result of living in halls they had 'learnt to be aware of other people and respect their opinions', to 'appreciate diversity and community', to 'give and take' and to 'be independent'. On a practical note, some resident students had also got together and formed study groups. Imagine, then, if a little structure was added to this and the learning potential channelled. For example, SDAS is planning to fund and launch its first living-learning residence community, focused on an international house concept that brings together international and home students in a structured programming environment (e.g. via culture nights, language sessions, 'Ask An In-houser', 'Global Gourmet' and discussion groups to heighten cultural awareness and global understanding (www.provost.ucsd.edu/roosevelt/ihouse). Other living-learning communities, focusing on the environment or on well-being, for example, can also be considered and faculty staff actively engaged in the delivery of these programmes.

Conclusions

Had cost not been an issue (the service salary budget has more than doubled as a result of the restructure and subsequent mergers), and had there not been a need to get the basics in place first (i.e. developing and embedding a credible, functional, effective structure), then more capacity would have been put into the structure and job roles to focus on learning agendas. It is difficult, for example, for the full-time Residence Life Adviser responsible for the residences and residential student teams across five campuses (up to a 90-minute drive apart) to focus on programming activities and creating living-learning programmes when student crises and disciplinary situations need to be prioritized on an almost daily basis. Similarly, the Health and Well-Being Advisers, two full-time staff in post for nearly two years, have been absorbed in handling an ever-increasing number of complex counselling and mental health cases, putting new appointment and monitoring systems in place and rationalizing the well-being services for three newly merged institutions; developing pro-active, student development-focused sessions, for obvious reasons, has not been the priority.

That said, the potential to promote the seamless learning environment in these two areas is there; the changes can and will continue. As Kezar wrote, change is 'essentially never seen as complete because there are always ways to improve processes' (Kezar, 2001, 66).

The change processes within Student Services continue, albeit in an incremental and transitional rather than a transformative way, adapting to an ever-changing landscape of national, regional and corporate agendas. Indeed, the constant evolution of the SDAS structure and organic developments (e.g. the creation of a fourth specialism and the absorption of FE work, more students and courses) is testimony to the robustness and agility of the new structure to respond, adapt and expand within an institution that went on to secure taught degree awarding powers and university title and then merged with two other institutions to create the University of Cumbria. There is only one constant in higher education – change. Organizational restructures have to factor that in, if resources are to be used effectively and new structures are to be fit for purpose over time.

It could be argued, however, that Hopkins' 'candy shop', with its wealth of student-orientated services and development-focused programmes, remains something of an enigma, a distant star. However, this says more about resourcing than it does about values and mindset. Indeed, the change processes have begun to dissolve the boundaries and raise aspirations, such that the University of Cumbria is now favourably placed to engage more fully in the 'learning reconsidered' debate, not just in terms of co-developing curricula, of which there are emergent examples, but also in terms of team teaching, service–faculty-inspired learning communities and co-creating a framework of measurable learning and developmental outcomes. In this respect, UoC is no further away from realizing a co-curricular, faculty–service approach to student learning than many of its American counterparts; there, perhaps, lies the sequel.

References

Association of Managers of Student Services in Higher Education (2007) Putting Learning Reconsidered into Practice. In *Learning for Leadership: leadership for learning, AMOSSHE Annual Conference, 18–20 July, 2007,* www.amosshe.org.uk/content.asp?ContentID=21.

Aynsley-Smith, S. (2002) Widening Participation and Student Support, *Learning and Teaching in Action,* **1**, www.celt.mmu.ac.uk/ltia/issue1/student_support.shtml.

Fuller, T. and Haugabrook, A. (2001) Facilitative Strategies in Action, *New Directions for Higher Education,* **116**, 75–87.

Guskin, A. E. (1996) Facing the Future: the change process in restructuring universities, *Change,* **28** (4), 26–38.

Hopkins, K. (2001) Outsourcing: an English perspective, *New Directions for Student Services,* **96**, 51–9.

Kellogg, K. (1999) Collaboration: student affairs and academic affairs working together to promote student learning. In *ERIC Clearinghouse on Higher Education Washington DC,* www.eric.ed.gov/contentdelivery/servlet/ERICservlet?accno=ED432940.

Kezar, A. (2001) Organizational Models and Facilitators of Change: providing a framework for student and academic affairs collaboration, *New Directions for Higher Education,* **116**, 63–74.

Kuh, G. D. (1996) Guiding Principles for Creating Seamless Learning Environments for Undergraduates, *Journal of College Student Development,* **37** (2), 135–48.

Layer, G. (2002) Widening Participation: the national challenge, *Learning and Teaching in Action,* **1**, www.celt.mmu.ac.uk/ltia/issue1/layer.shtml.

Layer, G., Srivastava, A. and Stuart, M. (2002) *Achieving Student Success: an analysis of HEI widening participation strategies and the proposed impact on student success*, Higher Education Funding Council for England.

Mielke, P. L. and Schuh, J. H. (1995) Ethical Issues Related to Restructuring, *New Directions for Student Services*, **70**, 75–86.

The National Association of Student Personnel Administrators and the American College of Personnel Association (2004) *Learning Reconsidered: a campus-wide focus on the student experience*, NASPA and ACPD.

Office for Standards in Education (2008) *A Primary Initial Teaching Training Short Inspection Report 2007/8*, www.ofsted.gov.uk/oxedu_reports/download(id)/97626/(as)/70128_322930.pdf.

Schmidt, N. and Kaufman, J. (2007) Learning Commons: bridging the academic and student affairs divide to enhance learning across campus, *Research Strategies*, **20**, 242–56.

St Martin's College (2004) *Corporate Plan 2004–9*, St Martin's College.

St Martin's College (2006–8) *Employability and Skills Matrix*, unpublished.

Taylor, S. H. and Matney, M. M. (2007) Transforming Student Affairs Strategic Planning into Tangible Results, *NASPA Journal*, **44** (1), 165–92.

Thomas, L., Quinn, J., Slack, K. and Casey, L. (2002) *Student Service: effective approaches to retaining students in higher education: full research report*, Institute for Access Studies, Staffordshire University.

Universities UK and Standing Conference of Principals of Colleges of Higher Education (2002) *Student Services: effective approaches to retaining students in higher education*, http://bookshop.universitiesuk.ac.uk/downloads/services.pdf.

Woodard, D. B. Jr, Love, P. and Komives, S. R. (2000) Organizational Change, *New Directions for Student Services*, **92**, 61–70.

4

From learning to learner: the role of Learner Support Services in the Bradford student experience

SARA MARSH

Introduction

This chapter discusses the development of Learner Support Services at the University of Bradford, in the UK. The particular nature of our institution and its students is explored, with an emphasis on the relationship between the student body and the institution's approach to learning support activities. In Bradford we have brought together a range of services into one directorate, with the aim of supporting the academic, professional and personal development of our students and staff. This creates benefits in terms of identifying common service aims, making services easier for clients to use and exploiting synergies between teams. The chapter seeks to draw some conclusions about the impact of our organizational changes on the quality of the Bradford student experience.

Bradford

The city

Bradford is one of the ten largest cities in the UK, with a population of just over 400,000. During the 19th century it became one of the major industrial centres in the north of England, producing wool and textiles from its many mills and factories. In the 20th century it became the focus for large-scale immigration, particularly from Pakistan, with migrant workers attracted to the jobs available in the textile industries. Following the decline in these industries Bradford has experienced a continuing need for economic regeneration, which has taken longer to develop than in neighbouring cities such as Manchester and Leeds but which is now well under way. Over 20% of Bradford's population is from minority ethnic groups, and 14% of the local population is Pakistani.

The University

The University of Bradford was established in 1966, its predecessors being the Bradford Institute of Technology and before that Bradford Technical College, which began life in 1882. The University's strapline is 'Making Knowledge Work', which has its roots in the University's industrial and vocational past while reflecting current aspirations in terms of knowledge transfer and student employability.

The student profile

In 2006–7 the University had 14,345 students: 67% were undergraduates; 88% were full-time; 50% had non-white ethnic backgrounds, with 20% of the total student body being Pakistani; and 38% were from the local area. We regularly recruit a high proportion of our undergraduates from lower socioeconomic groups. Around half the students who live locally are from minority ethnic backgrounds, and this reflects the cultural preference among the local Asian community for young people to continue to live at home while studying.

Background to the development of Learner Support Services

The University of Bradford is currently coming to the end of its corporate plan for 2004–9. At the beginning of this period the University was experiencing declining student numbers coupled with poor retention rates, and a relatively low average Universities and Colleges Admissions Service (UCAS) entry tariff (a points-based system that allows potential students to map their prior educational achievement across a wide range of qualifications in order to choose an appropriate course). The estate was in poor condition, with a number of 1960s and 1970s buildings beginning to show their age. Organizationally there was a perception of working in silos with insufficient co-ordination and communication between units.

The University reviewed its approach and has taken a number of steps to address these issues, including investing in an estates strategy and reviewing its learning, teaching and assessment strategies at institutional and school level. New initiatives have been developed to improve student recruitment, retention and attainment, with a particular emphasis on student engagement and the overall student experience. These include:

- bringing together support activities for learning, teaching and personal and professional development to create Learner Support Services (LSS)

- creating the Learner Development Unit (as part of LSS) with a focus on academic and personal skills development for students
- integrating student administrative support functions and establishing a one-stop-shop for related student enquiries, designated 'the Hub'
- developing a series of local support initiatives in academic schools, including personal tutoring and personal development planning for students
- reviewing the role, purpose and function of the Students' Union and its relationship with the University.

The University has made significant progress since 2004. The initiatives above are starting to make a difference, and the institution as a whole has become more proactive and engaged in reflection and review. The rest of this chapter will focus on the work of Learner Support Services (including the Learner Development Unit), outlining the composition and structure of this large and diverse directorate, and highlighting the opportunities and challenges it offers.

The composition of Learner Support Services

Learner Support Services (LSS) has developed following what has become a fairly traditional pattern of convergence. The Library and the Computer Centre had been jointly managed for a number of years, with Management Information Services and Career Development Services joining the planning unit some years later. This expanded service was known as Learning Support Services.

Following the review of student engagement discussed above, a number of smaller support units were brought together with a view to rationalizing provision, building capacity and improving services. Administrative functions such as accommodation, admissions, registry and student finance joined Academic Administration and now deliver their services via the Hub. The Counselling Service and Disability Office joined LSS.

During this same period three other key areas relating to teaching and training joined LSS. These are:

- the Teaching Quality Enhancement Group (TQEG), a small team of academic staff and learning technologists who promote educational development, lead the development of the University's learning, teaching and assessment strategy, and deliver a range of training and support initiatives to assist academic staff in improving the quality of their teaching

- the Graduate School, which is responsible for the provision of research skills training for postgraduate students
- Staff Development: formerly part of Human Resources, this small team delivers a range of personal, professional and organizational development opportunities for staff at all levels.

Finally, the new Learner Development Unit (LDU) was created and located within LSS. The main focus of this small team (four full-time staff with a range of part-time contributions) is to offer personal and academic skills support to all students, particularly in the areas of maths, numeracy and the use of English for academic purposes. The LDU liaises with the Language Unit over teaching English language skills to non-native speakers.

The new Learner Support Services thus comprises: Library, IT Services (including Management Information Services or MIS), Careers, Counselling, Disability, the Learner Development Unit, the Teaching Quality Enhancement Group, the Graduate School and Staff Development. It now represents an example of what might be described as 'superconvergence', where a core of Library and IT functions has been extended to include other elements of student and staff support.

The Society of College, National and University Libraries (SCONUL) identified the issue of 'superconvergence' as a key theme in its 'Top Concerns' survey in 2006. It is described as 'defining and implementing new organizational structures around academic support (wider than Library and IT convergence) by the integration of Library services with other areas of student support ("super-convergence")' (Enright, 2006). An example is given by Mary Heaney at Manchester Metropolitan University, who describes her experience of drawing together a range of student support services to improve student satisfaction and quality of experience as well as creating capacity to invest properly in learning and working spaces (Heaney, 2007).

Team structures

At the time of writing LSS is working towards defining its internal structure. We have proposed four divisions, aiming to bring together those teams which match most closely in terms of their main professional focus. These are:

- Library Services
- IT Services
- Centre for Academic Practice (TQEG, the Graduate School and Staff Development)

- Progression and Support (Careers, Counselling, Disability and the LDU).

There are of course significant overlaps in many areas, and for this reason the formal line management structure is supported by a system of matrix team-working to allow the effective delivery of services.

Library and IT Services have worked closely together for many years, and co-location of most members of these teams within one building has made this easier. Consideration has been given to merging these two teams into one; however, both are large teams in comparison with others in LSS and although there are synergies (e.g. around customer service and electronic information provision) there are also significant differences between IT systems and network infrastructure at one end of the spectrum and the collection development and information literacy teaching activities of the subject librarians at the other. Given also that they are both part of a much larger directorate now, it makes sense to retain these as distinct professional divisions for the time being, but with a shared customer service team providing front line support. The size, composition and management of the customer service team is under review at the time of writing.

Our other two proposed divisions are based on the main synergies between other LSS teams. The Centre for Academic Practice delivers and supports teaching, learning, training and development activities for staff and postgraduate research students. In Progression and Support the focus is on personal, academic and professional development for students, delivered through a mix of one-to-one advice and guidance, informal workshops and accredited taught modules.

Opportunities and challenges

This section outlines some of the key areas in which the new Learner Support Services has made a difference to service delivery and organizational development.

Capacity building

By drawing smaller services into the larger grouping of LSS we have been able to build capacity in these areas. For example, the careers information and reception desk handles initial enquiries on behalf of the LDU as well as offering some support to the Disability Office, while trainers in Staff Development and the TQEG are working together with those in IT services to create a common booking system for training courses.

LSS has been able to raise the profile of some of the smaller services now within its remit, for example the Graduate School and Counselling. Senior managers within LSS have supported the Graduate School in seeking clarity in its staffing model and funding arrangements, and the School is about to recruit some much-needed additional staff and to set up a steering group to provide stakeholder-led focus and direction for its activities. The Counselling service provides support to nearby Bradford College of Further Education as well as to the University. Since joining LSS a new service level agreement has been drafted with College staff, and again a joint steering group for this service is being planned.

The Library and IT Services have worked together for a long period, with a shared service point for front line enquiries. This is 'classic' convergence, and the opportunities and issues this presents have been rehearsed elsewhere (e.g. Akeroyd, 2007; Hanson, 2005). The new LSS offers scope to exploit new synergies between subject librarians (Library), learning technologists (IT) and educational developers (TQEG), both in integrating learning resources within the University's virtual learning environment, Blackboard, and in using blended learning techniques to deliver information literacy skills.

All of the constituent parts of LSS have gained from the opportunity to work more closely together and learn from each other's experience. One example is a recent workshop for all staff involved with teaching and training, at which a number of shared issues were raised and suggestions made for improving future communications. In our planning for new learning spaces we have been able to draw on the wide range of professional expertise available in the LSS senior team.

Service integration

Converged services offer the opportunity to integrate service provision at different levels with the aim of making it easier for customers to get the information and help they need. Within LSS our front line staff are crucial to the success of our service, and one of the challenges in our new structure is to ensure that we have the right mix of people and skills in these key roles. This means balancing generic customer service skills with specific knowledge of particular areas, and getting the right mix of professional and para-professional staff. The concept of the one-stop-shop where trained para-professionals are able to deal with 80% of all enquiries and refer the remaining 20% effectively to professionals (perhaps via an appointments system), appears ideal. However, we also have to bear in mind the wide range of services provided in LSS and take account of expected changes to our physical environment.

We already have a shared service point in the Library dealing with IT and information-related enquiries, and we are planning a refurbishment of the entrance level for this building which involves reconsidering the location and function of other service points including the reception/admissions desk, the security point, the inter-library loans desk and the main Library lending counter.

Promotion and communication

Learner Support Services is a large directorate incorporating a wide range of activities. As described above, these activities relate to each other in different ways, but have largely evolved as separate services. The new structure raises questions about how we promote ourselves and our activities. There is a tension between the desire to integrate services and provide a one-stop shop approach and the recognition that our customers understand concepts like 'Library' or 'Careers' more easily than a generic term such as 'Learner Support Services'.

The question of staff loyalty and professional allegiance is also relevant. It is easier and more natural for staff to associate themselves with their immediate team than with a larger organizational structure, but increasingly we are identifying opportunities for staff to work across teams (and to learn about each other, as described above) so as to develop a sense of belonging within the larger unit.

A cross-LSS public relations group has been established, which is active in planning joint induction and promotional activities. This group has created a small fan-fold leaflet listing the key elements of all LSS services, including opening hours, contact telephone numbers and workshop timetables.

Another cross-LSS team group looks after the LSS website. This site includes a page for each element of the service, but these have been branded consistently to include the strapline 'A department of Learner Support Services' and follow a consistent style (see www.bradford.ac.uk/lss). A shared web page listing all the workshops offered by the constituent parts of LSS now exists, with a common booking system for many of these.

Learning environment

As part of the estates strategy mentioned at the beginning of this chapter there are plans for new buildings and refurbishments which will allow LSS to co-locate services around two key buildings on campus.

Currently the Library, Computer Centre and TQEG share a building (known as the JB Priestley building), with Career Development Services, the LDU and

Counselling located next door in the Students' Union building. Other parts of LSS are distributed around various buildings on campus, including the Richmond building, which is the main administrative centre of the campus. This building also incorporates some academic areas and the student support Hub, as well as an atrium space with a coffee bar, some LSS-supported PCs and a range of informal seating.

At the time of writing our plan is to retain the Library and IT Services divisions in the JB Priestley building, incorporating MIS which is currently isolated from the rest of IT services. A new extension to the Richmond building will house the other two divisions (Progression and Support, and the Centre for Academic Practice) in a facility with the working title of 'Knowledge Exchange'. The latter will bring together key elements of our support activities for staff and students, and will incorporate a range of flexible technology-enabled bookable teaching spaces so as to increase opportunities for academic staff to engage with students formally and informally.

At a recent LSS consultation day, students told us that they liked the study facilities offered by the Library, but wished to be able to bring food and drink into the building so that they could take occasional breaks without leaving the building and losing track of their studies. They saw value in linking the Library building with the Students' Union building next door, as they felt this would increase footfall within the Union building. Although they would welcome some less formal study spaces within the Library, at the same time they were keen to maintain a clear distinction between work and non-work activities.

The Union worked hard to ensure a broad representation of students on the day of the consultation exercise. It was, however, noticeable that very few Asian students were present, despite this group making up a significant proportion of the student population at Bradford. At the time of the consultation the Union was concerned about the future of the Union bar. Given that many of our Asian students are Muslim and do not drink alcohol, it is possible that the event was seen to be related to the future of the bar and therefore not of interest to this particular group. There is a tendency for social life on campus to be divided between the Students' Union building (bar, sports, societies, etc.) and the atrium in the Richmond building. The choice of where on campus to locate different elements of LSS (and indeed the range of services offered by the Students' Union) will have an impact on how different buildings are used by student groups, and we need to be sensitive to these issues as we develop our plans.

Educating the whole student

The University of Bradford takes a holistic view of student support. The creation of LSS with its wide remit and the change of name from 'Learning' to 'Learner' Support Services, highlights the learner as an individual (and not 'just' as a Bradford student). It emphasizes that the role of LSS is to support the individual in their personal development as well as in their academic study and research. (The concept of the 'whole learner' has been discussed elsewhere, for example in the 'learning reconsidered' programme described in Chapter 3.)

The University's learning, teaching and assessment strategy for 2005–9 (www.brad.ac.uk/admin/acsec/QA_Hbk/LTAS.pdf) highlights a number of core educational outcomes which are embedded within the curriculum and supported outside formal teaching by LSS. These include:

- subject and professional expertise
- communication in an information age
- working effectively in teams and groups in the context of an increasingly diverse society
- independence and lifelong learning
- student success and employability.

Academic skills and personal development

While the teaching of subject and professional expertise is primarily the responsibility of the academic schools, Learner Support Services (in conjunction with the schools) supports academic and personal development for our students. Workshops and seminars on IT and information literacy are delivered by IT and Library staff, and an accredited module called 'communication in an information age' has been developed by one IT Services colleague. The workshops provided by the Learner Development Unit cover interpersonal skills as well as academic support for students, including for example time management, dealing with difficult people, managing meetings and handling stress.

Working with others and developing independence

The University places a particular emphasis on helping students work together in teams and groups. This is partly for pedagogical reasons, as we recognize the value of peer learning and peer support (Bradford is leading the group work strand of the LearnHigher Centre for Excellence in Teaching and Learning; see www.learnhigher.ac.uk/learnhigher/index.php/Learning-Areas/Group-Work/ Group_Work.html), and partly a reflection of our diverse student body and our wish to create a cohesive campus community.

One of the challenges in getting students to work in groups is that they tend to gravitate towards the peer groups they formed in school, especially when a high proportion of students come from the local area and continue to live locally. We need to find ways of encouraging students to work outside their established peer groups, and create opportunities for personal development while recognizing cultural sensitivities.

LSS works with the Students' Union to offer training and development opportunities for student course representatives, including a range of workshops and a residential weekend featuring team-building activities. Because of the nature of the student population at Bradford we have found that some students, especially female students from Muslim backgrounds, have not previously had many opportunities to interact with others outside the controlled environments of school and family. Providing 'safe' opportunities for such students to engage with others has been a key feature of our learner development work.

Employability

Students who are confident learners, who are able to use technology and who have a range of interpersonal skills are at an advantage when it comes to seeking employment. In addition to the generic skills taught elsewhere in LSS, Career Development Services teaches a range of accredited modules in support of employability and enterprise, and has close links with all academic schools. The employability rate of Bradford graduates has traditionally been high, but many of our students choose to remain in the Bradford area after graduating (over 40% of UK-domiciled Bradford students who found employment after graduating in 2007 are working in the local area). While this shows that our graduates make a valuable contribution to the local economy, it may also indicate a lack of aspiration to seek employment beyond the immediate local area. Consequently, many students continue after graduation to work in the kind of non-graduate local jobs that they may have had before starting university (or during study). Developing a culture of enterprise and entrepreneurship is especially important in Bradford, where an unusually high proportion of local employers are small- and medium-sized enterprises.

What difference has it made?

LSS staff views

All staff in LSS were invited to contribute their thoughts on how (if at all) the new
LSS structure had affected service delivery and their own experiences. Relatively
few responses were received, which may suggest that for many the new arrangements have yet to make very much difference. For a few, however, there has been
a significant impact:

From the Library:

> I thought this afternoon's meeting [of the LSS public relations group] was an
> excellent example of the wider LSS in action and the benefits closer
> cooperation can generate in terms of a more seamless coordinated service for
> the student. It is not only the joint planning, the picking up of snippets of
> relevant information from a range of different sources both inside and beyond
> LSS (instead of living in silos without knowing the relevant contacts), the greater
> promotional impact, more momentum with more ideas flying around and more
> bodies to contribute – it is also the sharing of good practice and the potential
> application of new technologies in other areas. So synergies and a joined up
> approach are the key benefits that I see.

From Staff Development:

> I feel really proud, when I'm out and about in Coaching and Emotional
> Freedom Technique (EFT) networks and circles, to say that [the University of
> Bradford] had me running EFT sessions for students on behalf of the Learner
> Development Unit (LDU). . . . [The manager of the LDU] and I have never sat
> in the same meeting in my 5 years at the Uni . . . but now that we are both on
> the LSS PR steering group we see each other regularly, and that's how the EFT
> sessions got set up. I think the big impact on me of the re-structuring (it's a
> concept rather than any particular structural outcome) is that I've received the
> message that the Uni is serious about doing whatever it takes to support student
> learners/meet their needs.

From IT Services:

> I think the integrated student workshop programme and [the promotional
> leaflet] would be good examples of how a number of separate units coming

under the umbrella of LSS has provided a more holistic service to students. The LSS Web Group and Promotions Groups might also be good examples of how we have pooled resources/experiences.

From Counselling:

I have always been aware as a counsellor working within an educational setting that there is a raft of support for students that clients can tap into or be directed towards. This sometimes sits uneasily with counsellors who think that they must sort all problems out with the client and do not see themselves as part of a greater whole. However it is also sometimes difficult to be part of the greater whole! The move . . . to LSS has provided an opportunity for the Counselling Service to redefine itself within the University as it has moved from being within a department that 'supports' in a 'looking after' way into a department that considers the support needs of someone as a learner in a holistic sense. Thus psychological difficulties are considered alongside difficulties with writing essays, accessing IT facilities, wondering what career to pursue or finding a particular article, and are not partitioned off as something 'other' that only the few 'suffer' from. It has also expanded *our* referral options, so that we no longer mainly refer to those departments we are familiar with . . . but have an increased confidence and knowledge in referring students on for study skills, computer problems, careers advice etc. Conversely the Counselling Service team has become more familiar to colleagues, and understanding of the nature of counselling will improve as the departments inter-mix through meetings etc. This all has to be good for the service, for LSS, for the University as a whole – and not forgetting of course the many clients who come to us.

And a note of caution in relation to change management from the Learner Development Unit:

My feeling is that the most important thing for LSS, as it has such a crucial front-line service role for students, is that any change be addressed and managed in an emotionally intelligent way. This would mean that there is transparency in every decision, allowing people to feel heard and have their say. This avoids tendencies to thrash out tough opinions or express anger and disagreement behind closed doors. Many feelings like this only leak out into attitudes conveyed to LSS's clients. . . . Perhaps some . . . staff are looking forward to a period of stability and calm once [structural changes are] resolved, allowing them to fulfil their roles without the added burden of 'living in a state of flux'.

Student and external views

As yet there has been no formal evaluation of the impact of Learner Support Services on the student body. However the University has scored well in each of the first three years of the National Student Survey, and scores relating to learning resources have compared well with those of our comparison institutions. Student numbers have increased in recent years, average UCAS entry tariffs have improved and levels of employability are higher. A working group on student retention has been set up, and figures to date show improvements in most areas. Although it is difficult to ascribe these changes to any one development, they do follow on from the review of student engagement discussed in the early part of this chapter, which led to the creation of Learner Support Services and the establishment of the Learner Development Unit, along with the Hub as a focus for student administrative support.

The University underwent a Quality Assurance Agency institutional audit at the end of 2007, and the final report acknowledges the strength of the University's learner-centred approach:

> The University is strongly committed to a student-centred approach to resources and services. Support systems are well-understood and valued by students, who also confirmed that they have access to sufficient library and IT resources. The University offers a very high quality of support to its students. The University's strategic and co-ordinated approach to the development of student engagement and support is identified as a feature of good practice in this audit.
>
> (Quality Assurance Agency, 2008, para 30)

The report also notes the effectiveness of the LSS consultation with students over building plans affecting both LSS and the Students' Union.

Conclusions

This chapter has explained the institutional background leading to the formation of Learner Support Services at the University of Bradford. A focus on student engagement and the student experience has resulted in a learner-centred approach highlighting the personal development of the 'whole student' alongside the academic and professional learning required by the academic programme of study.

This approach is particularly relevant in Bradford, where the student body is diverse (culturally, socially and in terms of educational background) and where the emphasis on group and peer learning is as relevant to students' personal and professional development as it is in the pedagogical context.

The chapter has described some of the ways in which the new Directorate of Learner Support Services is capitalizing on its own diversity in order to build capacity, improve service integration, promote and deliver services and plan for new learning environments. Feedback from LSS colleagues demonstrates that the integration of different professional groups is already having a positive effect on those individuals and the way they situate themselves and their services within the broader context of LSS. There will always be uncertainty over organizational restructuring, and staff are bound to feel anxious, both when changes happen too quickly and when everything seems to take far too long. However, it is important to seize the tremendous opportunity for creativity and innovation that is generated when groups of dedicated, passionate and yet reflective staff come together from different professional backgrounds, and are able to challenge one another in a supportive context to create something new which incorporates the excellent qualities that all bring to the table yet as a whole offers far more than the sum of its disparate parts.

To this extent Learner Support Services has the opportunity to model as an organization the kind of peer-supported learning that we are seeking to promote within our student body. We have moved from a 'traditionally' converged service including Library and IT Services to one which incorporates experts in academic teaching and learning and in personal, professional and organizational development. We have the ability to improve services to staff and students by sharing professional expertise, and we have the enormous advantage of being able to grow and develop as an organization by sharing, reflecting, challenging and growing internally. This is a powerful tool for change management, and one that we look forward to exploiting to the full.

References

Akeroyd, J. (2007) Taking stock of convergence, *Library and Information Update*, **6** (1–2), 50–2, www.cilip.org.uk/publications/updatemagazine/archive/archive2007/janfeb/takingstockofconvergenceakeroyd.htm.

Enright, S. (2006) SCONUL Representatives' Top Concerns 2006, *SCONUL Focus*, **37**, www.sconul.ac.uk/publications/newsletter/37/17.pdf.

Hanson, T. (2005) *Managing Academic Support Services in Universities: the convergence experience*, Facet Publishing.

Heaney, M. (2007) *Towards Superconvergence at MMU*, paper presented at the SCONUL summer conference 2007 in Birmingham, www.sconul.ac.uk/events/agm2007/presentations/heaney.ppt.

Quality Assurance Agency (2008) *University of Bradford Institutional Audit, December 2007*, RG 358 04/08, www.qaa.ac.uk/reviews/reports/institutional/Bradford08/summary.asp.

Part 2

Transformation through delivery: engaging learners by reshaping the learning environment – physical, virtual and temporal

5

Next-generation learning spaces: built pedagogy in action

PHILIP COHEN AND JEN HARVEY

We shape our buildings and afterwards our buildings shape us.
(Winston Churchill, quoted in Space Management Group, 2006a, 3)

Introduction

Founded in 1887, the Dublin Institute of Technology (DIT) is one of the largest higher education institutions (HEIs) in Ireland. It has 22,000 students in six faculties and occupies some 40 buildings around inner-city Dublin. During the next five to ten years, the Institute will move to a new single campus at Grangegorman – a brownfield site of 75 acres on the north side of the city.

In preparation for the move, the DIT Learning, Teaching and Assessment Strategy Committee established the Learning Spaces Group (LSG) and directed it to 'consider the implications of the student-centred "new learning paradigm" on learning spaces, as DIT moves towards Grangegorman'. The Group comprised 17 members: a broad cross-section of staff and students from across the Institute. It reported in November 2006 (Dublin Institute of Technology, LSG, 2006).

This chapter provides the context to the Group's report and content from the report itself, and describes what followed from it. We discuss the application of pedagogical theory to learning space design in one particular institution, and offer a toolkit for others wishing to follow the same path. The practical nature of the work is evident throughout.

Context

Building Ireland's Knowledge Economy set out the country's action plan for the promotion of research and development investment from 2004 to 2010. It called for a step change in such activity, particularly in the enterprise sector, in order to sustain employment and competitiveness in an increasingly global economy 'with the aim of improving knowledge, skills and competence, within a personal, civic, social and/or employment-related perspective' (Irish Government, 2004).

This move from a post-industrial information society to a knowledge society places increasing emphasis on the development of 'soft' generic skills such as communication, team-working and lifelong learning. Consequently, the *National Development Plan 2007–2013* identified as a priority for Ireland the need 'to embed key skills such as learning to learn and ICT, to develop higher order thinking skills' (Irish Government, 2007).

The impact of learning space design

Buildings often reflect the learning and teaching approaches of their time. Thus, the many large lecture theatres on university campuses manifest the traditional notion of pouring content into students' heads; with an expert authority figure at the front, providing knowledge to passive recipients. An active collaborative learning philosophy, on the other hand, would be more likely to be evidenced through interactive studio spaces and small group break-out rooms, where students share and create new knowledge through social engagement.

Torin Monahan (2002) first coined the phrase 'built pedagogy' when arguing that 'the way in which space is designed shapes the learning that happens in that space' (Van Note Chism, 2006). This view was supported subsequently by reports from the Joint Information Systems Committee (JISC) and the Space Management Group (SMG) in the UK and EDUCAUSE in North America. In addition, a number of studies have specifically linked learning space design to student retention and achievement (National Learning Infrastructure Initiative, 2004).

The building and renovation of learning spaces represents one of the largest capital investments for HEIs. There is a need, therefore, to understand what constitutes effective design and how learning space can better become 'a physical representation of the institution's vision and strategy for learning' (JISC, 2006, 6). For example, if the intention is to produce information-literate, team-playing, problem-solving graduates with effective communication skills, then this should be evident not only within the design of the curriculum but also within the design of learning spaces and other supporting infrastructure.

Many traditional standard classrooms appear sterile and unstimulating; seating arrangements do not allow for peer-to-peer exchanges and the technology does not provide individual access to information as required. In order to address such issues, JISC (2006, 3) recommends that the design of learning spaces should be:

- *flexible*: to accommodate both current and evolving pedagogies
- *future-proofed*: to enable spaces to be re-allocated and reconfigured
- *bold and creative*: to energize both staff and students
- *supportive*: to develop the potential of all learners
- *enterprising*: to make the space capable of serving different purposes.

Like most other HEIs, DIT has a student population that is becoming increasingly diverse. Innovative learning, teaching and assessment practices have emerged in response, building upon educational research and learning theories. The design for the new campus at Grangegorman, therefore, has to sustain the present character of the Institute and predict its future as well.

Changing technologies

Information technology has changed what we do and how we do it. New and evolving technologies facilitate anytime, anywhere learning, making it possible to study off-campus – in work, at home or elsewhere. 'Blended' learning, a mixture of face-to-face and IT-supported learning, has become commonplace in parallel to the rollout of institutional virtual learning environments. At the same time, wireless technologies have started to blur the boundaries between academic and social arenas, enabling more intensive, well-serviced use of space for teaching and learning. With imaginative design, therefore, the same space can be deployed flexibly to accommodate multiple uses. These emergent technologies, however, will not result in significant reductions in overall space utilization; instead, more smaller and more adaptable spaces will be required in future.

Technology provides opportunities for students to take greater control of their own learning – designing projects, sharing ideas and planning future work. It has the potential to enhance participation in the classroom by increasing student engagement through the use of simulations, games or problem-based learning, with students engaged in these activities working in teams around small tables (and able to see each other) and creating highly interactive dynamic learning environments.

Small break-out rooms situated beside larger flexible spaces facilitate both private and shared collaborative study. Ubiquitous wireless networks mean that students can readily search for information on the internet, engage in joint project work or use learning objects to illustrate specific points. Facilities that have wireless keyboards and mice make it easy for students to present from where they sit. Mobile technologies and PDAs may well replace these in years to come.

Considering technological requirements early on will ensure that maximum benefit can be obtained from longer-term investment in physical space design and management. Thus, an institution's pedagogical aims will need to be clearly identified prior to any support infrastructure review if current, and indeed future, aims are to be achieved.

In addition, timely, appropriate support will need to be in place to facilitate and encourage any necessary changes in practice. An e-learning support team was established at DIT in 2002, to assist academic staff in the optimum use of technology to foster student learning. Most programmes now offered by the Institute have an online presence and increasing numbers utilize blended learning. As a priority, stakeholder groups have been involved in the design of new physical and virtual learning spaces so they might better serve innovative course delivery.

Institutional demands on space

HEI space demands in the future will be affected by the mix of full-time and part-time learning, the extent of off-campus or work-based learning and changes in subject preferences from science, technology and languages (SMG, 2006b).

Most learning spaces are currently defined by their designation as lecture theatres, laboratories or studios, for example. Space is controlled and usage measured through timetabling schedules, hours of class use, seating arrangements and predetermined learning activity. As a resource-saving issue, however, there is a drive for HEIs to manage existing space more efficiently rather than develop additional space. This might be achieved by extending the working day, shifting space ownership from departments to the institution as a whole, establishing centralized timetabling systems and generally using space more flexibly. Institutions are also working to reduce the number of contact teaching hours and encouraging students to engage in more self-directed learning.

At DIT, the LSG recommendations and Grangegorman planning activities have stimulated discussion relating to the availability of different kinds of learning spaces, both centrally and in faculties. However, one challenge already facing the provision of non-faculty spaces relates to their long term upkeep, since funds would need to be re-allocated to ensure regular maintenance and renewal.

Changing pedagogical practice

In recent years, various initiatives have been established to develop and evaluate changes in pedagogical practice that support learners better. Centres of Excellence in Teaching and Learning (CETLs) and Teaching and Learning Research Centres have been established in the UK while the Strategic Innovation Fund (SIF) in Ireland supports a national 'change agenda' across HEIs. Outcomes from all these projects will be employed to direct and promote the effective implementation and use of learning environments and to inform the next generation of learning tools and support services.

Increasingly, as more self-directed learning approaches are utilized, students will spend more of their time outside formal classes. Frequently, these informal learning engagements are more meaningful as students and their peer groups explore academic work or other topics. Spaces that encourage social interaction and impromptu meetings can contribute to personal and professional growth. A positive recent trend, therefore, has been the recognition of learning space as distinct from teaching space – particularly the provision of generic learning space that addresses a range of different needs and enables different ways for students to work, including unstructured or independent working.

This trend is particularly noticeable in the planning of libraries and learning resource centres, where increasingly space is provided for students to work together in groups. Many libraries now have relaxed prohibitions on noise, food and drink to produce more congenial surroundings and 24-hour opening is becoming the norm, for parts of buildings at least (SMG, 2006a).

Although new student-centred curriculum models have evolved, there seems little suggestion that the use of lectures will reduce in the near future (SMG, 2006b). The lecture is still considered a cost-effective way of teaching large numbers of students, particularly in their first year of study. Indeed, some HEIs are now building new larger lecture theatres, as increased student numbers resulting from modularization mean that existing lecture theatres are too small. More creative design of these spaces (e.g. horseshoe-shaped layouts for better eye contact) and easier-to-use technologies such as electronic voting systems mean that lectures can now incorporate more interactive learning opportunities.

Supporting changing practice

While the provision of informal learning opportunities has the potential to realize a truly student-led rather than teacher-led approach, new learning spaces will not in themselves promote collaborative inquiry in students. There is need to educate all students and staff (both academic and support staff) about the effective use of such spaces and about optimum pedagogical practice. Strategies need to be implemented at the same time to support changes in learning, teaching and assessment practice that will promote greater interaction, creation of more cohesive campus communities and feelings of ownership – both of space and of learning activities (see Chapter 6).

Appropriate academic development for all staff will help provide a baseline knowledge of learning theories, methods of delivery and instructional design to ensure they have the necessary skills to provide constructively aligned curriculum design. Timely continuing professional development (CPD) will then encourage appropriate changes in practice as new technologies emerge.

Students also need to understand how best to use the new opportunities available. Some of them will have experienced student-centred learning before higher education and they may have little fear of technology. However, they will not necessarily be proficient with that technology or with academic writing, information literacy or cognitive skills. Learning how to learn within a new environment may be the most important lessons that HEIs provide, by enabling students to experiment with, develop and be assessed upon key transferable skills embedded within subject-based curricula.

With so many possible options, it is a significant challenge to plan and then manage new dynamic learning spaces that function effectively by motivating learners and teachers alike. Smith (2008) identified a number of strategic design and operational issues related to learning spaces, revealing widespread use of personal technologies both on and off campus and a growing requirement for spaces that facilitate collaborative and social learning to support individual needs.

Oblinger (2006) argued that institutions can create learning spaces that will transform their ability to teach current and future students by taking the following actions:

- identify the institutional context
- specify learning principles meaningful to that context
- define the learning activities that support these principles
- develop clearly articulated design principles
- create a set of requirements
- determine a methodology for assessing success.

Such actions are now being implemented in DIT as part of the Grangegorman planning process and, more immediately, in the work of the Informal Learning Spaces Group (see below). In addition, new academic staff in the Institute are now required to undertake the Postgraduate Certificate in Third Level (HE) Learning and Teaching. Further CPD courses are provided for all staff to ensure they are equipped with the skills to embed student-centred approaches in their teaching.

This section has considered various factors that currently influence the design of learning spaces (see Appendix 1). It was within this context that the DIT Learning Spaces Group did its work. Key findings from the LSG report are presented next.

Key findings of the DIT Learning Spaces Group

The LSG worked quickly, with three sub-groups investigating physical spaces, pedagogy and change management respectively. Their findings were edited to produce a final report (Dublin Institute of Technology, LSG, 2006) that included recommendations for both the Grangegorman Planning Group and others preparing submissions to the overall planning process.

The recommendations are shown in Appendix 2. Reflecting the speed of their compilation, they are indicative and functional rather than exhaustive and refined. Despite this, the Group was successful in having them placed high on the planning agenda.

The issues identified here and in the appendices are intended to serve as pointers for others reviewing their own learning spaces. The presence of queries in the text below indicates that some issues were not resolved by the LSG or subsequently.

Variety of learning space provision

Different students will have different needs, as will the same students at different times:

1   It was recognized that learning opportunities must be afforded through a variety of spaces, including spaces for informal or social learning as much as those designed for formal learning.
2   There is considerable variation between faculties and subjects as regards preferred size of class groups.
3   Additional work is needed to determine the ideal mix of class sizes, particularly given the possibilities provided by modularization to combine groups of students.
4   An institutional decision is required regarding the effective maximum size of groups, taking into account a range of issues such as pedagogy, resourcing and student experience.

5   Additional work is needed to ascertain the genuine requirements for specialized spaces (e.g. dedicated laboratories). These are the most inflexible and the most expensive spaces to provide.

Design standards for learning spaces

High quality benchmarked standards for all learning spaces should be established and maintained:

1   The DIT environment should be fully accessible to all. This will impact upon aspects of design such as signage, and provision of assistive technology and wheelchair access.
2   All spaces that are used for learning and teaching should have a minimum provision of learning technology equipment.
3   The standards are to be informed by potential learning activities and learner needs (e.g. small group work, individual private study spaces) rather than just class sizes per se.
4   An appropriate balance needs to be struck between subject or course identities and integrated institutional approaches, in order to facilitate multidisciplinary programmes and integrated projects.
5   Flexibility rather than inflexibility of space design needs to be prioritized, so that learning is not limited by lack of available facilities.
6   There should be a move away from inflexible classroom furniture – for example, desks are to be more comfortable, with multi-use options.
7   All furniture is to be appropriate to higher education adult learners.
8   The location of learning spaces and the proximity of different learning spaces is important if a range of different kinds of learning is to be encouraged.
9   Design of learning spaces should be undertaken by professionals with recent expertise in the design of such spaces. It must be informed by pedagogically sound practices and up-to-date standards.

Shared space

The sharing of learning spaces is to be actively promoted:

1   There are potential conflicts between formal and informal learning, learning and social space, and quiet and noisy areas. What needs to be managed? Who will manage it? And how?

2   There are issues around access to staff. Should there be separate and/or shared spaces for staff and students? Can staff be more available to students at certain times?

3   Should we classify spaces as, say, Type A (all uses) or Type B (only specific uses)? Or have multiple uses of the same spaces, perhaps by integrating different subject disciplines, entirely or partially?

4   The use of space for formal or informal learning will change over time – different rooms at different times will be used for different activities. Thus there will be a continuum of use that requires maximum flexibility of facilities.

Management of learning spaces

What needs to be done, by whom and how?

1   The initial allocation and continuing control of learning spaces should be determined by means that are both equitable and transparent to all the DIT community. Who should control this process, and should it be done centrally or locally?

2   There is clear need for an effective central timetabling system that is directed by learning activities.

3   Should access to learning spaces be 24/7 or limited? To some or all spaces? And should different people have different rights of access?

4   How is such access to be controlled? Is there a cost-effective smart card? What are the health and safety issues?

5   There is a need to provide technical (especially IT) support for students and staff, and to think more about just-in-time support for off-campus and independent learners. This could be provided by students or online or both.

6   Learning materials and other resources must be readily accessible and easy to use for all learners and staff at all times.

Pedagogy

In order to put pedagogical theory into practice:

1   Appropriate policies to support changing pedagogical practice must be developed, building upon existing DIT best practice where possible. Changes need to be implemented in the short-term, as evaluated pilot studies.

2   Technology and other resources should be driven by pedagogical concepts and planned. Who are the DIT students of the future and how might we best address their needs? Pedagogical changes should be in line with those needs and future allocation of funding (e.g. for mature students and non-traditional learners).

3   Learning spaces must be managed according to pedagogical need.

Support infrastructure and training

Staff and students should be trained to use new methods in new spaces:

1   The training of staff (both academic and support staff) and students in the appropriate use of learning spaces is essential, especially as regards optimum use of non-formal learning spaces. There may be a need to encourage take-up of such training.

2   Evaluated pilot spaces should be funded in order to promote changes in practice now, rather than waiting for the future. These pilots should include training, as above.

3   The use of students employed as tutors or mentors to their student peers works successfully elsewhere. This should be actively investigated at DIT.

4   There is a need to make explicit and promote best practice that will assist in the transition to Grangegorman, such as catering for non-traditional groups and providing support that will attract new student groups.

5   Early adopters within DIT should be encouraged to disseminate throughout the Institute the lessons learnt in pilot studies.

Management of change over time

Change is the only constant:

1   There will be a continuing need to make incremental changes – building on current best practice – as we move towards Grangegorman.

2   Changes to pedagogy and learning spaces are interlinked. Will they happen together or must one precede the other?

3 Will increased access to laptops, WiFi, and PC kiosks mean reduced need for PC laboratories? If so, will the space and other resources released be used for informal learning spaces?

4 DIT should create its own solutions, learning from examples elsewhere.

5 There may be a need for culture change in some parts of the Institute to overcome 'us and them' 'silo mentalities'.

6 All staff and students must engage now with the potential that arises from the move to Grangegorman.

7 Managing pedagogic change – as well as change to administrative and other processes – has to be central to the activities of any DIT change unit.

Informal Learning Spaces Group

As noted above, the original remit of the Learning Spaces Group was to consider the design of learning spaces 'as DIT moves towards Grangegorman'. Members of the Group were invited to present their report to a number of Institute committees in early 2007. Shortly afterwards, their recommendations were endorsed by senior management and adopted as policy by the Grangegorman Project Team. In particular, it was recognized that there was need for change in the short term, before any move to the new campus.

Formation

In May 2007, the present writers took the initiative and convened a new ad hoc group to progress the development of 'informal' learning spaces at existing DIT locations. Informal spaces were chosen because they were few in number at the outset, they were central to the promotion of more student-centred learning, they could be located in underutilized space and they promised relatively quick, high-profile success for modest outlay.

The self-styled Informal Learning Spaces Group (ILSG) met irregularly. It had no formal terms of reference, no earmarked budget and its membership was fluid. However, it was able to achieve much in its first year and much more was expected for the future. At the same time, working in parallel, the DIT Learning, Teaching and Assessment Strategy Committee initiated a number of projects to support student development of 'key skills towards employability' through the creation of accredited modules embedded within subject discipline programmes.

The work of the new ILSG was informed by recent literature relating to the effective design of learning spaces (EDUCAUSE, 2008; JISC, 2006, 2008; SMG,

2006b; Temple, 2007) and by the experience of other institutions such as the University of Auckland's Kate Edgar Centre, Glasgow Caledonian University's Saltire Centre, the Warwick University Learning Grid and Sheffield University's Information Commons.

Modus operandi

Initially, members were invited to join the Group through personal contact. As the work progressed, and word spread, others were keen to join of their own volition. Nobody was turned away. Thus a small number of dedicated enthusiasts – staff and students – came together from a variety of professional backgrounds, concentrated on practical outcomes and got things done.

Early on, ILSG evolved some rudimentary guidelines:

1   One size does not fit all. A range of different spaces would be developed in order to test different ideas.
2   The Group would develop at least one new informal learning space in each of the existing main buildings, in order to maximize their impact.
3   Some spaces may be more successful than others. This was both inevitable and welcome since the work was part of the Grangegorman development process and valuable lessons could be learnt from supposed 'failure'.

Funding

As noted above, the Group had no specific funds to implement its proposals, but several members were budget holders in their own right and they used resources at their disposal where they could. The real breakthrough, however, came towards the end of the financial year when bids were invited for capital expenditure. The Directorate of Academic Affairs at DIT encompasses a number of academic support services, all reporting to the same senior manager. By working together, the heads of those services secured €30,000 for a joint bid to finance the implementation of informal learning spaces across the Institute.

With the Academic Affairs funding as a lever, it was possible to secure further matched funding from most of the faculties – for spaces that were of direct benefit to their own students – and from the central Buildings Maintenance and Information Services departments. Altogether, approximately €90,000 has been spent so far.

An additional source of support was the Strategic Innovation Fund. This Irish government initiative invited bids for proposals for 'new approaches to enhancing quality and effectiveness within higher education' (Strategic Information Fund, 2008). An application for funding was submitted for a project to evaluate the effectiveness of informal learning spaces and to plan for their wider adoption. The bid was successful and at the time of writing a one-year post to undertake the research is to be advertised.

Sample spaces created

A number of the informal learning spaces are described below. Most of those implemented to date have been relatively inexpensive and occupy existing space that was underutilized previously.

Mountjoy Square: 'the Purple Place'

The basement area of this building accommodates a canteen and other student facilities. One end has been delineated by painting the walls a distinctive purple colour and introducing low movable screens. Benching and two blackboards have been fixed to the walls, WiFi and three PCs have been installed and casual seating and tables have been provided. The space was immediately popular and christened 'the Purple Place' by the students themselves. The name has stuck and the branding replicated at spaces elsewhere.

Aungier Street: Java City and lecture theatre crush areas

Part of the ground floor of the Aungier Street building is occupied by a large coffee bar, with one half of the area comprising low casual seating. Students naturally congregate here and sometimes undertook group discussion work here previously. By the simple addition of WiFi access, this group work has greatly increased.

Two small lecture theatres on the upper floors have relatively large crush areas at their entrances, used occasionally for providing refreshments at conferences but largely unused and neglected. Both areas now have casual seating and low tables, WiFi, and artwork fixed to the walls to differentiate the space. Use of these areas for informal learning has been disappointing to date and promotional activities are being considered to make students more aware of them.

Kevin Street: snackery and annexe foyer

This 1970s building has a large soulless canteen, with a mezzanine 'snackery' serving light refreshments. Existing tables with benches seat six to eight students. The addition of WiFi access, a small number of desktop PCs and some casual seating has transformed the snackery into a vibrant internet café, which is popular with students for both group and individual study.

Outside the canteen is a foyer that serves as one of the main entrances to the building. It has a small shop in one corner and was generally cluttered with a plethora of ATMs and vending machines, some redundant. The area has been tidied, the machines reorganized and PCs have been installed on stand-up benches for quick access to e-mail, student timetables and similar information.

Bolton Street: PC kiosks and courtyard

An in-house carpenter designed and constructed a number of kiosks to house standard desktop PCs here. These are located at strategic points throughout the building – near entrances and outside lecture theatres – in space that was previously under-utilized. The kiosks are extremely popular, with queues of students waiting to use them at busy times.

A courtyard to the rear of the building has been selected as an external learning space, with WiFi access and patio furniture, including umbrellas. The area is sheltered and already popular with smokers so it is expected to be heavily used whatever the weather.

Rathmines: student common room and foyers

Having learnt from experience in other buildings it is planned to install a mix of WiFi, casual seating and bench-top PCs. Students here have seen developments elsewhere and are demanding their own enhanced facilities. This in itself is taken as endorsement of the work done at the other sites.

Work continues

The ILSG completed its first phase of work within a year. All the main buildings had informal learning spaces functioning or planned, and the original Purple Place was about to be launched officially.

Simple observation shows that all the new spaces are well used and informal comments from students are overwhelmingly positive. The SIF project referred to above will enable formal evaluation of all the spaces, to ascertain what works best and what can be improved. Then the Group will be able to refine guidelines for future developments. Meanwhile, further spaces will be created, wherever opportunities arise and whenever funding allows.

Conclusions

A number of important lessons have been learnt from the work so far.

Both the initial LSG and its successor the ILSG comprised a diverse group of staff – from a range of central support services and academic disciplines – and students, based at different sites around the Institute. Some had a history of working together already, while others did not. However, they all shared a common interest, a willingness to collaborate and a positive attitude to change.

Progress to date has been uneven. Undoubtedly, quick wins have been achieved with the informal learning spaces while other, bigger changes have been slower. Some basic principles, however, have been accepted by the Grangegorman Project Team and it is hoped the master plan for the new campus will make them explicit.

The ownership of space is highly political, with great sensitivities surrounding its use. This militates against large-scale changes and raises questions about ongoing management of recent developments.

Changes to physical space have not been easy. However, they have proved much more successful than changes to pedagogical practice and institutional culture generally. In order to maximize benefits from developments in space utilization, it is important to implement pedagogical developments at the same time.

Further research is needed to evaluate use of the new spaces and to identify better the support requirements of each.

Difficulties aside, early evidence from the ILSG pilot projects indicates significant engagement by students. They use the space responsibly and demand more. This is hugely encouraging for believers in student-centred approaches to learning.

Acknowledgements

We thank our colleagues on both the LSG and the ILSG, as well as the students and staff of DIT generally, for their enthusiastic participation in this work.

References

EDUCAUSE (2008) *Learning Space Design Constituent Group*,
www.educause.edu/LearningSpaceDesignConstituentGroup/5983.

Irish Government (2004) *Building Ireland's Knowledge Economy: the Irish action plan for promoting investment in R&D to 2010*,
www.entemp.ie/publications/enterprise/2004/knowledgeeconomy.pdf.

Irish Government (2007) *National Development Plan 2007–2013, Transforming Ireland: a better quality of life for all*,
www.ndp.ie/documents/NDP2007-2013/NDP-2007-2013-English.pdf.

Joint Information Services Committee (2006) *Designing Spaces for Effective Learning: a guide to 21st century learning space design*, Higher Education Funding Council for England, www.jisc.ac.uk/uploaded_documents/JISClearningspaces.pdf.

Joint Information Services Committee (2008) *Planning and Designing Technology-rich Learning Spaces*, Higher Education Funding Council for England,
www.jiscinfonet.ac.uk/infokits/learning-space-design/more.

Learning Spaces Group (2006) *Report to Learning, Teaching and Assessment Strategy Committee*, Dublin Institute of Technology.

Monahan, T. (2002), Flexible Space and Built Pedagogy: emerging IT embodiments, *Inventio*, **4** (1), 1–19, www.torinmonahan.com/papers/Inventio.html.

National Learning Infrastructure Initiative (2004) *Leading the Transition from Classrooms to Learning Spaces*, EDUCAUSE.

Oblinger, D. G. (ed.) (2006) *Learning Spaces*, EDUCAUSE,
http://net.educause.edu/ir/library/pdf/PUB7102.pdf.

Smith, R. (2008) *Designing Spaces for Effective Learning*, Higher Education Funding Council for England, www.jisc.ac.uk/uploaded_documents/Ros%20Smith.ppt.

Space Management Group (2006a) Space Management Group report 2006/10, *Impact on Space of Future Changes in Higher Education*, SMG,
www.smg.ac.uk/documents/FutureChangesInHE.pdf.

Space Management Group (2006b) *Space Management Project: summary*, SMG.

Strategic Information Fund (2008) *Strategic Innovation Fund*, www.hea.ie/en/sif.

Temple, P. (2007) *Learning Spaces for the 21st Century: a review of the literature*, Higher Education Academy,
www.heacademy.ac.uk/assets/York/documents/ourwork/research/Learning_spaces_v3.pdf.

Van Note Chism, N. (2006) Challenging Traditional Assumptions and Rethinking Learning Spaces. In Oblinger, D. (ed.), *Learning Spaces*, EDUCAUSE, 2.2,
www.educause.edu/learningspacesch2/11900.

Appendix 1 Potential drivers for change in space usage

	Reduced use of space	Changed use within existing space	Increased use of space
Changes in institutional planning and management	Extended teaching day/week/year Improved space management tools Increased student:staff ratios leading to unit space savings Revised staff working arrangements, including teleworking Outsourced infrastructure functions	Restructuring of functions Changed mix of teaching and research Enhanced community use of facilities	New central infrastructure functions, e.g. quality assurance and marketing Increased student and staff numbers Increased research needs, of staff and students Higher standard and/or more extensive student facilities New health and safety or access demands
Changes to learning and teaching	Increased use of distance learning Workplace-based learning	New teaching methods, including IT use and blended learning New mix of student group sizes More flexible use of space Changed approaches to library use More social/informal work space	Changed subject requirements
Changes in subject disciplines	Reductions in the size of workshop and laboratory equipment	Changed equipment needs	New research fields, requiring specialist facilities

Source: Adapted from Space Management Group (2006a) (with permission)

Appendix 2 Recommendations of the DIT Learning Spaces Group

1 The Grangegorman campus should both accommodate and epitomize a student-centred learning paradigm, as outlined in the DIT *Strategic Plan 2006–2009*. This will require a cultural shift now plus practical changes in the short and medium term, based on current best practice.

2 Support pedagogical development and improvement. Policies relating to pedagogy and learning spaces should be implemented in parallel.

3 Consultation with all stakeholders, including students, should be paramount at all stages of the planning and implementation process.

4 Spaces have to be easily accessible by all, including those with disabilities.

5 A range of learning spaces that are bookable by both staff and students should be provided for different types of learning (formal and informal), some with 24/7 access.

6 A robust, transparent and equitable room booking system is essential, to engender confidence among staff and students that appropriate space will be available when required.

7 Learning spaces must accommodate formal timetabled events but we must plan also for the informal non-timetabled use of space for independent learning. A significant percentage of space should be allocated for this purpose.

8 Learning spaces should embrace the following key concepts:
   • flexibility
   • access
   • comfort
   • electric power
   • technology
   • information access (e.g. tv, radio, internet)
   • variable lighting control
   • sustainability
   • ambience – comfortable, well-designed, welcoming
   • 'decentredness' (rejecting notions of the 'sage on the stage').

9 Spaces should be flexible in order to accommodate different types of learning activities (e.g. in terms of furniture arrangement and/or network access). Spaces should be transformed easily, according to current and future needs.

10 All learning spaces should be designed to include a standard level of technology – to be specified in line with best practice, founded upon pedagogical principles. All spaces should be wireless-enabled.

11 Provide efficient, low-cost and environmentally friendly printing and photocopying services.

12 Facilities, equipment, management and organization should not be a barrier to space usage. All spaces should be seamlessly available, with appropriate support as required.

13 Top slicing of resources – setting aside a central fund of money that all departments contribute to – will encourage shared usage, and will finance ongoing maintenance and upgrading.

14 All learning spaces should be centrally managed and operated in order to optimize effective usage. A high proportion should also be student-managed.

Accountability for space is necessary, with the possible introduction of notional charging for usage.

15 A balance should be achieved in terms of the distribution of different kinds of learning spaces, according to pedagogical and faculty objectives (i.e. a 'fit for purpose' approach). Draw upon best practice internally and externally to encourage implementation and change.

16 Staff and student training for optimum use of learning spaces should be explicit, integral and continuous.

17 A central DIT area is required, to act as a resource centre with examples of best practice.

18 Develop different virtual learning spaces providing personalized and managed learning opportunities. Make available a range of different programme and support options to facilitate choice for students.

19 Encourage the involvement of past students by enabling their access to appropriate spaces and activities.

20 Offer a variety of restaurants, coffee shops, bars, sports halls, theatres, exhibition spaces and outdoor areas for disseminating, collaborating and sharing learning.

21 Provide spaces for reflection and the practice of different religions.

Source: Learning Spaces Group,
Dublin Institute of Technology (2006)

Place, pedagogy and people: learning facilitation in flexible learning spaces

MARGARET WEAVER AND HANNAH HOUGH

Introduction

Many institutions are fundamentally reconsidering the role of space and its impact on student learning and tutor engagement, and are configuring their learning environments accordingly. It is timely to reflect on progress and to listen to students, supporters and tutors who are using such spaces, in the context of widening participation, new curricula and pervasive learning technologies. This chapter will critically examine one of these 'voices', that of the supporter of learning, and aims to reveal how learning spaces are influencing the student experience in UK higher education. Using the Learning Gateway at the University of Cumbria as an exemplar, the authors concentrate on the support designed for that space and the views of a team of learning facilitators. Their personal reflections demonstrate the ways in which the space has, or has not, been conducive to learning. Implications for the future will be drawn out specifically highlighting the opportunities for innovative support roles and partnerships made possible by effective learning facilitation.

Context

There has been a transformation in the conception of space and its role in student learning, influencing the redesign of our most fundamental academic structures: institutional, physical, pedagogical and virtual. Consequently libraries, common rooms, corridors and even the outdoors are all part of an extended and holistic learning environment that fundamentally redefines universities and colleges in the 21st century as learning leaves the confines of the traditional classroom. Further and higher education institutions are utilizing space in diverse ways to remain effective and competitive, and to more readily engage students (Joint Information Systems Committee, 2005). Many educational systems are embracing the change from school to university, and the 'philosophical shift' (Malenfant, 2006) that accompanies the introduction of such developments. Most would agree it is a significant cultural change. Staff who support learning in our new learning spaces are central protagonists.

The global rethink of learning space and its role in education emerged from a reconsideration of the characteristics of future learners, particularly their use of and attitudes to technology (Oblinger and Oblinger, 2006; Watson, 2007). It recognized that student-centred learning is complex, situated and possibly more fulfilling when active pedagogical approaches promoting deep rather than surface learning are adopted. In the UK, Dearing was first to suggest that networked learning and access to ICT for learning and teaching would become pervasive (National Committee of Inquiry into Higher Education, 1997). It has become so, with the result that the relationships between space and learning, technologies and learning, and learning and support are converging, impacting on student, tutor and supporter roles.

To understand this phenomenon more fully and how place, pedagogy and people might connect, it is helpful to reconsider briefly their respective positions in higher education before describing how one institution, the University of Cumbria, responded to this agenda in the UK.

Place: the discourse on learning spaces

The discourse on learning spaces spans several cognate areas – education, psychology, architecture, the built environment and the arts – and is dominating the literature of academic support professions, notably librarianship.

Organizational theory offers insight into the complexities of spatial and psychological relationships in organizations. Hatch and Cunliffe explain how space and hierarchy are closely connected, as exemplified by the Hawthorne experiments of the 1950s, which found that an improvement to a person's working environment (such as better light) and/or being observed, had a positive effect on work productivity. Further, Hatch and Cunliffe make clear the link between the built environment and power, whereby organizations use space as a cultural symbol, or manipulate physical artefacts (including technology) for material expressions of some form of control (Hatch and Cunliffe, 2006). This view is given credence by Caldwell's observation of the 'movement of librarians away from locations and functions that express their power' (Caldwell, 2006). Latterly some of that power has been devolved to students through implementation of 'third age' learning spaces offering opportunities for institutions to engage with students in ways that did not previously exist.

Hatch and Cunliffe also observe:

Movement in space causes humans to associate certain experiences with particular places which in turn allows physical structures (built spaces) to evoke meaning for their occupants.

(Hatch and Cunliffe, 2006, 222)

These meanings and experiences are the subject of this chapter, as contextualized by learning spaces and by the supporters of learning at one institution whose voices to date have been largely undiscovered and undocumented.

Technology-rich learning spaces

The term 'technology-rich learning space' has developed in UK further and higher education to describe a conceptually different 'classroom' in which active learning takes place using appropriate learning technologies, and is student-centred rather than tutor-centric. These spaces might be located in libraries, teaching blocks, study halls, student accommodation or corridors, connecting their inhabitants virtually via wireless and online learning environments. They fundamentally redefine the university 'campus' including service delivery, support and ways of working.

Often space configurations are founded on a judgment of whether to build new premises or to adapt existing premises; in many cases the decision is not straightforward. Strategic capital build programmes and value for money frameworks, and the need to optimize space utilization (Space Management Group, 2007) and reduce costs, can be tangential to enhancements in learning and teaching, and particularly its measurement (Roberts and Weaver, 2006). So, as one might expect, there have been a variety of implementations across the sector.

Commons and collaboration

In the USA the shift referred to earlier is epitomized by the rise of the Information Commons (IC), latterly termed the Learning Commons, and there are many descriptions of its approach (for a helpful overview and origins of the IC, as conceived by Beagle, see Spencer, 2006). Sinclair suggests that Commons 2.0 is extending the IC concept with a focus on collaboration, wireless connectivity, social software and 'human-centred' design (Sinclair, 2007). In Australia the design, demonstration and evaluation of three distinct types of learning environment are currently being evaluated: fourth-generation libraries, collaborative learning centres and advanced concept teaching spaces (University of Queensland, 2006).

In the UK the Joint Information Systems Committee (JISC) is leading the debate on learning space and its integration with institutional priorities, ICT infrastructures and student perspectives (JISC, 2006). A recent report by the JISC concerned with the design and management of open-plan technology-rich learning and teaching spaces suggests there are several 'commons' denoting the 'sociality (and orality) of learning' (Watson, Anderson and Strachan-Davis, 2007, 9). See Chapter 13 for an analysis of the Information Commons at the University of Sheffield, UK.

The evolving student experience

The boundaries between student social behaviour, home life, academic study and use of IT are blurring as the 'net generation' enter higher education (HE). This is equally true for mature students who already balance work and family commitments and for whom using IT enables the juggling of many requirements: 'The differentiating factor may not be so much one person's generation versus another; the difference may be in experience' (Oblinger and Oblinger, 2006, 11).

How can staff working in these new environments successfully mediate this diverse experience so that the individual student benefits irrespective of prior engagement in learning or with technology?

One way is to consider the design of support roles at the conceptualization stage of any space project. McDonald mentions the need to include the 'oomph factor' and employ the architectural drama that underlies psychological elements concerned with student learning (McDonald, 2006; Watson, 2007). The authors of this chapter contend that support for users of the space similarly needs to have the 'oomph factor' and be outcome-focused.

As alluded to in Chapter 1, space redesign can itself be the catalyst for change. For example, Watson describes how the creation of the Saltire Centre at Glasgow Caledonian University led to structural change by converging the formerly separate departments of Library, IT and Student Services to allow 'holistic . . . delivery of the student experience' (Watson, 2007, 255). Church outlines how the Information Commons at the University of Capetown resulted in a restructure and a continuum of service that provided 'synergy between the user support skills of (library) reference staff and production skills of media staff' for one-stop-shop referral and guidance (Beagle, 1999, quoted in Church, 2005, 78). What these examples demonstrate is a universal commitment to a comprehensive convergence of resource to better facilitate student learning and a desire to think about multi-disciplinary team working in the new HE learning environments. Academic libraries are in an ideal position to broker new partnerships between other student-centred services as long as they have flexibility of approach and are prepared to adapt (Church, 2005). Sinclair puts it succinctly: '. . . the ability to work together and understand each other is critical to our collective future' (2007, 6).

These examples demonstrate a universal commitment to a comprehensive convergence of resources to better learning, and a desire to think about multidisciplinary working in the new HE learning environments.

Pedagogy: discourse on the learning environment

The science of learning and the role of the learning environment in student learning is a contested area. What we can be sure of is that technology and the students themselves are transforming the conditions required for learning (see also Chapter 1).

The changing learning environment

While the research literature in relation to learning styles and learner conceptions has matured since the 1980s, and terminology has been clarified and accepted, research into the effect of the changing learning environment on students and approaches to learning has been slower to emerge. There is not yet a common definition of what constitutes a learning environment, despite many studies into student perceptions of it and into the role of technology as a mediating factor.

To fill this gap, the term 'blended learning' is being used to describe a hybrid model of learning that encompasses a mix of traditional teaching, online learning and independent problem-based learning (Bliuc, Goodyear and Ellis, 2007). These developments are radically changing the learning landscape, not least in the area of learner support, and the facilitation of learning is acknowledged to be taking place without tutor intervention as students become self-regulated learners. As a result learning facilitation is taking on more prominence, from a wider range of perspectives, than the previous 'remedial' support which has been the focus to date – as commented on by others in this book (see Chapter 3).

Self-regulation is also a recurring theme in the educational literature and is very much linked to the competence model of higher education, which relates to ability to perceive certain actions and patterns through a variety of lived experiences:

> Regardless of the teaching method or educational arrangement used, variation must be present in the learning environment in dimensions corresponding to the aspects students have become capable of discerning. (Bowden and Marton, 1998)

The flexible learning spaces emergent in further and higher education are indeed providing this differentiation – through the features of their space and its technology, through their mix of formal and informal facilities and through the staff and peer support given and received by students. One might also assume that active learning facilitation and dialogue can assist learners to discern their learning tasks more readily.

These reconsiderations refocus the role and remit of the academic library and support services, and serve to legitimize their integration into the wider learning environment; they are undoubtedly having an impact on staff roles. While there are many accounts of the former, to date little has been written about the nature of these new roles in our blended libraries and learning spaces, or indeed their value to student learning, which we define in this context as learning facilitation.

People: the discourse on learning facilitation in an HE setting

There is no consensus on what higher education institutons (HEIs) mean by learning facilitation, although in the further education sector the term is better understood. Lifelong Learning UK (LLUK) – the independent employer-led skills council responsible for the professional development of staff working in further and higher education and libraries – has developed a role profile for learning support practitioners (LLUK, 2007).

However, this draft profile does not encompass the pedagogical skills needed for support in new learning spaces, focusing as it does on supporting the pastoral, welfare and core skills of students that are needed for progression and transition across the education system. The British Learning Association (BLA) takes an even broader view, identifying three variables that impact on how learning support for adults is implemented: the type of organizations involved, the location of the learners and those involved in the support. The BLA suggests that timely tailored support is necessary – the so-called 'human touch' (BLA, n.d.).

A broad sweep of the literature on learning support in higher education reveals that learning support does not exist as a strong discipline in its own right. It appears to fall between the traditions of various professions in HE such as librarians, IT support professionals, career advisors and study skills professionals, each with its own view and professional standpoint. However, this does not mean that it is not happening on the ground.

The case study below focuses on the 'voice' of one such support role – the learning facilitator, a role specifically created by one institution.

Pedagogy into practice case study: the Learning Gateway at the University of Cumbria, UK

The University of Cumbria is in the north-west of England, and was recently formed from three HEIs. These three institutions have been through a major transformation, following the publication of Sir Martin Harris' report in September 2005 proposing the creation of the University of Cumbria from 1 August 2007 (Harris, 2005). The University's base is in Carlisle, near the border with Scotland; it serves a largely rural population of 490,000 and seeks to raise aspirations to higher education on the west coast of this region. Around half the county is designated as National Park or Areas of Outstanding Natural Beauty. Factors such as the dispersal of communities, the economic profile of Cumbria and its problematical geography and communications mean that many of the traditional ways of conceiving student learning are no longer appropriate.

Design concept

The Learning Gateway, opened in April 2006, embodies the vision for flexible learning in Cumbria. The Learning Gateway is one of the first spaces in the UK, if not the first, to embody collaborative learning principles (Weaver, 2006, 124), and to interpret these through the design and ethos of its space, suggesting rather than imposing how the space might be used. It was included as a case study of innovative learning space design in the JISC InfoKit that brought together exemplars of technology-rich space implementations in further and higher education establishments in the UK (JISC, n.d.).

The aim of the space is to offer complete flexibility, combining comfort, social and informal space alongside more formal settings with embedded ICT, and to support academic staff in experimentation with blended learning delivery on and off campus. The design recognizes that students are not passive in their learning and have varying needs, often studying at a distance. The building is predicated on the assumption that a space with learning at its centre would have a distinctive look and feel and would have a positive impact on students and how they learn. It is also student-owned space, with wireless connectivity, laptop loans, real-time video conferencing, streaming and interactive polling, and a mix of social, community and open areas to foster collaborative working and informal groupings. A team of learning facilitators with newly constructed job roles provide support, managed within Learning and Information Services (LIS).

Adaptive implementation

The key to any effective learning environment is responsiveness to learners' needs. The Learning Gateway has continuously evolved over the two years it has been open. Ongoing evaluation of the user experience (for both students and staff) by survey, facilitator interviews, feedback forms and formal liaison with academic departments has provided the facilitator team with a wealth of information. Procedural amendments have improved the service to visitors of the Gateway, and many comments have given the learning facilitators an insight into the roles and responsibilities that will have the greatest impact upon those requiring support.

As expected, a large amount of time was invested shortly after the building was opened on the practical implementation of the technologies. Many new systems required troubleshooting, and changes were made to ensure continued resilience of the services. Flexible use of technology can bring unexpected issues around compatibility, and these had to be resolved very quickly, which required technical skills throughout the facilitator team and good links with technical support. Some changes have been led at the institutional level, developing the service to meet the requirements of the institution and departments within. Expectations of the applications of the building have varied greatly among potential stakeholders. Various cross-service partnerships have developed to integrate this concept space into existing norms on campus, while also driving step change in learning and teaching.

Numerous conferences and experimental days have been hosted within the Gateway space – a use not envisaged to this extent at the outset. Traditional conferences, such as the University Teaching and Learning Fest, the North West Academic Libraries Conference and the Higher Education Academy Health Sciences and Practice Festival of Learning, have taken advantage of the technologies in the flexi rooms and large social spaces within the building. External groups choose to use the space for meetings and celebrations, enjoying the environment of the building and the adaptive furniture that can be used for most occasions. The Gateway has also enabled the development of more innovative events such as digital art showcases, which have displayed new digital forms of art throughout the building and transformed the Gateway into an art gallery for the evening, enabling students studying at the University to exhibit their work to the public. Links with the Events Office, Catering and Estates have been essential to ensure a professional service for both internal and external events.

On a day-to-day basis the staff and students working within the Gateway have dreamt up their own uses for its flexible spaces, from building tepees, timing paper helicopters as they fell from the top floor and clearing the furniture for drama exercises, to planning projects on the interactive whiteboards, watching and discussing videos and speed dating for a 'get to know each other' session.

The flexibility of the space clearly promotes innovative learning and teaching for all users. New ideas bring new puzzles for the support staff in the building to solve. Offering the furniture and tools is just the first step: there then follows a cycle of experimentation and discovery as the environment is explored. The relatively new role of learning facilitator must evolve and develop alongside the learners.

There are many ways in which the building could adapt further, with new technologies, new spaces and new partnerships, but each new concept requires careful planning and evaluation to ensure that it will truly add value to the space, and specific attention must be paid to how this can be taken forward by the support team, and how the staff can work together to sell the new concept and mentor the users of any new pedagogical application.

Evaluating the learning facilitator experience

Roberts and Weaver outline the importance of critical evaluation studies to assess the impact of technology-rich learning spaces, pointing to the prize of gaining new insights into the learner perspective (Roberts and Weaver, 2006, 96). This chapter extends this work by presenting the lived experiences of learning facilitators (the Gateway team) and their ongoing engagement with the Learning Gateway through a series of qualitative encounters.

The learning facilitator voice: 'No two days are the same . . .'

The role of the learning facilitator is clearly both challenging and exciting, with daily revelations as the cultural shift in learning unfolds. The staff within this role may have arrived from a library/information professional, educational or technological background, but all three skills sets are essential. This multifaceted role develops continuously, requiring enthusiastic dedication to the pedagogical underpinning of these changes in learning. This section investigates several key elements of this new position within the information service, drawing on comments made by the facilitation team at the University of Cumbria.

The lack of structure and history to the learning facilitator role means that we have had to, and continue to, create an identity within LIS and the University.

The creation of the Learning Gateway at the University of Cumbria led to an initial culture shock because it was so different from existing provision. Many services and teams already established in the institution needed to re-evaluate their roles, as the Gateway concept overlapped with many existing structures. This was intended; the Learning Gateway would not be effective if it did not draw upon and extend existing practices in higher education (e.g. connecting online learning and group study facilitation). The space was designed to enable these processes and act as a catalyst. The role of the facilitators was clear on paper, but in practice how would these facilitators interface with learning technologists and lecturers?

At an institutional level the Head of LIS ensured that the Learning Gateway was debated by all the major committees and embedded in the University's learning and teaching strategy, to facilitate continued buy-in and understanding from senior management, students and academics. Interest and understanding grew most strongly, however, when students and staff used the facilities and support, and commented on their intrinsic value.

> *Initially people were unsure as to how to use the space and what the Learning Gateway staff were there for. We suffered an identity crisis and we have worked to promote the service and the building.*

Over time, the learning facilitators developed their own role, complementing the existing processes around them. Many discussions took place to clarify boundaries where one service stopped and the facilitator service began; this not only led to effective collaborative working but helped to identify the responsibilities that the learning facilitators needed to focus on.

Discussions with academic staff enabled the facilitators to envisage ways in which their work could support lecturers and tutors, promoting the assets of the building for flexible working, encouraging enthusiastic staff to become innovative champions for the space, supporting the development of the service and advocating the benefits of the learning space to their peers.

> *We have built up a rapport with our regular users, both staff and students.*

Once the initial phase of advocacy had passed, many regular users were seen within the building. Some students enjoyed working in a social environment on the ground floor; others tucked themselves away in the quiet private study areas at the top of the building. These regular visitors were a valuable resource for the promotion of the building, bringing friends and colleagues with them and engaging more people with the service available.

The team requested users to complete a survey, investigating the common uses of the building and ways in which the service could support them further. It was found that many of the initial users were not capitalizing on the technology within the building. The space was being effectively used but the interactive white boards and polling software was undiscovered.

Working with an academic or student over a long period of time, and seeing how their skills and enthusiasm for the technology grows, is very rewarding.

Although the Gateway facilities were publicized across the campus, many users were hesitant about experimenting within the flexi rooms. This demonstrated one of the major cultural shifts required within the institution: students and staff had not previously had equity of access to hi-tech study spaces and students could not book rooms independently of lecturers, so it took a while for them to see the benefits.

The facilitator role was key to this change, with helpful staff moving around the building, encouraging students to try the technology and use the rooms for their work. As the students developed trust in the facilitators and confidence in the services on offer they began to experiment, with positive results, as they were keen to learn new skills in which they could see real application and value to their studies.

At the start of the new academic year we tried a new approach to raise our visibility to students. Integrating the 'Introduction to the Learning Gateway' into the learning advisors' sessions with PCGE students ensured that we were able to advertise our training sessions effectively to a captive audience. This worked brilliantly!

A series of training workshops were created, designed to take first-time users through the basics of the equipment and introduce more advanced users to interesting features of the technologies on offer. An emphasis on practical experimentation during the sessions empowered the users to gain the practical skills needed and encouraged peer support during workshop exercises.

Each session had a clear pedagogical focus, giving examples of how the different tools could be used for different aspects of teaching and learning. This was intended to encourage greater use of the equipment and more interactive, flexible learning scenarios that could be embedded within course curricula.

Being successful in our bid for the University 'Enhancing Learning and Teaching' project has created a great opportunity for us to develop closer working relationships with academics. We are really looking forward to working collaboratively with them to embed interactive whiteboard technology effectively within their teaching sessions.

Academic applications of the Learning Gateway facilities have highlighted the necessity of partnership between the learning facilitators and the learning advisors (subject liaison staff) within LIS. It is taking time for the importance of flexible learning to take hold within certain areas of the university. The champions and early adopters are already using the space so it is critical that the facilitation team finds new routes to promote the service.

'Buddy' sessions take place between the two sets of LIS staff every month to keep the two teams up to date with each other's actions. This has been a key partnership for promotion of the service. Learning advisors sit on academic committees and build links with course teams that the facilitators cannot. This not only encourages staff to visit the Gateway team but also leads them to consider flexible learning methods within their course developments. Gateway training is now embedded into key courses at the point of need to equip students with the skills required for effective engagement with non-traditional learning.

Expectations of our skills and role have grown and continue to do so.

It is positive to see that the complexity of enquiries in the Gateway has increased. Many staff are beginning to think of innovative applications for the technology – some of which the facilitator team had not previously considered. Professional development plans have been followed to ensure that all members of the team can provide parity of support to all users of the building but the long-term vision of the role keeps on growing, and with it the skills set needed by the Gateway staff.

The team is keen to continue developing and is committed to further promotion of the true potential of the building, and to responding to service demands in a timely way. The university recognized the work of the learning facilitators by awarding the team a teaching fellowship in April 2008. The reflection and review process undertaken by the team is thus becoming embedded in practice and, as alluded to by Lindsey Martin in Chapter 10, is a significant element in team development and role negotiation.

We now have a 'blog' in order to keep visitors to the website updated on the 'goings-on' in the Learning Gateway. It is exciting to be able to reach our users (and potential users) in this way.

To encourage first-time users of the building to try something new, and to give regular users new ideas, the Gateway team maintains a weblog of all the interesting pedagogical activities taking place within the space. The facilitators keep a reflective log of the different scenarios they see and support, and share the most exciting ones through the website. The team has received many positive comments about this resource and enjoy sharing exciting case studies of flexible learning events (University of Cumbria, n.d.).

The entire Learning Gateway website is currently under review, the aim being to organize the existing information into an intuitive pedagogical structure. The team also hopes to include video clips, audio files and interactive photographs to fire the imagination of potential users.

Room bookings have increased and we regularly source alternative places for users to access the space and technology they need.

The success of the facilitator role in the Gateway is evident, as students and staff are jostling for space at peak times. The team is conjuring up new ways of using the space to enable access to the facilities for all at busy periods. This by no means suggests that the job is done; the team must continue to grow and respond to users' demands on a daily basis.

There is also only one Learning Gateway at the multisite University of Cumbria. It is not feasible to replicate the team across all sites, but as the learning technologies are introduced into classrooms and study spaces across the institution the team has a new role: a role of leadership and dissemination. This is a challenge the team are ready to take on.

We are at an exciting time in our development; we have taken the first steps and have worked hard to get a strong set of training materials together for face-to-face sessions based in the building. We now need to get out to different campuses and are addressing how to reach distance learners and staff at remote campuses who we may never meet.

Conclusions

Higher education institutions that support blended learning have very different learning environments depending on their institutional context, space planning strategy, learning and teaching strategies and culture. There is growing fusion of the physical and virtual spaces we occupy, at work, study or leisure, and consequently the services we offer to our communities are also changing. The latter are increasingly defined by updated notions of studentship informed by a reconsideration of what constitutes a holistic learning environment and the learning support within it. This chapter has argued that both are significant shapers of the student experience.

We conclude that roles designed to embrace the pro-active and individualistic nature of learning, via facilitative practice in redesigned learning spaces, have the potential to assist experimentation by students, tutors and ourselves. We have evidence that the space is indeed a motivating factor for academic staff, students and learning facilitators alike, encouraging them to try out new tasks and engage with each other differently through the space and the technology.

There are more voices to uncover, however, and we intend to continue to research the precise nature of the dialogue between all stakeholders. As this book attempts to demonstrate, librarians and other professional groups are responding positively to the new paradigms of 21st-century learning, changing the way they think and work and diversifying their roles in order to remain at the forefront of student enhancement services. Understanding the new pedagogies of place will determine the library's future role and influence.

References

Beagle, D. (1999) Conceptualizing an Information Commons, *Journal of Academic Librarianship*, **25** (2), 82–9. (Quoted in Church, J. (2005) The Evolving Information Commons, *Library Hi Tech*, **23** (1), 80.)

Bliuc, A.-M., Goodyear, P. and Ellis, R. A. (2007) Research Focus and Methodological Choices in Studies into Students' Experiences of Blended Learning in Higher Education, *Internet and Higher Education*, **10**, 231–44.

Bowden, J. and Marton, F. (1998) *The University of Learning: beyond quality and competence in higher education*, Kogan Page.

British Learning Association (n.d) *10 Steps to Develop Learner Support: a guideline through the key issues*, BLA.

Caldwell, T. (2006) Future Shock, *Information World Review*, **225** (June), 19–22.

Church, J. (2005) The Evolving Information Commons, *Library Hi Tech*, **23** (1), 75–81.

EDUCAUSE (2005) *Learning Space Design in the 21st Century*,
www.educause.edu/ir/library/pdf/nli0446.pdf.

Harris, M. (2005) *Initial Proposal for a New University of Cumbria*,
www.hefce.ac.uk/NEWS/hefce/2005/cumbrep/#dwnld.

Hatch, M. J. and Cunliffe, S. (2006) The Physical Structure of Organizations. In
Hutch, M. J. and Cunliffe, S., *Organization Theory*, Oxford University Press.

Joint Information Systems Committee (2005) *E-spaces Project*,
www.ldu.bham.ac.uk/other/espaces.shtml.

Joint Information Systems Committee (2006) *Designing Spaces for Effective Learning: a
guide to 21st century learning space design*,
www.jisc.ac.uk/whatwedo/programmes/elearning_innovation/eli_learningspac
es.aspx.

Joint Information Systems Committee (n.d.) *Planning and Designing Technology-Rich
Learning Spaces*, www.jiscinfonet.ac.uk/infokits/learning-space-design.

Lifelong Learning UK (2007) *National Occupational Standards for Learning Support
Practitioners: learning support role description*,
www.lifelonglearninguk.org/documents/learning_support_roles_draft_nov07.p
df.

McDonald, A. (2006) The Ten Commandments Revisited: the qualities of good
library space, *Liber Quarterly: The Journal of European Research Libraries*, **16** (2)
104–19.

Malenfant, C. (2006) The Information Commons as a Collaborative Workspace,
Reference Services Review, **34** (2), 279–86.

National Committee of Inquiry into Higher Education (UK) (1997) *Higher
Education in the Learning Society* (Dearing Report), HMSO,
www.leeds.ac.uk/educol/ncihe.

Oblinger, D. (2006) *Learning Spaces: e-book*,
http://net.educause.edu.ir/library/pdf/pub7102.pdf.

Oblinger, D. and Oblinger, J. (2006) Is It Age or IT: first steps to understanding the
Net Generation, *California School Library Association (CSLA) Journal*, **29** (2)
(Spring), 8–16.

Roberts, S. and Weaver, M. L. (2006) Spaces for Learning and for Learners:
evaluating the impact of technology rich learning spaces, *New Review of
Academic Librarianship*, **12** (2), 95–107.

Sinclair, B. (2007) Commons 2.0: library spaces designed for collaborative learning,
EDUCAUSE Quarterly, **30** (4), 4–6.

Space Management Group (2007) *Implementing Space Management Guidance*, UK Higher Education Space Management Project, www.smg.ac.uk/documents/Implementing%20SMG%20Guidance%202007.pdf.

Spencer, M. E. (2006) Evolving a New Model: the information commons, *Reference Services Review*, **34** (2), 242–7.

University of Cumbria (n.d.) Learning Gateway, www cumbria.ac.uk/services/lis/learninggateway/home.aspx.

University of Queensland (2006) *UQ News Online*, 6 June 2006, www.uq.edu.au/news/index.html?article=9803.

Watson, L. (2007) Building the Future of Learning, *European Journal of Education*, **42** (2), 255–63.

Watson, L., Anderson, H. and Strachan-Davis, K. (2007) *The Design and Management of Open Plan Technology Rich Learning and Teaching Spaces in Further and Higher Education in the UK*, www.jisc.ac.uk/media/documents/themes/elearning/approved_learning_spaces_case_studies_vers1b.doc.

Weaver, M. L. (2006) Exploring Conceptions of Learning and Teaching Through the Creation of Flexible Learning Spaces: the Learning Gateway – a case study, *New Review of Academic Librarianship*, **12** (2), 109–25.

7

Flexible delivery in action: the case of the University of the Highlands and Islands

FRANK RENNIE

Introduction

The University of the Highlands and Islands (UHI) Millennium Institute is trying to create a new university serving the Highlands and Islands of Scotland, a huge area with the second-lowest population density in Europe (after Lapland). The UHI is based on a model of federated academic partners (established colleges of further education and some specialized research centres) located across the north and west of Scotland, which have added higher education to their curriculum. As a result the UHI delivers a mixture of further education (FE), higher education (HE) and research degrees, and a mixture of face-to-face campus-based tuition, attendance at an affiliated local learning centre and tuition that is wholly or partly online for students who are remote from their teaching campus. In order to attempt educational equivalence for learners, student support must cover a variety of delivery formats, and needs to cope with students migrating between different formats during their educational career. This chapter deals with some responses to that challenge, including online library access and social networking for postgraduate students.

The context

The UHI Millennium Institute in the Highlands and Islands of Scotland is a distributed HE institute spread over 15 academic partners and more than 50 local learning centres, covering in excess of 40,000 km^2 of northern Scotland, including over 90 inhabited islands and some of the most sparsely populated corners of mainland UK. Since 1993, the UHI has focused on bringing HE opportunities to people in geographically dispersed locations throughout the Highlands and Islands of Scotland, and, by recent extension, to other parts of the UK and Europe (Hills and Lingard, 2004). The students are typically cast as 'remote students' (i.e. remote from the main teaching campus), but the essential point is that students do not need to leave their home area in order to pursue their studies. As a federated network of 15 existing colleges and research centres, the UHI is spread over a very wide geographical area with the second lowest population density in Europe. There is no university within this large region, although a number of higher education institutions in other parts of the country have supported students in the region through distance and distributed learning.

The UHI offers access courses in further education and vocational training, right through to undergraduate and postgraduate degrees. The vocational courses are generally validated by the Scottish Qualifications Authority (SQA) and this extends into level one (HNC) and level two (HND) of many degree courses. The undergraduate degrees have been validated by the Open University Validation Service (OUVS) and the research degrees by the OUVS and also by the University of Aberdeen, but the UHI hopes to move to the validation of its own taught degrees within the next few months.

There is some specialization of subjects among the different colleges, but most degree courses are delivered jointly across the UHI network. The aim of networked courses is to ensure that wherever the student is located, a range of courses can be studied. Thus distributed learning (as defined below) represents an attractive solution to enable the UHI to deliver educational resources in diverse formats (usually, but not always, digital) throughout the region. A key characteristic of UHI is therefore the networking of courses, such that students in any location can study courses delivered from other parts of the network. These courses may have an element of face-to-face contact, but increasingly they are offered using a range of advanced technologies that can supplement or replace face-to-face tuition.

Furthermore, the UHI aims to be responsive to the local (region-specific) context of education, and reflects this in its choice of curriculum and research foci. Examples of this include the masters degrees in managing sustainable rural/mountain development and in archaeology, as well as undergraduate degree programmes in Gaelic and North Atlantic studies, cultural studies, Nordic studies or rural and remote health issues.

From this context it can be seen that the UHI has a strong interest in the support of distributed learning systems that are flexible enough to permit easy access to multimode educational resources over a wide geographical area covering small rural communities on islands and mountainous locations. Even in a higher education institution such as this, however, there is a great diversity of perception regarding the definition, function and design of distributed educational resources, so some clarity is required. Among the plethora of definitions of distributed learning in the academic literature, there is little common ground. For some, the practice is synonymous with distance learning and e-learning (e.g. Oblinger, Barone and Hawkins, 2001); for others it is identical to the term 'blended learning' (e.g. Bonk and Graham, 2006). While 'blended learning' is also a contentious term, it generally refers to a combination of face-to-face and online learning (such as using e-learning to complement classroom activity or vice versa). A recent study of the undergraduate experience of blended e-learning in the UK (Sharpe et al., 2006) comprehensively explored recent literature and practice, to come up with some key recommendations to guide future policy, practice and research. This report forms important background reading to the present chapter, but a slightly wider interpretation is taken here (see Figure 7.1) to accommodate the facts that:

- blended learning may take place on one campus (i.e. without geographical distribution)
- distributed learning, although combining distance and e-learning, may not necessarily include any face-to-face activity (as is normally implicit in the term 'blended learning').

In UHI terms, distributed learning can be thought of a form of the latter that is also geographically distributed.

For the above reasons, it is useful to explore the example of the UHI with regard to innovative student support systems. Some of the solutions attempted by the UHI are becoming fairly mainstream elsewhere in the HE sector, while some are unique to the region, but the combination of geographical, technological, subject-specific

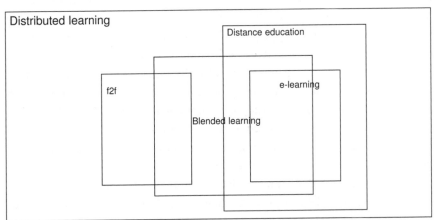

Figure 7.1 The relationship of e-learning to distributed learning (Mason and Rennie, 2006, xvii)

and administrative complexities provides a rich area for experimentation and innovation.

The HE and FE mix

This is a complex and multifaceted issue. As stated, the UHI is largely built upon a partnership of pre-existing colleges of FE largely offering vocational and pre-degree courses, and this continues to form a major proportion of the work of the network. In an average year, around 65–75% of the total number of students are studying at FE level, but in the UHI the figures are slightly complicated by the fact that students studying for Higher National Certificates and Diplomas are considered to be HE students (unlike in most of the rest of Scotland). This is because many of the UHI degree programmes have been designed on a '2+1' basis – two years of HND study followed by a third year of study to take the student to degree level.

Owing to the fact that many of the courses were operational in the partner colleges before the federation of the UHI, there are several variations of student support for different disciplinary areas. In the simplest case, where a module is taught only to students on the same campus, student support needs are dealt with in a conventional way, but this is not generally the case for the UHI. More commonly, a module is taught in a conventional face-to-face format by a number of academic partners, and there has been increasing convergence to support these students through 'subject networks'. A subject network is a sort of virtual department, within a particular faculty, that attempts to standardize certain issues – assessments, student support, access to resources, etc. – regardless of where students are geographically located in the UHI network. The key aspect of a subject network is that it provides a unifying structure to bring together all courses in a discipline area (e.g. engineering or Gaelic), regardless of the geographical location of the campuses delivering the courses. Some staff initially feared that such 'rationalization' might lead to job redundancies, but these have largely been avoided through re-deployment into other areas, such as the development of new courses, translation of existing courses into a distributed format and the development of research activities. In the UHI context, where high quality networked delivery is evidenced, it is often the case that academic and support staff numbers grow in order to support the resulting student growth.

This has led to the development of a particular style of course delivery at the UHI called 'network delivery' whereby different modules in a course can be delivered by staff geographically scattered in any of the 15 academic partner colleges, to students who may be based in one or more of the academic partners. Again, the type of support will vary with the subject discipline and possibly the location of the student's main campus. It is normal, for instance, for an entirely new (to the academic partner) subject area to be more networked and generally pool more resources than a subject area previously traditionally taught separately, in a parallel fashion, by each of the independent academic partners. There is also a distinction between the more academic subjects that lead to degree awards and the more practical, vocational awards that are below degree level. Even among modules that are at SQF (Scottish Qualifications Framework) level seven (HNC) or eight (HND), those covering more academic subjects that articulate with a degree level tend to be more enthusiastic supporters of networked delivery and shared resources, particularly of pooled networking technology. In part this may be attributed to the pre-existing culture in the academic partners, as they move from being an independent college focused largely on FE to being part of a federated network of colleges with a much wider offering, from non-vocational short courses, through all the levels of FE and HE, to doctoral and postdoctoral research degrees. The range of subject areas and levels, and the geographical and administrative complexity, means that a one-size-fits-all solution is neither desirable nor possible. The rest of this chapter looks at some of the different solutions that are being attempted to support HE students throughout the UHI network.

Working with the constraints of geography

The first thing that needs to be pointed out is that the UHI has a high proportion of adult learners (over 50% are over 25 years of age) and around 57% (headcount) of students are part-time learners. Although all of these students may be attached to a particular academic partner, the student may not physically attend that partner college, but rather could be studying from home, from work or from one of the many local learning centres used by the UHI. As students are frequently located in remote areas of the Highlands or Islands, the UHI has invested in an extended network of over 100 local learning centres across the region, where students can go to access course materials and receive support from the local learning facilitator. These local learning centres range from simple access to a computer and desk-space in the premises of a local organization (e.g. a school, a community hall or the office of a voluntary body) to sophisticated, purpose-built learning centres with dedicated classrooms, IT access, a small library and perhaps local staff. In some cases the local learning centres have been built by the academic partners of the UHI (the constituent colleges and research centres), while other learning centres are housed in premises leased from community organizations or the local authority. Many small communities seem to regard the location of a local learning centre in their village as a key factor in local economic and social rejuvenation. No doubt the economics and value of running a local learning centre will change over time. As broadband access becomes more ubiquitous and affordable, and learners obtain better access to online resources and communications applications from their own homes, perhaps the local learning centre will become more important as a study space and a social space to meet other local learners – but this is for the future.

The UHI has invested heavily in developing a range of learning resources and means of communication that allow learners spread over a wide geographical area to utilize a variety of technologies that suit their skills and lifestyles, such as print, virtual learning environments, audioconferencing, videoconferencing, Skype and face-to-face tutorials.

The UHI has invested in videoconferencing as a major technology to link the various colleges, both as a teaching medium and for administrative purposes. The UHI is currently the heaviest user of videoconferencing for HE in the EU, and accounts for more than half of all the use for educational purposes in the UK. Most of the big committees at the UHI, from the executive board, the research committee and the quality assurance committee to the network teams of academics at each of the academic partners, routinely conduct their regular meetings by videoconference. In addition, many courses include subject tuition, research seminars and/or presentations via the videoconference system. An interesting spin-off has been the adoption of videoconference technology by other agencies and government departments in the region, and by a number of community and voluntary organizations seeking to make use of the UHI videoconference network to link with their own geographically dispersed collaborators. The UHI maintains its own telecommunications hub in Shetland to service the entire network. Such heavy use comes with a price tag that is evaluated not simply in monetary terms (there are limited slots available, and there is a lack of flexibility for students outwith learning centres), and despite the excellent videoconferencing service provided many course teams have recently begun to move away from the videoconference to use other, more flexible, networking systems. Clearly there is a trade-off between the convenience and the disadvantages of videoconferencing that will vary its relevance to different situations and different subjects. New generations of desktop-to-desktop videoconferencing are extending its flexibility further for some users and courses, and the optimum use of videoconferencing for teaching and support services continues to be a fertile area for practical research.

New technology: solutions and problems

From a very early stage in the development of the UHI there has been a realization that the intelligent use of new technology can offer a solution to the problems of low student numbers at any one locality and the wide geographical scattering of learning and teaching localities. The first UHI networked degree was the undergraduate programme in rural development studies, which morphed from a 'traditional' face-to-face course based at one academic partner to a networked degree, available online with tutor support anywhere in the UK (Rennie, 2003). This has been followed by degrees in a number of different subjects at undergraduate and postgraduate level, some restricted to delivery at a few academic partners, while others are available throughout Europe (Price and Rennie, 2005).

Due to the difficulty of defining a 'typical' programme, we should be clear about what we mean by an 'online degree' and about the nature of online support for students at different levels. An online degree, for instance, does not involve students being plugged in to a computer environment with no regular tutor contact. A common feature is for learners on a networked course to be offered a variety of technological solutions to replace reliance upon traditional face-to-face tuition, in a more flexible manner than requiring all students around the network (or at home) to adhere to rigorously fixed classroom timetables.

In this context we speak about 'distributed education' as being a delivery style that enables us to cater for both the geographical distribution of participants and the physical distribution of resources and support across a range of different media. It is also significant that rather than simply focusing on student 'entitlements', the UHI is also careful to consider student equivalence – students on the same course should have a broadly equivalent learning experience. Note that this need not necessarily mean the same learning experience for each individual. A key part of this philosophy is that while students and staff may have access to the same pool of technological applications and resources, students may elect to select options that they are most comfortable with. Obviously there are financial and administrative limits to this, but an example might be that all students on a degree module, whether attending campus or working from home at a location remote from the teaching campus, will receive their main tuition and academic support via the institutional virtual learning environment (VLE). In the 15 years or so since the formation of the UHI, the VLE has evolved from FirstClass to Blackboard and WebCT, had a brief flirtation with CLAN, a customized open-source software built on Bodington, and recently gone back to Blackboard7, although we anticipate moving to an open-source solution such as Sakai within the next few years. While the VLE provides the common platform for all students on the module, additional support media may vary depending upon the learning situation and/or level of e-literacy of the learner. For example, the VLE provides a discussion board facility that is used to develop threads of information on key themes and develop dialogue among the learners, but some learners may supplement this by sending one-to-one e-mails to a tutor in order to avoid what they might regard as embarrassing comments/questions on an open forum. Normally this e-mail correspondence drops off as students acquire more confidence in themselves and the VLE technology. In addition, individual tutors/modules might employ instant messaging, live chat sessions at a pre-arranged time and/or Skype to facilitate real-time video, audio and/or textual communications to support students. Similarly, there may also be some tutor–learner contact by telephone (individual and conference calls) to supplement the VLE/e-mail and to clarify key concepts. There are potential difficulties, not just in the costs accrued in replicating the same teaching materials in a number of different ways, but also in overloading tutors with multiple communications channels. In practice, however, the VLE discussion boards provide a unifying platform which is supplemented by other support media if and when appropriate.

Although some courses still use videoconferencing as a medium of tuition, there is a recognition that this technology is not a panacea for communicating with remote students, and must be used strategically for key tasks. Specifically, although videoconference sessions can foster social intimacy and stimulating dialogue, there are other, less expensive ways of achieving this when it is not imperative that learners see tutors and/or each other (Mason and Rennie, 2008). From initial enthusiasm for videoconferencing for regular distance teaching, many tutors have moved towards less intensive use of the videoconference, for intermittent sessions such as keynote presentations, seminars and/or learners' verbal assessments. Some tutors have abandoned the use of videoconference sessions for their modules, on the grounds that rather than providing flexibility the videoconference ties students to a relatively small number of key locations and times, and moved to the use of desktop video through Skype (straight to the user's own computer) or the use of video-streaming or webcasting of recorded visual presentations that can be accessed asynchronously and repeatedly. This is particularly significant in rural and island communities where geographical difficulties and/or severe weather may impact upon the reliability of ferries or the ability to drive over 20 miles to the nearest learning centre. Interestingly, the videoconference is still the favoured technology for specialist, highly interactive sessions such as research seminars and team meetings, involving a small number of like-minded specialists from scattered locations in the UHI or local learning centres. Some work has also been done on the provision of counselling services via videoconferencing (although this is still the subject of debate between practitioners), and some work is in hand to use the medium to support postgraduate research students who are based at locations remote from their supervisor(s).

Student support issues

Students are supported with reference and reading materials on a similar distributed basis. Each academic partner has its own library and employs its own library staff, with some also supporting small collections of resources in certain local learning centres throughout the Highlands and Islands. There is also a small, centralizsed library support team (including a specialist e-librarian) to assist the work of the individual college librarians. Learners can access the full UHI library catalogue online, which allows them to search the details of the resources at each centre, request a resource and have this delivered through the internal interlibrary loan system. The usual forms of UK inter-library loan also exist at each different academic partner.

Due to the fact that UHI students are distributed across a wide geographical area, reliance upon a single, large library serving the whole of the UHI was recognized as being both undesirable and impractical. As a result, academic partners that lead certain areas of the curriculum tend to be regarded as the key repository for the hard copies of the relevant specialist resources – for example, in Gaelic, oceanography, rural development or health studies.

This is supplemented, where appropriate, with electronic resources that may have wider relevance for other curriculum areas, such as electronic journals and e-books for science, social science and education. These electronic resources have the advantages that they can be accessed from any computer by staff or learners with the appropriate password, and that users in different locations can access the online resource simultaneously. There is also a UHI facility for key texts to be digitized from specialist sources not normally available to students, especially those on networked courses. This is particularly useful for tutors on networked courses, who can e-mail them to students scattered over large geographical areas. The UHI central library team provides this service.

Three limitations are:

1   Electronic journals and books are frequently expensive to purchase.
2   Not all relevant journals and books are as yet automatically published in electronic versions.
3   As the UHI is still in the early stages of its formation, with a strong culture of individually autonomous colleges, the UHI as a whole is in a transition

phase as regards collective agreement on which services and resources should remain the responsibility of the individual academic partners, and which should be centrally provided by the network as a whole.

A good example of the latter is that several course teams adopted a course design that included attaching digitized copies of key papers and chapters to the relevant 'learning sessions' on the VLE. In traditional parlance this would be equivalent to making a photocopy available to accompany a particular point made in a lecture. The advantages to students are obvious, but there are also benefits for tutorial staff in knowing that their students are being directed to good quality materials (even out-of-print classic texts) that are accessible regardless of the learners' physical location. In the last few years, copyright checking and digitization tasks have been passed from the individual colleges to a centralized library support unit. It is intended that other support services and resources should also move in this direction, although because of the sensitivity of some individual colleges these moves are likely to be slow and consensual rather than top-down.

General student support and guidance services are a case in point, as each academic partner, rather than the UHI as a whole, is generally responsible for the support of the students they enrol. Each academic partner may have slightly different procedures, so to ensure consistency for the higher education UHI students in different colleges there are moves being made to prepare a set of 'core' criteria for the UHI, with individual academic partners having the option to add to, but not remove from, these criteria. An example of this might be a common 'baseline' health and safety policy for students, with individual colleges being able to add additional clauses that are relevant to their own specialist areas (e.g. in dealing with safety precautions for laboratory work, for handling radioactive materials, for field work or for work placements).

The evolving role of staff

Developing such a distinctive, federal institution as the UHI has resulted in considerable debate between teaching and learning practitioners. A key strength in this organizational development has been the success of the student support mechanisms that have developed in the FE colleges on which the UHI structure is based. Many of the strengths of this provision (as evidenced by HM Inspectorate of Education review reports for the constituent colleges) have been built on FE and developed to encompass HE students as this aspect of provision has expanded – in terms of both student numbers and different modes of course delivery. Examples include the development of the student advisor role, access to specialist student support staff on each campus and the secondment of experienced student support practitioners to central co-ordinating roles with the UHI executive office on UHI-wide student support initiatives. Frequently, the administrative staff in local learning centres act as mentors to students at that centre to provide general support and generic academic advice, as well as a local face to help liaise with academic tutors elsewhere in the network. The changes can be challenging for all staff: lecturers who no longer lecture but tutor online, administrative staff who no longer have paper copies of registers but need to track students across the network, and support staff who now add 'technology skills' to the list of student support issues that they deal with. Consequently, a heavy investment has been made in staff development and training at all levels, although apart from on the strongly networked courses, much of this has been done in the context of the work of individuals at each academic partner, rather than taking a consistent approach across the UHI, but moves are being made in this direction.

The nature and extent of library provision varies between UHI academic partners but a key strength is the close involvement of librarians from each academic partner in the strategic planning and development of course provision, and their representation on the UHI learning and teaching committee.

Two further aspects of curriculum planning are significant in terms of supporting students on networked programmes. First, it is important to include library and student support staff in the early stages of curriculum design as part of the course team. This ensures that appropriate resources and services can be targeted at both face-to-face and off-campus students. Second, an initial course induction for students embarking on networked degrees is particularly significant in easing students into HE, and in maintaining a good course retention rate. For adult returners to HE, the first six weeks of any course can be particularly challenging. When this is combined with an innovative use of a mix of technologies, an initial induction can be crucial in enabling the learner to access course materials and develop their learning style and skills to make best use of these resources.

There is no 'one size fits all' approach that will provide effective learner support at induction. The key is to acknowledge that all learners should be entitled to high quality course induction, and that the form this induction will take will vary depending on the location of the learner and the mode of their particular course delivery. Course teams need to utilize an induction model that best meets the often varying needs of their new learners. Examples of approaches used to support remote learning students across the Highlands and Islands of Scotland include residential induction at the lead college where the course is based, and new students being invited to a central location near to their place of residence (a local learning centre or an academic partner) to meet with course staff. The course leader and/or tutors can provide induction at these sites and other members of the course team (academic and support) can videoconference into the meeting when applicable. Online and CD-based support materials have also been made available and provided as reference material for students.

The UHI is currently experimenting with a new generation of student support tools and methods that will facilitate greater student social connectivity. One of the obvious disadvantages of the distributed, decentralized model of the UHI is that while students have the advantages of studying close to their home, and having a vibrant connection with their home community, it can be difficult to socialize with fellow students on the same course (or faculty) who are geographically distant. Various methods have been investigated to provide students with an independent forum for discussion and group socializing that need not be specifically related to the academic content of their course. These experiments have included dedicated non-course discussion boards, group mailing lists, access to videoconference time that is unsupervised by staff and, more recently, the employment of the Elgg social networking software to facilitate group interaction online. Elgg is an open-source software application, customized by the UHI, that allows participants to create their own profile, select friends and set up different communities of interest. In common with other, more mainstream, social networking software, the application allows participants to post pictures of themselves, create blogs and hyperlinks to other resources, and to search for/add other participants as 'buddies', but within the protected framework of the UHI firewall. This software has great potential for peer-group support and social learning within the UHI structure, but it is still too early to judge the success of this initiative.

Conclusions

Supporting courses with online resources, online interaction and tutor contact is now a standard feature of many, if not most, Western universities, whether the institution teaches largely at a distance, face-to-face or a blend of the two (Paulsen, n.d.). Unlike the Open University, the UHI in not primarily a distance teaching institution, but due to the geographical distribution and demographics of its students (a small, scattered population, with a high proportion of learners being mature, employed, part-time students) it has invested considerable resources developing technologies to support students in distributed education. With a variety of combinations of support, students can study individually in their own home, access online library facilities, participate in teleconferencing, engage with online activities and work with web-based assessment processes.

What makes the UHI distinctive is not the formulaic application of new technology, which is after all employed by many other institutions, but the strategic application of conventional face-to-face support in collaboration with a range of new technology that is offered in a flexible combination to most efficiently minimize the natural constraints of the region. Increasingly, courses are using blogs, wikis and e-portfolios, in order to provide students with a rich experience of intellectual life and social networking. These are offered not just to 'remote' students, distant from the teaching campus, but to all students, regardless of their chosen mode of study. Via extensive questionnaires (now often online), students provide information about their means and time of access, ownership of technology, training needs and interests in using technology for their learning. Considerable investment has been made in the provision of induction for new students, both campus-based and remote, to ensure that they receive adequate support for course orientation, as well as in the use of the relevant technology for their course. Undoubtedly there will be further modifications to the range of support facilities for UHI students – for instance, as the economics of local learning centres change, and the cost of home computers comes down, there may well need to be a re-appraisal of the function of such centres. Perhaps their current technological function will be replaced by a more social-learning function; perhaps the new generation of desk-top video technology will prove to be more flexible and effective for student needs than the current videoconferencing network. Undoubtedly, changes in VLE design and the availability of electronic library resources will require a re-assessment of hard-copy resources and the requirements of classroom-type accommodation for learners, but the unique geographical situation of the UHI means that, for the foreseeable future, the nature of student support will involve clever combinations of both old and new technology that will enable flexible and responsive distributed learning solutions tailored to the needs of learners in the region.

References and further reading

Bonk, C. and Graham, C. (eds) (2006) *The Handbook of Blended Learning*, John Wiley & Sons.

Hills, G. and Lingard, R. (2004) *UHI: the making of a university*, Dunedin Academic Press.

Mason, R. and Rennie, F. (2006) *eLearning: the key concepts*, Routledge.

Mason, R. and Rennie, F. (2008) *The eLearning Handbook: social networking for higher education*, Routledge.

Oblinger, D., Barone, C. and Hawkins, B. (2001) *Distributed Education and its Challenges: an overview*, American Council on Education, www.acenet.edu/bookstore/pdf/distributed-learning/distributed-learning-01.pdf.

Paulsen, M. F. (n.d.) *An International Analysis of Web-based Education*, www.nettskolen.com/pub/artikkel.xsql?artid=131.

Price, M. F. and Rennie, F. (2005) MSc Degrees in Managing Sustainable Mountain/Rural Development at the University of Highlands and Islands, *Planet*, **14**, (June), 22–4, www.gees.ac.uk/pubs/planet/p14/mpfr.pdf.

Rennie, F. (2003) The Use of Flexible Learning Resources for Geographically Distributed Rural Students, *Distance Education*, **24** (1), 25–39.

Rennie, F. (2007) Understanding Practitioners' Perspectives on Course Design for Distributed Learning, *European Journal of Open, Distance and E-learning*, www.eurodl.org/materials/contrib/2007/Frank_Rennie.htm.

Ross, C. (2000) *Video-counselling: a report of a pilot study in the University of the Highlands and Islands Project* (UHI/SFEU Learning Environments and Technology Report).

Sharpe, R., Benfield, G., Roberts, G. and Francis, R. (2006) *The Undergraduate Experience of Blended E-learning: a review of UK literature and practice*, www.heacademy.ac.uk/assets/York/documents/ourwork/research/literature_reviews/blended_elearning_full_reviews.pdf.

8

The integration of physical and virtual environments to support HE learners: a European perspective

PETER BROPHY

Introduction

Although the title of this chapter offers a 'European perspective' (and that is not, incidentally, intended as a political comment on Britain's position within the continent!) it has to be stated at the outset that European library and learning resource provision is very far from heterogeneous. There is a plethora of perspectives and practices across Europe. Physical and virtual environments are as varied as any other social and cultural expression across the countries of the European Union and surrounding states. What cohesion and common purpose can be found is largely based in our common cultural heritage, so far as that extends, and in the funding programmes of the European Commission. With the expansion of the European Union, new perspectives have been introduced and new cultural resources made accessible. Pedagogically, Europe is a disparate continent, with constructivist approaches evident, at least in theory, in many countries but a much more didactic paradigm evident in others. Change happens slowly, even where there is widespread use of information and communication technologies (ICTs). Furthermore, rhetoric is not always accompanied by action!

The European Union has the stated aim to become 'the most dynamic and competitive knowledge-based economy in the world capable of sustainable economic growth with more and better jobs and greater social cohesion, and respect for the environment' (the Lisbon Strategy – see http://europa.eu/scadplus/glossary/lisbon_strategy_en.htm). A mid-term review of the Strategy painted a rather gloomy picture of progress but the basic strategy was confirmed. Significant funding for educational initiatives continues to be made available through programmes such as Erasmus, Leonardo da Vinci and Comenius. However during the last ten years the availability of funding for European library initiatives has diminished considerably, with the loss of the libraries R&D programme within successive Framework Programmes (see also below).

The European Commission's strategy to boost the digital economy, within this context, is known as i2010. It contains a number of programmes of at least partial relevance to library and learning resource services, including the Digital Libraries Initiative, which has two strands, one concerned with cultural heritage and the other with access to and preservation of 'scientific' information. An overall aim is to move towards a European Digital Library (EDL), based on existing shared activity by the major national libraries. An experimental service was launched under the title Europeana (www.europeana.eu/) in 2007 and the service is expected to be fully launched in late 2008, focusing on digitized material from the major libraries, museums, galleries, etc.

In the education sector the first major milestone was the Bologna Declaration of 1999 (http://ec.europa.eu/education/policies/educ/bologna/bologna.pdf), which committed the 29 signatory countries to align their higher education systems to create 'a European space for higher education in order to enhance the employability and mobility of citizens and to increase the international competitiveness of European higher education'. The major requirements were a move to a common framework for first and masters-level degrees, and subsequently doctorates, and compatible credit transfer systems. Although progress has not been consistent, considerable changes have been achieved in many countries, with three-quarters of the EU member states reporting at least 60% of students enrolled on compliant courses by 2007.

In 2007 the European University Association issued the *Lisbon Declaration* (the habit of naming these various documents after the city in which the relevant meeting took place causes endless confusion!) with the title *Europe's Universities beyond 2010: Diversity with a common purpose* (www.eua.be/fileadmin/user_upload/files/lisbon_convention/lisbon_declaration.pdf). This agreement declared that the central task 'is to equip Europe's populations – young and old – to play their part within the Knowledge Society, in which economic, social and cultural development depend primarily on the creation and dissemination of knowledge and skills' and urged all European universities to develop a stronger student-centred focus. Alongside this emphasis there is concern to build the research capacity of Europe's major universities – only Cambridge (at second place) and Oxford (tenth) feature in the widely accepted Shanghai Jiao Tong University's table of the world's top 20 universities (http://ed.sjtu.edu.cn/rank/2005/ARWU2005_top100.htm). The University of Utrecht is the highest-ranked non-UK institution in Europe at 41st.

European Commission programmes

A considerable amount of innovation in Europe is funded under one or other of the European Commission's research and development programmes. Of these the most important for libraries and learning resource services are probably the ICT part of the Framework Programmes and eContentPlus.

The ICT Programme sets out a series of 'challenges'. Under the heading 'Digital Libraries and Content' – which received over 200 million funding for 2007–8 – the following target outcomes have been identified. It is worth quoting them in full because they illustrate the priorities which the European Commission, and its expert advisers, regard as critical for research and development in this area:

For digital libraries:

a) (Medium term) Large-scale European-wide digital libraries with innovative access services that support communities of practice in the creation, interpretation and use of cultural and scientific content, including multi-format and multi-source digital objects. They should be combined with robust and scalable environments which include semantic-based search capabilities and essential digital preservation features. Particular attention is given to cost effective digitization processes and to the use of digital resources in multilingual and multidisciplinary contexts.

b) (Long term) Radically new approaches to digital preservation, such as those inspired by human capacity to deal with information and knowledge, exploring the potential of advanced ICT to automatically act on high volumes and dynamic and volatile digital content, guaranteeing its preservation, keeping track of its evolving semantics and usage context and safeguarding its integrity, authenticity and long term accessibility over time.

For technology-enhanced learning:

(c) (Medium term) Responsive environments for technology-enhanced learning that motivate, engage and inspire learners, and which can be embedded in the business processes and human resources management systems of organizations. They support the transformation of learning outcomes into permanent and valuable knowledge assets. Focus is on the mass individualization of learning experiences with ICT (contextualized and adaptable to age, situations, culture and learning abilities), through pedagogically-inspired solutions for competency, skills and performance enhancement. Activities integrate pedagogical and organizational approaches and exploit, where relevant, interactivity, collaboration and context-awareness. Interdisciplinary research should deliver a convincing and theoretically sound body of evidence as to which approaches are effective and under which circumstances.

(d) (Long term) Adaptive and intuitive learning systems, able to learn and configure themselves according to their understanding and experience of learners' behaviour. Cross-disciplinary research on the synergies between learning and cognition in humans and machines should lead to systems able to identify learners' requirements, intelligently monitoring progress, capable of exploiting learners' abilities in order to let them learn better, and able to give purposeful and meaningful advice to both learners and teachers either for self-learning or for learning in a collaborative environment.

(ftp://ftp.cordis.europa.eu/pub/fp7/ict/docs/ict-wp-2007-08_en.pdf)

A considerable variety of projects has been funded under these (and similar, earlier) objectives. Areas covered include personalized lifelong learning environments (e.g. in the GRAPPLE Project; www.grapple-project.org/) and the use of games for education (eMapps.com under Framework 6, http://emapps.info/; and 80Days under Framework 7, http://cordis.europa.eu/fp7/ict/telearn-digicult/telearn-projects-80days_en.html). UK bodies like the UK Office for Library and Information Networking (UKOLN; www.ukoln.ac.uk/), the Centre for Educational Technology Interoperability Standards (CETIS; http://jisc.cetis.ac.uk/) and the Centre for Research in Library and Information Management (CERLIM; www.cerlim.ac.uk/) have significant involvement in EC programmes, often taking a leading role.

The level of integration between UK developments and these major European programmes, for example in shared services, is somewhat inconsistent. In some areas, for example in work on digital curation, there is close collaboration between UK and EC activity – in this case staff from the UK's Digital Curation Centre (DCC) play leading roles in the major CASPAR (Cultural, Artistic and Scientific knowledge for Preservation, Access and Retrieval – www.casparpreserves.eu/) integrated project while the British Library provides the focus for PLANETS (Preservation and Longterm Access through NETworked Services). Both are multimillion-euro initiatives. However, this leadership in research and development does not always extend to the actual services rolled out in UK universities. As an example, use of the Information Environment Service Registry (IESR;

http://iesr.ac.uk/), which is based on earlier international work by various bodies including UKOLN, has not taken off to the extent that might have been expected.

The eContentPlus programme had a budget of just under 150 million for the period 2005–8. The programme is designed to 'make digital content in Europe more accessible, usable and exploitable' and includes work on geographic information systems, educational content and digital libraries. The 2008 call for proposals set out the following objectives to be addressed in the educational content area:

- Facilitate the use and reuse of open educational resources.
- Facilitate the co-existence, use, reuse and exchange of existing professionally produced educational content and user-generated educational content in real contexts of use.
- Foster the educational use of digital libraries of content held by cultural institutions.
- Make it easier for users (both individuals and organizations) to find and use existing digital educational content that matches their learning and skills development needs.

For the digital library part, the equivalent requirements were:

- The actual content should be accessible and retrievable at item level.
- The users and their needs should be at the centre of the approach proposed.
- The proposal should demonstrate its capacity to contribute significantly to the achievement of the programme objective and to contribute to the advancement of the European Digital Library (EDL).
- The test and validation of the proposed solutions should be done within the EDL.
  (http://ec.europa.eu/information_society/activities/econtentplus/docs/call_2008/7_en_annex1_2008_wp.pdf).

This emphasizes the importance being attached by the Commission to the EDL as the core vehicle for delivering cross-European digital library services.

Virtual learning environments

During the last ten years there has been a noticeable shift across much of European higher education towards using virtual learning environments (VLEs) rather than simply experimentating with them. WebCT and Blackboard (now owned by the same company, of course) and Moodle appear to be dominant, although there is a considerable range of other platforms in use: ATutor, Sakai and DOKEOS are examples, while more generic platforms like Lotus Domino and FirstClass are used by some institutions. Although there is much discussion, at least among library staff, about the need to link digital library services into VLEs, there is as yet limited evidence of deep integration.

It is also apparent that many European universities are experimenting with the use of learning support software outside the VLE. Social networking systems like Facebook are being used within this context, although there is as yet a lack of robust experience. Similarly, there is interest in collaborative tagging and folksonomies – types of user-generated metadata applied to digital materials by a group or community.

A few examples of inter-university use of VLEs for collaborative learning are starting to emerge. Nunnington and Eilander (2005) report on a project called 'The European Challenge' which linked seven universities using Blackboard. They comment:

> The unprecedented usage of both the learning resources and the communication tools compared to control courses is confirmation that distance is no longer a barrier to learning and that high levels of motivation can be achieved where students are in control of their learning.   (Nunnington and Eilander, 2005, 53)

However, it is also quite clear that, while open universities have moved towards fully virtual delivery and there are plenty of examples of projects and experiments which use the approach, this is not the norm. Far more common in Europe is an approach based on blended learning, whereby a planned mix of online and face-to-face activity is provided.

Student services

While in the UK there has been considerable interest in recent years in coordinating and in some cases converging library, computing and other academic-related departments with the student services function, this is not apparent in the rest of Europe. A major reason is that in general what are called student services in continental Europe are mainly concerned with managing student finance and administering regulations. Lazerson and Bateson (2007) comment, in a paper from the Central European University in Hungary:

While student affairs and services are highly developed and sophisticated units in higher education institutions in North America and in the United Kingdom, universities in continental Europe have been slower to identify this area as an institutional objective for improvement. Concerns about adequate student support services emerged only recently in the context of the Bologna process, and initially in the framework of international student mobility and competition in student recruitment. (Lazerson and Bateson, 2007, 5, 6)

It seems likely that it will be some time before the broader range of student services commonplace in the UK and US systems becomes widespread across Europe.

Repositories

Considerable interest has been expressed in the development of learning object repositories, although there is little evidence of their widespread use, at least in terms of their use for repurposing objects, which is their primary justification. At the pan-European level there has been activity in developing shared services, of which the most prominent is the Learning Resource Exchange (LRE; see http://lre.eun.org/), a federation of learning resource repositories primarily developed within the CALIBRATING eLearning in Schools (CALIBRATE; http://calibrate.eun.org/) and Metadata Ecology for Learning and Teaching (MELT; http://info.melt-project.eu/) projects with support from the European Commission's Information Society Technologies (IST) and eContentPlus programmes. LRE is part of the Global Learning Objects Brokered Exchange (GLOBE; see http://globe.edna.edu.au/globe/go), an international consortium. However, language is a significant issue. McCormick and Li (2006) report in a study of learning object re-use, admittedly in the schools sector, that 'the match to the curriculum and the supply of sufficient LOs in national languages presents real problems for a European-wide repository of LOs'.

One of the pressing issues in this field is to achieve a greater degree of standards compliance. For example, although the Institute of Electrical and Electronics Engineers (IEEE) Learning Object Metadata (LOM) is treated as a standard there are a variety of application profiles in use (see Godby, 2004). The plethora of standards (in addition to LOM, consideration needs to be given to Dublin Core, IMS QTI, SCORM, OAI-ORE, etc. etc.) means that institutions need to put systems in place to hide these complexities from end users if they are to be encouraged to deposit material and reuse it. In addition, copyright restrictions have sometimes created at best uncertainty and at other times an unhelpful barrier. Although Creative

Commons licences are commonly used across most of Europe, not every country recognizes them in its legislation.

There is also evidence that e-print repositories are developing quickly although, as ever, the country-by-country coverage is patchy. Van der Graaf (2007) reported that significant progress had been made in just over half the 27 European countries surveyed, although seven submitted a report indicating that no examples had been identified. Clearly this has a significant impact on the accessibility of current research materials, especially in countries where English is not the main language of publication.

Infrastructure

Just as the delivery of learning is becoming predominantly blended, there is evidence from across Europe that the infrastructure of learning is following the same path. New library, learning resource and other buildings are still being erected, but alongside this the infrastructure for virtual delivery is being extended rapidly.

As far as physical infrastructure is concerned, there are frequent reports from LIBER (Ligue des Bibliothèques Européennes de Recherche/Association of European Research Libraries) on new buildings which show that libraries continue to attract significant investment and are often designed as the centrepiece of the campus. There is little evidence that this perception of the physical library is changing. A notable emphasis is on the development of 'green' libraries which maximize the use of natural light and use other measures to minimize their impact on the environment. The architecturally striking Robert de Sorbon library at the University of Reims in France is a good example of this approach (see http://bbf.enssib.fr/sdx/BBF/frontoffice/2007/01/imprimerdocument.xsp?id=bbf-2007-01-0068-012/2007/01/fam-dossier/dossier). It is also noteworthy that there has been a trend towards much more sensitive restoration and/or expansion of notable academic libraries – an example is the Science Library at the Arenberg Campus of the Catholic University of Leuven (see www.gsd.harvard.edu/people/faculty/moneo/projects.html#arenberg).

Virtual library and learning centre developments also continue apace. Twente University in the Netherlands, for example, claims to have put in place the most extensive wifi hotspot in Europe (Portier, 2006).

Professional education

The state of librarianship and related education is as varied as any other feature of provision across Europe. The northern European model tends to dominate, although southern European countries also have well-developed systems of training in place. Juznic and Badovinac (2005) surveyed both established and new member states and found considerable homogeneity in curriculum and approach. They observed:

> The extension of the LIS schools' curricula to include teaching information management and technology, and the convergence within information studies, librarianship, archival studies, media studies, book studies, record management, has brought changes to all LIS schools in the countries observed. (However) some schools continue to have strong ties to traditional library school education.
>
> (Juznic and Badovinac, 2005, 183)

Co-operation

Just as in the UK there is a strong element of collaboration in service provision, notably through the Joint Information Systems Committee (JISC), so many other European countries have developed regional and national services and structures. These recognize that the days of individual service development are long gone. In a global information marketplace there is plenty of room for individual experimentation and innovation, but mainstream services need to be a shared enterprise. This is true whether we are talking about access to the periodical literature, provision of metadata or the software needed to support the VLE.

While many cooperative schemes are national in scope there is significant international cooperation in Europe. For example, Electronic Information for Libraries (eIFL), an initiative of the Open Society Institute (OSI), focuses on the needs of developing and transition countries, and has launched many programmes that impact on the newer member states of the European Union such as the Baltic states. Its programmes include collective licence negotiation, building national consortia and advocacy in respect of intellectual property rights, open-access and open source software for libraries. In this last instance it is supporting a programme to roll out and support migration to an open-source integrated library system.

JISC itself has good relationships with cognate bodies in Europe, notably with SURF in the Netherlands, through initiatives like the e-Framework (www.e-framework.org/) which is heavily involved in advising institutions on systems interoperability across the whole range of higher education services. Another initiative, the Knowledge Exchange, involves Denmark's Elektroniske Fag-og

Forskningsbibliotek (DEF), Germany's Deutsche Forschungsgemeinschaft (DFG) and, again, the SURF Foundation in the Netherlands.

Innovative services

There are of course very many different innovations taking place across Europe and it is impossible even to summarize them in a short chapter. The following examples are illustrative of the kinds of provision which have been put in place.

Greece: HEAL-Link

HEAL-Link (Hellenic Academic Libraries Link) is a collaborative venture to address Greek academic libraries' need for wider access to the journal literature in the face of budgetary pressures, which were leading to significant subscription cancellations. After a fairly short period the decision was taken to switch away from print towards electronic only subscriptions, not least on grounds of cost. Hormia-Poutanen et al. (2006) comment:

> Even without any publicity, there was hardly any resistance to switching to electronic resources only, and the usage statistics from the publishers demonstrate the high usage, which is continuously growing. The reason is that Greek universities moved from collections of 500 to 1,000 journals each on average to a collection of almost 9,000 peer-reviewed journals (including the open-access journals that have been added to the collection).
>
> (Hormia-Poutanen et al., 2006, 364)

Bearing in mind the highly didactic, teacher-centred nature of Greek higher education, this national initiative has been of great significance.

Germany: convergence of services

Considerable changes have taken place in the way in which German universities have organized their learning support services. A Deutsche Initiative für Netzwerkinformation (DINI) report in 1998 proved a significant point of departure for convergence by stressing the importance of networked information. The Deutsche Forschungsgemeinschaft (DFG) issued a position paper in 2006 which stressed the need for differentiation of roles within the national academic information landscape:

In the future, the range of information provision provided at individual universities and research institutions will increasingly be determined by that institution's profile and the priorities it sets for itself in research and teaching. As a prerequisite, integrated national digital information environments must be in place to provide access to a wide range of current literature, digitised primary sources, learning materials and virtual research networks, independent of time and space. At the same time, specialised research libraries and archives will come to play an even greater role as physical (i.e. non-virtual) settings for research for advanced and graduate research, especially in the humanities.

(Deutsche Forschungsgemeinschaft, 2006, 2)

This differentiation can be seen in developments like the eLearning Integration Programme, which has funded a converged library, learning and multimedia resource and IT service at the ICMC/IKMZ Brandenburg Technical University at Cottbus, described by Degkwitz (2006). In addition to a new building and new staffing structures there is a dual emphasis on what are called 'front office' and 'innovation office' functions. The former is concerned with all the user-facing services, providing interface functions such as help desks. The latter is responsible for a continuous programme of innovation. This can be contrasted with the emphasis on research support in other German universities and institutes.

Finland: the Tritonia Academic Library

The Tritonia Academic Library, situated on the coast of Finland at Vaasa, is an innovative joint project in which three universities (the University of Vaasa, the Åbo Akademi/Unit of Ostrobothnia and the Vaasa Unit of the Swedish School of Economics and Business Administration) share a learning centre. Although some problems were experienced with licence restrictions on electronic materials (which publishers relate to individual universities as a matter of policy), this appears to have been a very successful development. Palonen (2002) reported that Tritonia's 'modern and beautiful facilities have had great effect both on customer service implementation and on staff well-being'. The learning centre has responsibility for supporting the development of learning and teaching and provides advice and training on the use of ICT. It also produces digital learning materials such as video and animations for use within the Moodle VLE. Being in Finland it is not surprising that they also support delivery over mobile phones and PDAs!

Denmark: Danmarks Elektroniske Fag- og Forskningsbibliotek (DEFF)

Following an in-depth report looking at the needs of Denmark's universities, published in 1997, a secretariat was established to oversee the development of a series of high level services. By 1999 the vision had crystallized into plans for the development of three sets of services: a portal to provide web access to disparate services, access administration services to provide authentication of users and integration of catalogue services using Z39.50 and other protocols. Despite some difficulties – the Ministry of Education withdrew from funding after the 2001 general election – by 2003 DEFF had been permanently established through government funding. By then the original three strands of work had been expanded into six action lines: e-learning, e-publishing, licenses, portals, system architecture and user facilities (see www.deff.dk/content.aspx?catguid={8305457A-9A0D-4F8C-9C98-A3d7C671B166}).

The components in the current architecture are shown in Figure 8.1 (see also Öhrström, 2008). Readers familiar with the JISC information environment architecture (see www.ukoln.ac.uk/distributed-systems/jisc-ie/arch/) will note many similarities (although the latter has the user functions at the bottom rather than the top). In particular, clear separation of the different layers enables new services and functions to be added without disrupting other layers. Common standards are, of course, critical to this achievement.

As noted above, DEFF is heavily involved in collaborative initiatives in Europe through the Knowledge Exchange and within a variety of European Commission programmes.

Conclusion

The range of developments across Europe, and the pace of change, makes it very difficult to draw any general conclusions from either a student or a service provider perspective. Certainly students can expect to see more and more services delivered online. They can expect to encounter experiments in the incorporation of Web 2.0 services such as social networking into course delivery. They will undoubtedly be able to search a portfolio of content services from any location. However, the overall impression is not one of revolutionary change, but rather the accretion of new services within educational systems which change very slowly and which, with honourable exceptions, have not yet fully come to terms with the concepts of student-centred learning. Notwithstanding, there are pockets of innovation and some

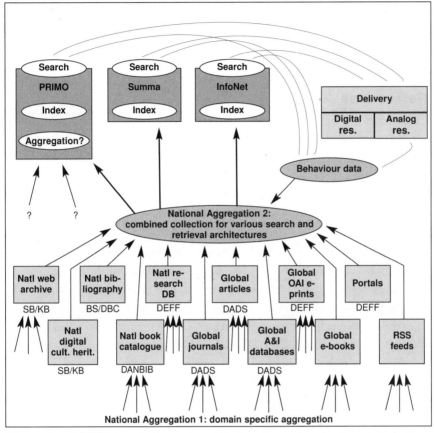

Figure 8.1 DEFF integrated search architecture (reproduced with permission)

of the major research and development programmes are producing results which are far-reaching in their significance.

So, where will all this activity lead? Just as in the UK, it is difficult to find clear images of the future but perhaps the idea of the 'learning mall', introduced by Wim Veen of the Delft University of Technology in the Netherlands at the Online Educa Conference in Berlin in 2005, gives a taste of things to come:

> The learning mall represents distributed electronic virtual knowledge centres equipped with personalized-learning delivery robots. Student, undergraduates, graduates, post-graduates and other experts will have access to these future distributed online libraries where 'just in time', 'just enough' and 'just for you' learning objects can be retrieved.
>
> (Veen, 2005)

Nevertheless, the final conclusion must be that if current trends are prescient, the human guide – teacher, librarian, educationalist, technologist – will still be central.

References

Degkwitz, A. (2006) Convergence in Germany: the Information, Communication and Media Center (ICMC/IKMZ) of Cottbus University, *Library Hi Tech*, **24** (3), 430–9.

Deutsche Forschungsgemeinschaft (2006) *Scientific Library Services and Information Systems: funding priorities through 2015*, www.dfg.de/forschungsfoerderung/wissenschaftliche_infrastruktur/lis/download/pos_papier_funding_priorities_2015_en.pdf.

Godby, C. A. (2004) What Do Application Profiles Reveal about the Learning Object Metadata Standard? *Ariadne*, **41**, www.ariadne.ac.uk/issue41/godby/.

Hormia-Poutanen, K., Xenidou-Dervou, C., Kupryte, R., Stange, K., Kuznetsov, A. and Woodward, H. (2006) Consortia in Europe: describing the various solutions through four country examples, *Library Trends*, **54** (3), 359–80.

Juznic, P. and Badovinac, B. (2005) Toward Library and Information Science Education in the European Union: a comparative analysis of library and information science programmes of study for new members and other applicant countries to the European Union, *New Library World*, **106** (3/4), 173–86.

Lazerson, M. and Bateson, R. (2007) *Innovation, Implementation, and Management in Higher Education*, Central European University Department of Public Policy, http://web.ceu.hu/dpp/courses/0708/innov.pdf.

McCormick, R. and Li, N. (2006) An Evaluation of European Learning Objects in Use, *Learning, Media and Technology*, **31** (3), 213–31.

Nunnington, N. and Eilander, H. (2005) The European Challenge, *CEBE Transactions*, **2** (1), 44–63, Centre for Education in the Built Environment, www.cebe.heacademy.ac.uk/transactions/pdf/NickNunnington.pdf.

Öhström, B. (2008) Denmark's Electronic Research Library: implementation of user-friendly integrated search systems in Denmark. In Brophy, P., Craven, J. and Markland, M. (eds), *Libraries Without Walls 7: exploring 'anytime, anywhere' delivery of library services*, Facet Publishing.

Palonen, V. (2002) The Tritonia Academic Library: new ways of organizing libraries, *Scandinavian Public Library Quarterly*, **35** (3), www.splq.info/issues/vol35_3/07.htm.

Portier, S. J. (2006) *Challenges for Higher Education in the European Context: presentation at the 1st European Sakai Day (Lübeck, Germany) September 7, 2006,* www.oncampus.de/fileadmin/inhalte/projekte/ref/esd_spr/portier_luebeck_20 06.ppt.

Van der Graaf, M. (2007) DRIVER: Seven Items on a European Agenda for Digital Repositories, *Ariadne,* **52,** www.ariadne.ac.uk/issue52/vandergraf/.

Veen, W. (2005) *2020 Vision: keynote lecture at Online Educa 2005,* www.global-learning.de/g-learn/downloads/veen-visions2020.pdf.

9

Scaling the ivory tower: widening participation pathways at the University of Manchester

Introduction

When the Labour government was elected in the UK in 1997 its major priority was 'education, education, education'. An ambitious target was set to engage 50% of the 18–30 age group in higher education (HE) by 2010. At the time the level was just over 30% but 80% of that figure consisted of students from more affluent backgrounds, indicating that young people from less privileged environments were least likely to engage in HE. Money was allocated by the Higher Education Funding Council for England (HEFCE) to HE institutions and targeted at raising aspirations and attainment among young people from lower-socio-economic backgrounds and minority groups, and also mature students. Like many institutions, the University of Manchester began a programme of activities which eventually included every faculty and school and also the University's cultural assets including the John Rylands University Library (JRUL). It is unusual for the library to be a major player from the outset in developing these plans.

This chapter describes the Library's scheme against this backdrop, including how it introduced young people to library systems and resources in their school years and encouraged them to use one of the world's major research libraries in their studies – both to improve their potential to engage in higher education and also to encourage them to consider the University of Manchester as a destination for that education. The scheme meant working with a wide range of other agencies both internal and external, allowing staff to forge new partnerships, not least with learners. In conclusion the success or otherwise of the University's widening participation work is evaluated, including the library's contribution.

UK widening participation strategy

Following government imperatives, most higher education institutions (HEIs) began programmes for widening participation (WP). Money was allocated via HEFCE partly through the so-called 'postcode premium', allocated to HE institutions per capita accepted from low participation neighbourhoods (LPNs) that are generally accepted from government statistics to contain a population perceived to be at a disadvantage. 'Aspirational funding' was also available, particularly to Russell Group universities who had a higher percentage than average of students from private and state grammar schools, and little tradition of accepting students from the broader state school system (see www.hefce.ac.uk/news/HEFCE/2000/widecon.htm; the Russell Group is an association of leading UK research-intensive universities committed to maintaining the highest standards of research, education and knowledge transfer).

Universities could also bid for funding from HEFCE to begin projects aimed at encouraging young people from poorer backgrounds with potential to consider HE options. There was often a distinction in the rationale posited for WP initiatives between the older established universities, such as Manchester, and the newer universities created in 1992. In the former, WP programmes were often seen as raising aspirations so that young people would consider any HE institution as a destination, not necessarily the institution running the programme. In the newer universities WP programmes were often considered as part of the recruitment process, and participants in the programmes were seen as potential recruits. The University of Manchester considers both outcomes to be part of its strategy.

Since 2003 WP funding has been channelled on a regional and sub-regional basis through the Aimhigher partnerships. Established in April 2003, Aimhigher seeks to encourage more people into higher education, particularly those from under-represented groups. Emphasis is placed on co-operative schemes between HE, further education (FE) and schools (see www.direct.gov.uk/en/EducationAndLearning/UniversityAndHigherEducation/DG073697).

The model used by Aimhigher for its work with partner institutions follows a route of raising awareness, aspiration and attainment, continues with encouraging application and admission and then concludes with retention. Schemes are allocated funding if they meet one or more of these aims and include collaboration with partner institutions. Although the University of Manchester receives Aimhigher funding, much of its work is now embedded in the infrastructure of the organization and the library is seen as crucial to the success of its goals.

Widening participation begins

In the early days of widening participation the University of Manchester began a targeted access scheme (TAS) whereby young people from deprived areas, whom it was thought could benefit from higher education, were selected by their schools to take part in the programme. At first there were 30 pupils from each of the three schools involved in Manchester. Eventually all 23 Manchester high schools were involved, as well as other schools in the Greater Manchester area.

The scheme used student volunteers from the University to act as mentors. The programme started with young people in Year 9 (age 13/14 years); the university students went into schools to talk about their experiences in HE and to offer advice and guidance. Many of the student volunteers saw the scheme as a chance to help young people like themselves. The scheme continued into Years 10 and 11 with curriculum and study skills support and also a very popular social programme. Student progress was monitored into sixth-form college and FE to continue the early work. The parents of the young people were also involved from the beginning. Without parental support many of them would not consider higher education, so it was important that the idea of HE as an 'ivory tower' was countered. Consequently both parents and young people were brought on visits to the University to make it seem a welcoming place. The student mentor scheme grew into the student ambassador scheme, which now recruits over 300 student volunteers each year to visit schools, act as mentors and help run University activities like campus tours, master classes and summer schools.

Widening participation at the new University of Manchester

In 2004 the Victoria University of Manchester and UMIST (University of Manchester Institute of Science and Technology) merged to form the new University of Manchester and the library was given its current name – the John Rylands University Library or JRUL. The president of the new University, Professor Alan Gilbert, was determined to make the University of Manchester one of the most important and respected research universities in the world and the strategic plan Towards Manchester 2015 was published. One of the nine goals, entitled 'Widening Participation', was 'to make the University of Manchester the UK's most accessible research-intensive university'. The WP work done at the University of Manchester has been recognized as one of the most successful programmes of its type in the UK.

The University Library role

The JRUL was involved right from the beginning. A member of staff was identified to take the lead role within the library and to liaise with the WP office and faculties involved in WP activities. This responsibility has grown, with the postholder actively seeking collaborative work both within and outside the university. The appointment of a WP co-ordinator in the university library is considered unique among HE institutions in the UK. This strategic focus through one individual has been considered a major factor in the success of WP initiatives in JRUL, as staff outside the library and outside the university have a name for easy contact.

Library schemes and initiatives

As previously mentioned, parents are thought to be influential in young people's decisions about higher education. At the initial TAS sessions, held in the evening on the campus, tours of the library were organized for parents and they also had tours of the historic John Rylands Library on Deansgate in the city centre. They were amazed at the size of the library and the resources on offer to students. One parent commented after a tour: 'Our son is of mixed race and at an inner city school and he knows now that he can attend university in the future and we, as his parents, expect him to.'

During the first summer of the scheme the young students spent a day at the University and did a study project in the library, using library resources to find information on famous Manchester graduates. A variety of other events were organized by the Widening Participation office of the University in collaboration with faculties, local schools and the library, including day visits, two-day seminars, master classes, debating days and summer schools for a week in early July.

For several years around 180 Year 11 (age 15/16 years) young people from across the north-west region came to spend a week at the University, experiencing student life both academic and social. As part of their week they did a major research project in the library using JRUL resources. Each of 20 groups covered a different topic, mostly involving current political, economic or health issues. Topics included the use of psychology in solving crimes, whether mobile phones damage health and the problem of population increase. Each group had to find at least one book, one journal article, one newspaper article and one website to inform their discussion and they all produced a poster and gave a two-minute presentation on their topic at the end of the week. In the summer of 2004 this scheme was expanded by combining with the UMIST (University of Manchester Institute of Science and

Technology) summer school in preparation for the merger of the two universities in October 2004. There were over 220 participants in that year.

The final session was attended by parents and senior members of the University. The students wore graduation robes and were given achievement awards. One of the Manchester participants in the 2000 summer school commented:

> Experience in the library was very beneficial. I realized how big it was and how much information it contained. The tour around the John Rylands Library opened my eyes to the size of a university library. We did some activities in and around the library which provided me with experience of how to get around and use the library in the most productive way. It is the heart of knowledge especially on a campus university and I am grateful that it wasn't new to me when I arrived at [University].

Widened access through collaboration

Gifted and talented programmes and Excellence in Cities (EIC) initiatives have been funded by central government and run by local education authorities to encourage the most gifted pupils and prevent them becoming 'turned off' by education through boredom. For several years the JRUL had an advanced English group using library facilities. Schoolchildren from Years 5 and 6 (age 9–11), who were achieving at higher standards than their age group, attended extra sessions on Saturday mornings in the library. The University was seen as a neutral location and it was also exciting for the parents to bring their children to the University.

The Manchester Excellence in Cities (EIC) project also collaborated with the University to provide a summer school for gifted and talented schoolchildren from Years 6–9 (age 10–14). It was run for three years and the schoolchildren were involved with a project called 'Tomb Team', studying aspects of Egyptian life. The children took part in activities with the Manchester Museum, the Whitworth Art Gallery, Jodrell Bank and the JRUL. They did research in the library, saw original Egyptian papyri, investigated artifacts at Manchester Museum, mummified an orange, produced a diary of their experiences and wrote and acted in a performance related to what they had discovered. This rich learning project is to be repeated in the summer of 2008.

In October 2003, through the Museums, Libraries and Archives North West, a half-term project was undertaken by children aged 10–14 based around themes in the children's novel *The Heartstone Odyssey* (Kumar, 1988). This project was a joint initiative between the Manchester Museum, the People's History Museum and the

JRUL. The book is a fantasy involving mice, an Indian dancer, journeys and an elephant. The children learnt about Indian textiles at the Whitworth Art Gallery in Manchester and journeys to Britain for immigrants from the People's History Museum; they decorated a cloak for an elephant and danced the story using Indian hand movements. Estelle Morris, at that time Minister for the Arts, was visiting Manchester Museum that day and dropped in to see the dancing. The children also kept a diary of their activities in a bound notebook with their name engraved on it, and these were shown to parents at a final session. The children kept them as record of their work.

These collaborative schemes were very important in the development of WP at the library. Colleagues from the Manchester Museum and the Whitworth Art Gallery, as well as WP staff from faculties and in schools, were able to see how the library could be part of projects, exploiting the full capacity of combined cultural collections through co-operation. It is unusual for a university library to be so involved with young learners but the experience of their enthusiasm and excitement is a welcome one for library staff.

Extending access to learners in schools and colleges

As WP became an integral part of the University's strategy, all departments were expected to take part and bid for funds for projects aimed at raising the aspirations and attainment of disadvantaged groups. As mentioned, Manchester Museum and the Whitworth Art Gallery had long been involved in activities aimed at young people but this was a new concept for the JRUL, and a scheme was proposed to allow access to young people from all backgrounds who were considering HE as a destination after school.

The scheme was first proposed by Diana Leitch, then Assistant Director and Deputy University Librarian, at a recruitment strategy meeting with senior members of the University. The Vice-Chancellor, Professor Sir Martin Harris, considered it an excellent idea and the scheme was launched in March 2001. The scheme allows reference only access to the JRUL for sixth-formers doing AS levels, A levels and Diplomas, for mature students on access courses and for the teachers and librarians who supported them from school sixth forms, sixth-form colleges and FE colleges across the north west. Access is allowed after 4 p.m. on weekdays and throughout weekends and vacations, except during May as this is the busy period for university students. As well as access to the printed stock and study space, the students are allowed to access the electronic journals and a few databases for which walk-in user access has been agreed with the license holders. User education is also provided to welcome school and college students to the library, because its size can be quite daunting on a first visit. Applications are processed via the partner school or college and not by individuals, although potential users are never turned away. The take-up has been successful and several schools bring subject groups to the library for a day, with an introductory session in the morning and the rest of the day spent researching their topics. This is seen as extremely beneficial for student course work.

Widened access with public libraries

Since JRUL's access scheme began, there has been interest from three local public library systems. Bury Public Library, on the outskirts of Manchester, launched its 'Passport to Learning' scheme in 2003 and JRUL became a partner, which allowed the public library to sponsor its readers for access tickets under the scheme. Nearby Stockport Public Library began a similar initiative, 'Key to Learning', in 2007. Most users of both schemes apply through the local colleges, but the opportunity is there for public library users to benefit. Negotiations are currently underway with Manchester Public Library for similar access.

Many areas in the UK have developed co-operative schemes which allow all library users access for reference to any designated library – usually public libraries, FE libraries, HE libraries and sometimes health libraries – under the Musuems, Libraries and Archives Council (MLA) Inspire initiative (www.inspire2.org.uk). Inspire is a national framework that encourages libraries in England from all sectors to work together so that they can provide better support for learners and potential learners. In the north-west there are schemes in Lancashire, Merseyside and Cheshire, but nothing formal has yet been developed for Greater Manchester.

Widening participation expansion at JRUL

In October 2004, when the universities merged, the library services – from the Joule and Precinct Libraries at UMIST and the library at Manchester Business School (MBS) – also merged. Following the publication of the new University strategy, JRUL began to expand its WP work. JRUL's strategic review 2006–10 followed the University's goals to show how it could support the University, and established key targets to measure success. Targets were set to increase school visits, issue more access cards and engage local schools and the community in visits to the historic John Rylands Library on Deansgate, Manchester, one of JRUL's many library locations. The latter was closed for three years for a £16 million renovation, re-opened in May 2007 and has always since its opening in 1900 been freely open to all – perhaps an early forerunner of widening participation in Manchester. A new strategic plan from 2008 is currently being discussed and targets for WP will be included.

Two current educational initiatives have also generated interest in the use of the library: the International Baccalaureate and the Extended Project Qualification, which is a compulsory part of the new Diplomas and an optional extra to the A level system. One local school in the pilot project used the JRUL resources extensively; several students presented their projects to university staff and were filmed by a team from the Department for Children, Schools and Families (DCSF). Many of the students said very gratifyingly on film how much help using JRUL resources had been to them in researching their projects.

The Manchester Access Programme

From September 2006 English universities have been allowed to charge variable tuition fees of up to £3000 per annum under the Higher Education Act 2004. Each university must submit an Access Agreement to the Office for Fair Access (OFFA). This document explains how the universities will use some of the extra income generated to assist low income families. Nearly 30% of the extra income which the University of Manchester received was used for this purpose, which was one of the most generous schemes for Russell Group universities, as confirmed by the Office for Fair Access (OFFA, 2008).

The University of Manchester's OFFA submission uniquely made several references to the library. It mentioned the appointment of a dedicated member of library staff, the Widening Participation Co-ordinator, to liaise with WP staff across the university. The library access scheme for school and college students was referred to, as were plans for a Manchester Access Programme (MAP) targeted at specific disadvantaged groups in Greater Manchester. This programme enrolled young students from lower socio-economic backgrounds, whose parents or carers had not experienced HE, on a two-year course with a view to them applying to the University of Manchester. Successful completion of the course was worth 40 UCAS points, which meant students would get a slightly reduced grade offer from the university than other students who had not done the programme. (UCAS is the central UK organization through which applications are processed for entry to higher education. Points are awarded for specific grades at A level, which universities use to offer conditional places at university.)

As part of the programme students submitted an academic assignment; they were offered a borrowing card for JRUL to assist them in their research. Introductory sessions on using the library were given to the whole group. In 2006, 95 MAP applications from young people resulted in 55 student enrolments at Manchester and 23 at other universities. In the *Annual Report on Widening Participation to the Office for Fair Access* (University of Manchester, 2007), a case study on support for students on the Manchester Access Programme by JRUL was highlighted.

During the early years of WP schemes many University staff wanted to be able to access statistical information to show whether their schemes were reaching the target audience and having an impact on applications to the university generally. In 2006 the University implemented a database to record all WP activities. Identification of deprived areas enabled the university to ensure that planned events benefited the target groups. The library also submits data to the database which allows for easy retrieval of the reporting information necessary for producing its annual reports to the university WP office and for the key performance indicators required by library management to be submitted in the JRUL's operational review. Submission of the annual report triggers a payment to JRUL from the WP budget, as the work done by the library is seen as extremely important. Although the access scheme run by JRUL is open to all school and college students, analysis of the school data shows that around 30% of the access scheme users come from schools and colleges in disadvantaged areas, mirroring national figures for widening participation.

Are widening participation schemes successful?

Recent statistics do show a small increase in the percentage of students from diverse backgrounds entering higher education. The original figure of just over 30% of 18–30-year-olds in HE in 1997 has now risen to well over 40%, but is still some way off the government goal of 50% by 2010. Less than a third of students from less affluent backgrounds are entering higher education, in contrast to their more wealthy peers. So, nationally, the large amount of government money used on the WP agenda looks on the surface to have had little impact. This conclusion may be a little unfair. The Higher Education Statistics Agency statistics (HESA, 2008) from which these results are derived are from 2006–7, as it takes time to compile such complex data. Also, since 2003 when the funding was channelled through Aimhigher, much stricter criteria have been used to ensure that money is channelled to targeted groups, so it may be several more years before the full impact of some of the WP work is seen. Another probable factor in the success or otherwise of WP has been the introduction of student fees and student loans. Stories in the media of students leaving university in debt do not encourage lower income families to see university as a viable option. New financial aid packages announced by the government could help to overcome this problem, but the complexities of the system may deter many young people.

Attitudes to WP in the UK diverge, demonstrating the variety of perspectives about students inherent in the class-conscious UK HE system. For example, an article in *Times Higher Education* on 22 May 2008 reported on a paper by a leading academic at a British university who claimed that the greater proportion of students from higher social classes at highly selective universities was not a sign of admissions prejudice but the result of simple meritocracy. This claim was rejected by the NUS (National Union of Students), the UCU (University and College Union) and Bill Rammell, Minister of State (Lifelong Learning, Further and Higher Education), Department for Innovation, Universities and Skills. The National Union of Students President responded thus:

> Of course, social inequality shapes people's lives long before they leave school, but the higher education sector cannot be absolved of its responsibility to ensure that students from all social backgrounds are given the opportunity to fulfil their potential . . . many talented individuals from poor backgrounds are currently not given the same opportunities as those from more privileged backgrounds. This problem will not be addressed as long as academics . . . are content to accept the status quo and do nothing to challenge the inherent class bias in education.
>
> (Attwood, 2008)

On the other hand, recent research by the Sutton Trust reported in the *Education Guardian* on 10 March 2008 has shown that 26% of students who attended summer schools specifically targeted at disadvantaged young people run by five universities funded by the Sutton Trust went on to obtain first class degrees, compared with the national average of 10.5% (Andalo, 2008).

The recently published HESA statistics indicate that the University of Manchester is performing above its benchmark for admissions from low participation neighbourhoods, and numerically it admits more entrants from less privileged backgrounds than any other Russell Group university, although there has been a decline in admissions from state schools and colleges. Possibly for this reason the President of the University, Professor Alan Gilbert, in a recent interim review on undergraduate education reported on the BBC news website on Thursday 15 May 2008, warned that Manchester is moving further away from its benchmarks for widening participation. He said: 'We aim to be an inclusive institution and therefore need to adopt more systematic measures to enable identification and selection of the best possible students from all educational backgrounds.' The piece was entitled by the BBC, rather sensationally, 'Manchester may lower entry grades' bringing possible accusations of 'dumbing down', but the text makes it clear that Professor Gilbert is actually advocating 'more sophisticated measures of academic performance to identify the most outstanding students' to enable the University of Manchester to pursue its widening participation goal.

Conclusions

All higher education institutions are committed to widening participation work, but the extent to which library services are involved in that work varies enormously. Pope (2007) produced an unpublished dissertation for an MA in library and information management for Manchester Metropolitan University entitled *Widening Participation: the role of university libraries in the North West*. She carried out interviews with staff in most of the region's universities and concluded that about half of the university libraries in the north-west had a clear commitment to supporting WP goals in their university, and the rest engaged in some activities on an informal basis but were focused on existing rather than potential students.

WP activities in JRUL have increased by more than 20% over the past three years, and the use of JRUL reference cards by school and college students has also increased dramatically. Students have had early exposure to the types of resources provided in a university library, which should enhance their information skills and provide them with the capability to progress into higher education and succeed. Despite early fears, increased access by prospective HE students has not impacted adversely on the core services of the library, and library staff have not found themselves overwhelmed by requests for information from external users; most of the planning work associated with the scheme is done by the Widening Participation Co-ordinator.

The WP work for the University of Manchester brings many benefits to the JRUL. It increases the library's profile within the University and shows the library's commitment to the WP initiative. The library access scheme even attracted national interest, with a mention in *Times Higher Education* on 8 October 2004 on the future of academic libraries (Fazackerley, 2004). Access to the library resources and library involvement in other university WP initiatives is intended to increase the likelihood of local students applying either to this University or other HE institutions. The scheme also contributes to the Department for Culture, Media and Sport's library agenda for more cross-sectoral co-operation (www.culture.gov.uk).

In conclusion, although the impact of WP programmes on the educational framework of the UK is yet to be proved, the University of Manchester schemes appear to be generating some success, and the school and college access scheme run by the JRUL in particular has proved to be very popular, as shown by its take-up and continued benefit to learners who have, with the library's help, begun to scale that ivory tower.

References

Andalo, D. (2008) Summer School Brings Degree of Success for Students, *Education Guardian*, (10 March), http://education.guardian.co.uk/print/0,,332883034-108729,00.html.

Attwood, R. (2008) Elite Institutions' Class Bias Simply Reflects Meritocracy, *Times Higher Education*, (22 May), 4.

BBC News (2008) *Manchester May Lower Entry Grades*, (15 May), http://news.bbc.co.uk/1/hi/education/7402737.stm.

Department for Education and Skills (2002) *Education and Skills: delivering results; a strategy to 2006*, www.dfes.gov.uk/aboutus/strategy/pdf/DFES-Strategic%20Framework.pdf.

Fazackerley, A. (2004) Adapt to Survive the Next Chapter, *Times Higher Education Supplement*, (8 October), 18–19.

Higher Education Statistics Agency (2008) *Performance Indicators*, www.hesa.ac.uk/index.php/content/category/2/32/141/.

Kumar, A. (1988) *The Heartstone Odyssey: Chandra's story*, Allied Mouse.

Office for Fair Access (2008) *Access Agreement Monitoring: outcomes for 2006–7*, www.offa.org.uk/about/publications/monitoring2006–07.

Pope, D. (2007) *Widening Participation: the role of university libraries in North West England*, MA dissertation, Manchester Metropolitan University.

University of Manchester (2005) *Towards Manchester 2015*, University of Manchester.

University of Manchester (2007) *Annual Report on Widening Participation to the Office for Fair Access (OFFA)*, University of Manchester.

Part 3

Transformation through integrative practice: learning from each other using research-informed approaches

10

Transforming ourselves: developing the multiprofessional team

LINDSEY MARTIN

Introduction

This chapter looks closely at the learning support roles and approaches that have emerged as a result of changes to support services as they reposition themselves within their institutions in order to anticipate or respond to the challenges of such change. Taking a UK perspective, it examines the new professional groups, their roles, skill sets and working practices, and the trend towards adoption of multiprofessional team approaches to supporting learners. It also discusses the perceived barriers, challenges and enablers to the establishment of such teams and the role that staff development must play in the evolution of individuals and teams. An institutional case study will describe how new approaches to learning and teaching have driven strategic use of staff development to create conditions where multiprofessional teams are an embedded feature of working life. The chapter will conclude with an exploration of how the emerging trend towards an embedded and contextualized academic literacies approach to learning support has created tensions as well as opportunities for new professionals and academics.

The changing learning and teaching environment

Although the context of change within higher education (HE) has been covered in detail by previous chapters, it is worth briefly revisiting themes that have been fundamental to the emergence and growth of learner support roles and approaches.

'Professionalization' of teaching and learning

Traditional teacher and classroom-centred practice has been challenged by what has been described as the 'professionalization' of teaching practice in HE in the UK following the publication of the Dearing Report (National Committee of Inquiry into Higher Education, 1997). The view of teaching as a serious, scholarly business has facilitated a shift in thinking around curriculum design towards learner-centred, social-constructivist pedagogical approaches.

The impact of technology on learning, teaching and academic support services

It is interesting to note that while a literature has emerged around how the introduction of online learning is effecting change upon the roles of academics and academic library staff, little is written that illuminates how this process of change has been successfully managed and sustained (Hunter, Clarke and Shoebridge, 2005). In particular, we know little about if and how academic libraries (and wider converged services) have managed to reposition themselves in order to anticipate or respond to the multiple challenges of what Beetham (2001) describes as the 'mainstreaming' of online learning within learning and teaching.

The emergence of the academic skills agenda

Despite the growing acceptance of constructivist approaches to learning and teaching, there remain tensions within an education system that is working towards achieving mass participation. Changing pedagogies does not, according to Haggis (2003), make the tacit details of academic study any clearer to learners. Haggis argues that it is unlikely that even the most well-educated post-school student arrives at university with the strategies or skills that will enable them to 'critique', 'argue' or 'structure', and as a result many students are 'pathologized' for their lack of study skills. Furthermore, the development of learners' study skills has not traditionally been the concern of academics, who consequently demonstrate little understanding of how such skills development can be integrated within the curriculum (Cotterell, 2001; Haggis, 2003). This deficit view of student skills has resulted in the rapid growth of professional support staff within universities, whose job is to 'fix' the skills 'problem' with what are frequently described as 'bolted-on' skills courses.

Convergence and integration

Whereas early examples of converged services were largely driven by the convergence of the technologies used in both libraries and computing services, latterly a learner-focused model of convergence has emerged that is less concerned with formal, structural convergence or technologies. It is interesting to note that the literature provides no examples of structural or informal convergence that include centres for academic study skills.

Fisher (2004, 79) describes the essential feature of successful convergence as 'planned and managed staff development appropriate to the identified needs of the individuals who deliver the support to staff and students alike'. In the early days of convergence in the HE sector, it was feared that 'de-professionalization' of roles and erosion of specialist skills would result. The reality, according to Abbott (1998, 321), has been that professional and specialist skills are required in even greater measure. The complexities of working within a formal converged service or across discrete support services have required staff to develop, in addition to task skills, a range of process skills: 'self presentation, marketing, persuasion, negotiation, team working, and the ability to communicate effectively with different professional groups'.

Four changing learner support roles

The preceding sections of this chapter have alluded to specific roles: the academic, the learning technologist, the academic skills adviser and the academic librarian. It is important to obtain an understanding of each of these groups' identity and role before turning to matters of team working, collaboration and staff development.

Academics

The role of the academic must be included in any discussion of learner support as changes to the academic's role have strongly influenced the development of the learner support professional. The use of the term 'professional' in relation to academics is interesting, as the literature presents two conflicting views. First, there is the view of the academic as experiencing identity crisis and loss of autonomy arising out of new corporate cultures within universities, where academics are increasingly 'managed' and, in their view, 'deprofessionalised' (Knight, 2002; Robson, 2006). Conversely, the professionalization of learning and teaching and the widespread use of technology have begun to change the traditional perception of the academic from a solitary figure immersed in their discipline and resistant to change, to more of a facilitator of learning. Greater breadth and complexity of programmes of study alongside the greater complexity of learner support needs in recent years have driven team approaches to learner support, resulting in a blurring of roles between academics and other learner support professionals (Armitage and O'Leary, 2003; Tait, 2003).

Learning technologists

Learning technologists are the newest group of 'new professionals' to emerge in HE and can, according to Beetham (2001), be categorized into three groups of staff:

- new specialists: multiskilled and peripatetic, but with learning technologies at the core of their professional identity
- academics who have incorporated an interest in learning technology into their professional identity or who have a formal responsibility for it within their academic role
- learning support professionals in non-academic (roles e.g. librarians and technical support staff) who do not define themselves as learning technologists, but regard learning technologies as the context in which they are now working.

There are no fixed routes to becoming a learning technologist, no acknowledged professional qualification or any prerequisite experience for entry to the profession. However, Oliver (2002) states that the new specialist category of learning technologist has developed a sense of its own identity, and there is also evidence that they are now employing strategies to support and demonstrate their own development (ALT, 2007; Armitage et al., 2004).

Academic skills advisers

There is an absence of literature on study skills advisers as a discrete group with a professional identity and a collective agenda for their ongoing professional development. While organizations such as Forum for Continuing Adult Education (FACE), ESCalate and Action on Access provide opportunities for professional networking, and discussion boards such as the Association of Dyslexia Specialists also provide an arena for networking, there is no organization or forum specifically for the professional development or interests of study skills advisers. As the least known and understood of the learner support professionals in UK higher education, there is clearly a need for them to publish case studies that describe the evolution of their roles, their professional development needs and their experiences of supporting learners and of working with other professional groups.

Academic librarians

Out of the four professional groups described, it could be argued that it is only academic librarians who have a longstanding professional identity and awareness. Certainly, they have long reflected upon and documented their professional evolution, as evidenced by the considerable literature on changing staff roles in academic libraries. In the past decade, much has been written in particular about the changing role of the subject librarian or information professional, who is widely regarded as being at the forefront of change and role development, requiring a broader skillset than before (Levy and Roberts, 2005; Pinfield, 2001).

The role of the academic librarian is increasingly regarded as growing closer to that of the academic and as related to the relatively new role of learning technologist. According to Bury, Martin and Roberts (2006, 25) this is 'particularly in the context of e-learning where information professionals have developed new approaches to supporting learners in the electronic environment, for example, using online tutorials and embedding e-resources into VLEs (virtual learning environments)'.

The emergence of multiprofessional teams

It is appropriate at this point to consider more closely what or who we mean by the multiprofessional team. These teams are often described as multiprofessional, multidisciplinary, hybrid, multiskilled and/or cross-functional. In addition to the four groups described previously, the list could also include educational developers and IT/computing staff. Multiprofessional teams should not, however, be confused with individuals or groups who simply consult or liaise together over a period of time. Rather, they have a defined membership and a shared aim, and the jobs and skills of each member complement those of other team members (Adair, 1996).

Little is known yet about whether multiprofessional teams have delivered any change in the support of learning and teaching. While multiprofessional teams are anecdotally viewed as effective at delivering change in learning and teaching, there is little evidence to support this contention.

Case study

The following case study aims to draw together the themes discussed in the previous sections by describing the role of staff development as an agent of change.

Context: Edge Hill University and Learning Services

Edge Hill University is located in the north-west of England, with 9000 students on a range of degree and diploma courses and a further 6000 on continuing professional development courses, particularly in education and health-related areas. Edge Hill has strong centralized academic support structures, enhanced by the formation of Learning Services in 2003, and incorporates learning resource centres and information provision, learning support, ICT user support for learning and teaching, e-learning development and support, media services and dyslexia support. The institutional VLE (WebCT), introduced in 1999, now supports over 400 courses delivered across the curriculum and currently has approximately 8000 registered users studying a range of courses, both undergraduate and postgraduate. Administration, development and support for the VLE and other learning technologies are managed within Learning Services by a team of learning technologists working closely with academic colleagues. As this is a converged service, a range of staff are actively involved in learning and teaching developments and delivery.

This case study focuses on academic liaison advisers who are library and information specialists, learning technologists and staff from the skills development team.

SOLSTICE: a conceptual framework for multiprofessional team working

In January 2005, Edge Hill was awarded Centre for Excellence in Teaching and Learning (CETL) status for its work supporting students. The bid for the award that established the centre was called SOLSTICE (Supported Online Learning for Students using Technology for Information and Communication in their Education). Integral to the bid was a claim that, as well as an innovative method of programme delivery, SOLSTICE was also a new structure of academic teams of academic and learning support staff working together to design and deliver programmes, particularly but not exclusively in the domain of online learning.

The importance of SOLSTICE as a key institutional driver of multiprofessional team development cannot be overstated. It provides the conceptual and structural framework and brokers opportunities where expertise, knowledge and skills are shared. While there has been blurring of roles, particularly in relation to pedagogy, the framework has safeguarded the professional distinctiveness of individual team members by establishing processes that ensure clarity of purpose, role and specific contribution.

The role of leadership, ethos and empowerment

The most crucial precursor to ensuring organizational readiness for change and development is leadership that visibly values learning (Waight and Stewart, 2005). Within Learning Services, this has been evidenced by the senior management's commitment to their own scholarship of learning and teaching and to the ongoing development of staff at all levels. Sue Roberts, Dean of Learning Services (2002–7), described this approach as providing strategic leadership at a service level: creating vision, direction and 'conditions for learning' for staff within the service.

The result of this form of leadership has been the emergence of a workforce that is reflective, flexible, collaborative and cohesive, with learner support and development at its core. The success of the service in responding to the challenges and opportunities created by convergence, technology and SOLSTICE is underpinned by research, scholarship and activities that have taken all the learning support professionals on a journey of development in terms of their contribution to learning and teaching.

The service-wide staff development programme

It was recognized in the early stages of convergence that there was a need to develop and prepare staff to take on new and changing roles. Staff development is therefore carefully aligned with the service mission, vision and values. In parallel with the staff development strategy, structural and operational changes were implemented to give staff time to learn new skills and take on new activities. Changes included new team structures, and remission from help desks, evening work and responsibilities of an operational nature. Considered use of the staff appraisal scheme ensured that individual roles were allowed to develop in a planned and strategic way.

Learning Services staff development activities can be categorized as follows:

- developing a people-oriented and participative culture: following the convergence with Learning Technology and Study Skills in 2003, a programme of events was introduced into the staff development programme that facilitated social interaction, sharing of experience and awareness-raising regarding the work of other groups of staff
- task-focused training in-house by specialist teams (e.g. in use of the VLE, in IT troubleshooting and in locating books and journals)
- process-focused training that includes personal development sessions on emotional intelligence, creativity and self as an e-learner, largely delivered by an external consultant who tailors her approaches to the local context

- wider University-accredited programmes such as the postgraduate certificate in teaching and learning support in HE
- externality: all outward-facing activity such as visits, benchmarking, professional networking and disseminating formal research and practice
- experiential learning through coaching, mentoring, job shadowing and projects undertaken by multiprofessional teams.

This case study now focuses on three multiprofessional team projects driven and framed by the SOLSTICE method, where staff were prepared and supported by the holistic approach to staff development described above. It aims to show how the projects have been developmental and have contributed to our understanding of how such teams can work effectively.

Example 1: research project into learners' use of technologies

The term 'multiprofessional team' here refers to six members of Learning Services staff with diverse research and professional backgrounds. Their project resulted from a successful application to Edge Hill's Research Development Fund in 2005, and aimed to understand student learning experiences in relation to learner support and the learning environment at Edge Hill, while illuminating student experiences of using learning technologies.

The project also researched the team's development process by capturing and reflecting upon its experiences during the forming and formative stages. It aimed to explore issues relating to the effectiveness and suitability of undertaking research within a multiprofessional team. As a result of this research project, three pivotal, interlinked, *team-shaping* factors were identified:

1 Team roles: a clear understanding of team roles was deemed absolutely crucial for effective team collaboration. However, it became evident from this project that members' professional roles had led to preconceived ideas about their roles within the team. Time devoted at the start to defining the project and sharing perspectives, together with the process of critical self-reflection and subsequent discussions, provided space for the team to renegotiate individual team roles.

2 Reciprocity: the success of this multiprofessional team greatly relied on notions of reciprocity, a shared desire and concern around giving something of value to the team effort. Members frequently questioned the ways in which they could uniquely and collaboratively contribute to the

project. For instance, one team member commented: 'I'm conscious that I feel I have not contributed a great deal in the developments so far.'

3   Communication: the study also found that strong social skills were absolutely crucial in the success of team communication, as was the use of a weblog (blog) for discussing, disagreeing and reflecting. The blog proved to be a highly successful tool for facilitating communication, ensuring processes were transparent and capturing personal reflections on what it felt like to be part of that team.

Our study into the multiprofessional approach provided us with an insight into the challenges and benefits of operating in such a team, and concluded: 'Learning in action has also allowed us to develop appropriate research skills in a way that is meaningful and productive' (Davey et al., 2006).

Example 2: Spring Board – enhancing academic study skills

While study skills advisers, learning technologists and information professionals have had considerable success in developing study, e-learning and information literacy skills within academic programmes, they have only tentatively begun to explore how the three skill sets could be brought together under the umbrella of 'academic literacies' (Lea and Street, 1998).

The Summer Enrichment Programme at Edge Hill provided an opportunity to combine these elements. Learning Services was asked to create a 15-credit module to enhance academic study and information skills. The brief requested tailored approaches and support materials that could be delivered to students using the institution's virtual learning environment, WebCT, to allow them to learn at their own pace and from a common platform. A multiprofessional team approach ensured that the module (Spring Board) was developed with an understanding of the technological, accessibility and pedagogical issues.

The team that created and taught Spring Board found the experience personally developmental. The brief cameos below have been provided by two of the team and describe their experience of working in a converged service and in this particular multiprofessional team.

Margi Rawlinson, Skills Development Co-ordinator

I have been the Skills Development Co-ordinator based in the Edge Ahead Skills Centre, Learning Services, for five years. The Centre provides both study skills and

SpLD (specific learning difficulties such as dyslexia or dyspraxia) support for students and staff. The diverse nature and geographical location of Edge Hill's student population make this a very challenging area to work in. It is interesting to note how roles such as mine are increasingly becoming more of a hybrid of academic support adviser and basic skills tutor, rather than study skills support adviser.

It's important to mention the impact of working together on Spring Board and other projects. I've gained skills in WebCT and ICT design and delivery. Even though I have teaching and assessing experience, I learnt about e-learning and what to be aware of – when to intervene and not in discussion support. We have also learned a lot from each other, such as general study skills and info skills (mine improved greatly when tutoring on Spring Board because I had to learn how to do effective searches, etc.). Finally, we need more collaboration via academic teams where we all learn from each other . . . I love it and it's the only way to work holistically!

Mark Roche, Learning Technology Development Manager

I have worked at Edge Hill since 2000, when I was Project Officer for the COMET project. After that I became a Learning Technology Development Officer and am now the Learning Technology Development Manager. Learning Technology was only brought into Learning Services in 2003, but I think it is important to say that there was close and successful collaboration between the two services before then.

When we became part of Learning Services, a lot of effort was put into integrating us into the service, which was good. We became involved in cross-service working groups and service delivery like student induction workshops. We had access to staff development that cuts across all layers of the service. It has been really helpful to talk to people outside of their roles and to build good working relationships outside of my own area.

As far as working on Spring Board is concerned, the team was able to build on relationships that already existed. It meant that we trusted one another to come through when deadlines were tight. It felt like there was a shared ownership of the project – it became more than just a job, it was a creative process and produced a better rounded product. I felt like I brought an expertise to the team, but equally, I learned a lot of new things, for example the application of academic quality processes and validation. Also, as a learning technologist, I create a lot of e-learning content and talk about 'chunking' and 'pedagogy' but this project gave me the opportunity to try them first hand and get direct feedback from my own experience and that of the learners.

Example 3: working in a new academic team to develop e-literacy

This final example describes a multiprofessional team consisting of an academic librarian (academic liaison adviser), a learning technologist and an academic working on a project to embed an online information literacy tutorial within the undergraduate health degree programme. All three professionals reported substantial development and changes in their role as a result. The academic liaison adviser felt that her role had changed through collaborative, cross-team project work and that her skills had developed at the same pace as those of staff in the faculty. The learning technologist's role demanded 'an outward-looking approach – becoming an e-learning "evangelist" in order to raise awareness of WebCT within the institution'. For the academic, the impact of e-learning was equally great: 'It has involved a reassessment of how I teach. It is about learning and has the potential to be inclusive, open, transparent and collaborative.'

Three very similar and enthusiastic perspectives emerged in relation to collaboration and teamworking, despite the different professional roles. In their own words: 'We can't work alone! We need to work as a team – faculty, academic liaison and learning technologists.' 'There's no need for me to work alone – people want to work collaboratively.' 'I couldn't work alone. Working with Adrian [learning technologist] and Rachel [librarian] is enjoyable and never a hassle.'

Case study summary

A strategic and joined-up approach to staff development within the service has established the conditions in which the SOLSTICE-enabled multiprofessional teams can flourish. In particular, the development of process skills has been viewed as of equal importance to the development of new task skills. Nurturing new teams by providing time to focus on the process of team development has been recognized and used to good effect. The success factors identified in the first example of multiprofessional teamwork can also be seen at work in the other two examples, namely: the creation of *trust and negotiated team roles*, the role of *reciprocity* in the social construction of team knowledge and skills, and the need for strong *social skills* and *transparent communication systems*. Paying attention to these factors has seemingly avoided the possible problems of territoriality and conflict identified in the literature (Roberts, 2005). What also emerges from the examples is that working and learning in multiprofessional teams is perceived as enjoyable, creative and productive of an outcome that is better than any that can be achieved individually.

Emerging trends in learner support

Academic literacies

This chapter has so far only touched on the influence of academic literacies on the learner support agenda. Much of the literature on academic study skills refers negatively to 'deficit', 'bolted-on', generic skills training compared to the 'embedded' academic literacies model where skills are developed as an integral part of the learner's programme of study. Wingate (2006, 459) asks whether 'the term "study skills" itself, trivializes learning' – and argues that 'much would be achieved if more academic staff could be encouraged to develop their students' learning within their regular teaching' (467). The literature suggests, however, that academics think they do not have the necessary skills to embed academic study skills, or that they do not have the time to do so. These tensions also apply to the integration of e-learning and information literacy within the curriculum.

The professionalization of teaching and learning has provided the conditions for academics to acknowledge the rationale behind the need to embed academic skills (or literacies) within their programmes of study. The practical application of embedding remains very tentative and there is not yet a consensus on how it should occur: there are merely suggestions based on individual practice (Haggis, 2003; Lea, 2004; Wingate, 2006). Convening multiprofessional teams to develop strategies and resources for embedding academic study, ICT and information skills seems an achievable and sustainable approach. From the point of view of academic librarians, skills advisers and learning technologists, working as multiprofessional teams towards an embedded model of skills delivery is essential as demand for their support exceeds their capacity to deliver. Such an approach offers the potential for learner support professionals to work smarter, not harder.

Staff development

The literature on team working of any sort tells us that effective teams do not emerge as a matter of chance (Adair, 1996; Bianey, Ulloa and Adams, 2004). Process is as important as output. Our emerging knowledge about the development and operation of Edge Hill's multiprofessional teams may be of benefit to others seeking to understand the ways in which effective multiprofessional teams might work. While we are still only at an early stage of understanding the process of facilitating effective teams, there are indications that the role of staff development is crucial in their success. Staff development has, however, changed from something that is 'done to' staff to being a highly participative way of learning new skills and knowledge that is tailored to strategic vision and planning.

Conclusion

The literature suggests that there is a significant trend towards multiprofessional teams comprising academics, technologists and librarians, but research into the involvement or otherwise of study skills advisers is minimal. Anecdotal evidence suggests, however, that specialist skills centres are beginning to converge with academic library and information services. Such convergence will provide more and improved opportunities for collaborating in multiprofessional teams. It is striking that, at this time in the UK, this group of learner support professionals has no voice and, seemingly, little legitimacy as a profession despite the growing demand for their services. An opportunity to gain an understanding of this group's working practices would be welcome. It is suggested that further research and discussion on the success factors for multiprofessional teams is now needed, to ensure that the trend of developing and working in such teams is based on recognized and informed practice.

References

Abbott, C. (1998) Personal Career Development in Converged Services, *Librarian Career Development*, **6** (3), 28–35.

Adair, J. (1996) *Effective Teambuilding: how to make a winning team*, Pan.

ALT (2007) *CMALT Prospectus: the Association for Learning Technology Certified Membership Scheme*, Association for Learning Technology, www.alt.ac.uk/docs/cmalt-prospectusv4.pdf.

Armitage, S., Bryson, M., Creanor, L., Higginson, C., Jenkins, M., Ringan, N., Newlans, B., Prescott, D. and Yip, H. (2004) *Supporting Learning Technology: relationships with research and theory*, Networked Learning Conference 2004, www.networkedlearningconference.org.uk/past/nlc2004/proceedings/symposia/symposium1/armitage_et_al.htm.

Armitage, S. and O'Leary, R. (2003) *A Guide for Learning Technologists*, LTSN Generic Centre e-Learning Series No. 4, Learning Teaching Support Network.

Beetham, H. (2001) *Career Development of Learning Technology Staff: scoping study*, Final Report, JISC Committee for Awareness, Liaison and Training Programme, www.jisc.ac.uk/media/documents/programmes/jos/cdss_final_report_v8.pdf.

Bianey, C., Ulloa, R. and Adams, S. G. (2004) Attitude Toward Teamwork and Teaming, *Team Performance Management*, **10** (7/8), 145–51.

Bury, R., Martin, L. and Roberts, S. (2006) Achieving Change Through Mutual Development: supported online learning and the evolving roles of health and information professionals, *Health Information Libraries Journal*, **23**, Supplement 1, 22–31.

Cotterell, S. (2001) *Teaching Study Skills and Supporting Learning*, Palgrave.

Davey, J., Kruger, S., Martin, L., McLoughlin, D., Roberts, S. and Williams, S. (2006) *Ethnographic Research Partnerships Within an Interdisciplinary Team at Edge Hill*, SOLSTICE Conference, www.edgehill.ac.uk/solstice/Conference2006/documents/39.pdf.

Fisher, B. (2004) Converging on Staff Development. In Oldroyd, M. (ed.), *Developing Academic Library Staff for Future Success*, Facet Publishing.

Haggis, T. (2003) Constructing Images of Ourselves? A critical investigation into 'approaches to learning' research in higher education, *British Educational Research Journal*, **29** (1), 89–104.

Hunter, R., Clarke, S. and Shoebridge, M. (2005) Change Management. In Melling, M. (ed.), *Supporting E-Learning: a guide for library and information managers*, Facet Publishing.

Knight, P. T. (2002) *Being a Teacher in Higher Education*, Society for Research into Higher Education (SRHE) and Open University Press.

Lea, M. (2004) Academic Literacies: a pedagogy for course design, *Studies in Higher Education*, **29** (6), 739–56.

Lea, M. and Street, B. (1998) Student Writing in Education: an academic literacies approach, *Studies in Higher Education*, **23** (2), 157–73.

Levy, P. and Roberts, S. (2005) *Developing the New Learning Environment: the changing role of the academic librarian*, Facet Publishing.

National Committee of Inquiry into Higher Education (1997) *Higher Education in the Learning Society* (Dearing Report), HMSO.

Oliver, M. (2002) What do Learning Technologists do? *Innovations in Education and Teaching International*, **39** (4), 245–52.

Pinfield, S. (2001) The Changing Role of Subject Librarians in Academic Libraries, *Journal of Librarianship and Information Science*, **33** (1), 32–8.

Roberts, S. (2005) New Professional Identities and Practices for Learner Support. In: Levy, P. and Roberts, S. (eds), *Developing the New Learning Environment: the changing role of the academic librarian*, Facet Publishing.

Robson, J. (2006) *Teacher Professionalism in Further and Higher Education: challenges to culture and practice*, Routledge.

Tait, A. (2003) Rethinking Learner Support in the Open University UK: a case study. In Tait, A. and Mills, R. (eds), *Rethinking Learner Support in Higher Education*, Routledge.

Waight, C. and Stewart, B. (2005) Valuing the Adult Learner in e-Learning: part 2 –
insights from four companies, *Journal of Workplace Learning*, **17** (5/6), 398–414.

Wingate, U. (2006) Doing Away with Study Skills, *Teaching in Higher Education*, **11**
(4), 457–69.

11

Not taught in graduate school: increasing student affairs' sphere of influence

SCOTT C. BROWN AND KENT PORTERFIELD

Introduction

Your campus is starting a new initiative. You have the knowledge and experience, but you do not get asked to participate. Student affairs and learner support professionals often find themselves at the perimeter of campus dialogues. What keeps them from realizing their potential on their campuses? How do we understand and impact organizational culture and help reshape it for the greater good? This chapter will help identify practical strategies to enlarge your sphere of influence on your campus, no matter what your position.

For some time higher education has been under increased scrutiny (American Association for Higher Education et al., 1998; Keeling, 2006). As a variety of stakeholders examine the college experience more closely, questions of greater accountability have brought attention towards learning (National Leadership Council for Liberal Education and America's Promise, 2007).

How does this context affect student affairs and learner support professionals? This is an unprecedented time of opportunity, in which the work of student affairs and other learner support areas and the current needs of higher education have become even more explicit and aligned. Institutions are asking: 'What do we want our students to know, value, and be able to do?' What can student affairs and other learner support areas do to advance these questions and become a bigger part of the dialogue? What new knowledge, skills and frameworks are needed to serve most effectively the holistic learning needs of our students? As professionals who support student learning both inside and outside the classroom, we need to put tool in hand, knowledge in head and wisdom in heart to help us help our institutions carry out clearly defined missions, goals and objectives (Brown, 2004a). All members of our learner support professions need to be able to enlarge and enhance their spheres of influence, regardless of position, on any type of campus.

However, what is required to move from this rhetoric to reality? What are the specific tools and guides? What are the specific barriers that keep these professionals from realizing their potential on their campuses? How do they shore up more 'political capital' to make change happen? How do they combine their shared strengths to operate out of a much broader base of influence? How do they understand and impact organizational culture and reshape it for the greater good?

This chapter will raise key questions and identify practical strategies to help professionals who support student learning increase their spheres of influence, with an emphasis on visioning, assessing situations within the campus context, making strategic alliances and implementing a strategy.

Visioning

In order to increase your sphere of influence, you will first need to develop an understanding and realistic picture of what an ideal role for you on your campus might look like, given your current position, area of responsibilities and campus climate. What are high but realistic goals for your area? If you were going to wave a magic wand, what would you like your ideal role on your campus to be? What initiatives do you want to be more involved in?

Example: visioning the ideal

One example of an initiative resulting from this type of visioning is the 'YourPlan' career program at Mount Holyoke College (MHC). Career centres have high aspirations to help students, but students do not always take the best advantage of their programs and services. There are many concerns about this lack of student engagement, which may lead to:

- limited self-awareness about their competences and values
- difficulty translating their college educations to the world outside the classroom
- not performing to their potential in application processes.

Mount Holyoke addresses these issues head-on by envisioning and implementing the 'YourPlan' program, a theory-based, developmental, four-year career curriculum that is cumulative, comprehensive, understandable and scalable (Brown, 2002, 2004b; Brown et al., 2007). The curriculum outlines expected career learning goals for each class year, and identifies specific tasks to help students achieve them.

Organizational resources, personnel and policies have been aligned towards the program, which is used as a springboard to deepen collaborations with key stakeholders (e.g. faculty, class deans and other student affairs staff). This program represents a full translation of theory to practice, and reflects a deep understanding of MHC's institutional culture and most pressing priorities. It allows the careers service office to fulfill its mission in ways that all stakeholders value, with a sustainable student services model. It also provides a concrete way to connect individual, mostly autonomous, programs/units into a more coherent whole.

Assessing your situation within the campus context

To make real progress towards your vision, you must have a clear sense of your situation within the campus context. To do this you must assess the campus culture, define campus priorities and manage your own situation.

Understanding your campus culture

One of the first and most important things to do is to deepen your understanding of your campus culture. Campus culture is incredibly powerful and very difficult to alter. What does your institution value? How do people interact? What symbols does the campus use to define its culture? What stories are told over and over again as a means to help others learn what your campus is like? What are the key themes and messages that are communicated on your admissions page or in a letter from your president? Culture is sometimes hard to define unless someone transgresses it. What is one thing a person can do at your institution that would trip a cultural landmine? How are significant conflicts resolved within the campus community? What are the 'unspoken' rules?

Although there are many different models for assessing organizational culture, Bolman and Deal (1991) suggest four frames for examining organizational issues and context: structural, political, human resources and symbolic. Of particular importance to considering culture is the symbolic frame through which organizational icons, symbols, stories, ceremonies, rituals and even common language are analysed and better understood.

Example: understanding campus culture

One learning experience about campus culture occurred early in Scott's tenure at MHC, when the Career Development Center (CDC) undertook the piloting of an electronic student portfolio. Although it was a powerful pedagogical tool with great promise, the CDC was not the right office at the right time to introduce this initiative. First, such a large initiative would have much deeper buy-in if it was 'co-sponsored' by a faculty member or academic administrative unit. Second, the institution did not feel urgency around the specific issues the portfolio was designed to address. Several key lessons were learned from this experience. To effect significant change beyond one's own unit and influence broader institutional priorities, understanding and appreciating institutional culture is paramount. Examining issues and opportunities from different organizational frames is a good way to gain this increased knowledge. Understanding how boundary-crossing ideas best germinate and gain traction on campus, knowing how to leverage carefully cultivated relationships and constantly representing the student affairs perspective in important campus dialogues are necessary actions of influential student affairs leaders, but they are difficult to achieve without a deep understanding and appreciation of cultural context.

Defining campus priorities

All of our own work has importance to us, but what matters most are the activities that conform to what the institution fundamentally needs from our offices. What is your institution's latest strategic document and how does your work connect to this directly? What keeps your president and/or your boss up at night? What does your institution's 'best self' look like? What are the barriers to this ideal and what is your specific role in realizing it? What are the roles of learner support professionals in helping to improve the quality of education for students and advance the goals of the larger institution?

Example: aligning with campus priorities

Most higher education institutions have strategic plans with defined strategic directions or specific vision elements. At Saint Louis University, strategic areas of influence (vision elements) which support the president's vision of being the 'nation's finest Catholic university' (Saint Louis University, 2008) include:

- a reputation of distinction
- a vibrant urban location
- a culture of high performance
- an affinity for the University's mission
- a global perspective.

Recognizing that opportunities and resources are largely dependent upon alignment, the Student Development division has aggressively pursued initiatives that directly and indirectly support these elements. An example of a Student Development initiative that supports the 'vibrant urban location' element of the University's vision would be the Grand Centre partnership, a collaborative with midtown St. Louis businesses and civic leaders that supports the arts district and promotes student engagement in the fine arts. Another would be an emerging student and academic affairs initiative, a 'centre of excellence' which will align service learning, servant leadership (leading by supporting others), community outreach/volunteerism and social justice pursuits into an integrated structure. The reality is that both of these initiatives have achieved greater support and notoriety because of their strong connection to and alignment with defined campus priorities.

Managing your situation

To be effective on campus, student affairs and other support professionals must engage in realistic self-appraisal. How are they regarded on their campuses? Why are they regarded in this way? How are you personally perceived on your campus? What are your perceived/actual strengths and weaknesses? How do you know? What problem(s) do you solve or contribute to solving for the institution? What do others on your campus think is the most important thing that you do? What are the issues that motivate the most influential 'players' on your campus? Recruitment? Retention? Development? Do you know of other comparable institutions that can be invoked to your advantage (competitive comparisons)? Are there benchmark data that people on your campus pay attention to and circulate widely?

Managing your situation means doing ordinary things, such as returning your phones calls and answering e-mails, extraordinarily well, and leading with 'yes' as often as possible when you field requests. Other ways to manage your campus situation well are through organizational efficacy, supervision, knowing your audience and contributing to the successful management of campus life issues.

Example: organizational efficacy

Having your organizational area operate at maximum efficiency is something all exemplary leaders hope to achieve. At Mount Holyoke College, the Career Development Center determined that the best way to achieve efficacy as a unit was to ensure that it aligned tightly with academic mission. Career Center staff introduced a new organizational framework that identified three learning outcomes

(Brown, 2002). This helped the Center, which was somewhat organizationally fragmented, to work more effectively. From the identified outcomes, the staff had a new lens through which to re-examine the organizational structure of the Center. Significant changes were made that increased Center efficiencies and staff ability to anticipate and respond to pressing institutional priorities. The Career Center became a much more prominent office on campus, and is now better able to negotiate and chart a path that fulfills its educational mission in an organizationally sustainable manner. With a more efficient structure in place, the talented staff have demonstrated a strong commitment to working with students and are better able to understand how their efforts fit within the larger institutional picture.

Example: supervision

Managing your situation well involves effective supervision of staff. Supervision is one of the most critical aspects of effective organizations (Janosik et al., 2003). An effective approach to supervision and professional development is to create a shared vision of organizational success, develop collective goals and harness your staff's individual and collective contributions towards those goals. Colgate University utilizes a performance evaluation process to appraise staff performance over the previous year, and to help staff develop clear, high, assessable goals connected to the larger objectives of the institution. The performance evaluation process helps staff develop workload efficiencies to accommodate any new responsibilities, and identify ways to manage shifting priorities (including reducing, eliminating and postponing projects); staff members must develop goals and plans to increase their desired skills, balance internal priorities with external demands and keep them tied to that which intrinsically motivates them. Some of the most important traits of a good manager are to establish a shared vision, connect staff to those collective goals and provide the individual support and guidance to help them be successful.

Example: know your audience

At Mount Holyoke College, the career centre adopted an 'educational entrepreneurial' approach; the staff were encouraged to have the 'hearts of educators, but the minds of entrepreneurs' (Brown, 2006, 28). A goal was to develop a deep understanding of the various constituents and stakeholders. There were competing and multiple priorities, as well as a need for more explicit feedback about how these different constituents and stakeholders defined success for the office. An external review was conducted to get honest and unvarnished assessment. Focus groups were also held, in which non- and low-frequency users of services were asked questions about their perceptions and what they specifically needed from the Career Center. Additionally, a faculty survey was used to gain impressions of the Career Center, determine what myths existed and learn more about what specific initiatives faculty found valuable. For example, through speaking with faculty (Brown, 2006), Career Center staff discovered that many faculty were bothered by how career services staff used the word 'learning' when communicating with others about programs and services. Once this issue was identified and understood, career service staff began using other words with similar meaning in their communications and interactions with faculty. This simple action helped improve faculty perceptions about the Career Center.

Example: campus life issues

Using the concept of self-appraisal in the context of examining an important campus issue, student affairs professionals at one institution decided to facilitate a new men's discussion group. The group was formed in response to a sexual assault incident, which had created a great deal of divisiveness within the campus community. Student affairs professionals volunteered to be some of the first members of this group, helping to increase membership among staff, faculty and students and to shape the group's discussions and activities. The group provided an opportunity for men from several generations to engage in frank discussions about how the negative consequences of male socialization have manifested in themselves, their families and society. This is just one small example of how student affairs can take a campus leadership role and provide a nuanced approach to a difficult issue – in this case, with a population that is difficult to reach.

Making strategic alliances

Who are the key players with formal or informal influence on campus? What is the organizational chart that does not appear on paper? What relationships have you developed that enable you to participate in important campus discussions? How are you working on connecting your work to the work of others? What are the opportunities to collaborate across difference? Who are some possible early adopters of more innovative, cross-boundary initiatives? What are some structures that you could facilitate which would create ways for people to connect? Making strategic alliances can be fostered by using the Socratic method to engage potential allies more deeply, as well as making efforts to create mutually beneficial collaborations.

Use the Socratic method

Often, student affairs and other student learner support professionals seek out allies on their campuses for the purpose of advancing a particular idea or initiative. This, in and of itself, is perfectly appropriate, but the seeking out of allies often ends up looking to others like the selling of your particular idea or solution, as opposed to genuinely working together with others to solve a problem or advance an idea. A softer approach, which often works better, is the use of what is typically thought of as a pedagogical technique called the Socratic method (Dye, 1996; Samples, 1998). Using the Socratic method, you would pose some thoughtful questions (as opposed to answers!) to your key stakeholders and partners.

You ask others a series of thoughtful, provocative and structured questions designed to take them down a particular path which further explores or examines the idea or initiative you are interested in pursuing. Through your questions, you are asking others to share their ideas, which is decidedly different from simply giving them your opinion or attempting to sell them your particular plan. Before you have suggested a possible answer or posited a particular approach to advancing the idea, you have more actively involved your potential allies. It is helpful to have studied real or imagined cases to test your own hypotheses, but the Socratic method is a technique that may allow you to engage in a more open dialogue with your colleagues, stakeholders and partners.

Ask key constituents (e.g. athletics staff, department assistants, student supervisors, the dean of students, trustees and other professionals) to provide advice on big projects, not only to strengthen ideas and allow opportunities for refinement and increased buy-in but also to leverage influence and, in some cases, resources to assist with program implementation. Also, you may want to consider proposing a pilot phase(s) before full implementation is to occur, as a means of gaining provisional support to move ahead with an idea. Avoid the 'all or nothing' proposition.

Collaborate

Example: learner support services collaboration

An example of learner support professionals collaborating can be seen when campus library professionals provide outreach support to their campus career centre (Hollister, 2005). The librarians at the University of Buffalo (UB) reached out to careers professionals who taught courses, helping their students develop career-related information literacy. The librarians demonstrated their value by providing tours of the UB libraries, and created 'library liaisons' to be a point of contact for the careers office. Librarians held information surgeries in the Career Center, and helped the

Center strengthen its own library with better information management and by weeding out-of-date resources. Additionally, the librarians helped the Career Center staff rethink their web presence, and even helped them think through their physical office redesign. This arrangement was mutually beneficial to both parties. Both departments served as resource and referral agents for each other, reaching more students.

Example: faculty collaboration

Faculty are obviously a key constituency group, and we need to work with them by understanding their needs and priorities, thereby enabling us to develop student affairs strategies that reflect these realities, including programming, resources and communication, and to develop critical relationships (Brown and Roseborough, 2007).

1   *Program planning and outreach.* At Mount Holyoke, a science faculty liaison program was developed by the Career Development Centre, which assigned a staff member to be the point of contact for every department and ensured that a direct line of communication was in place to enable the sharing of resources and joint planning of programs. Additionally, student affairs staff collaborated on an integrative program to help students reflect on their aggregate experiences, culminating in a banquet with faculty, class boards and class deans. Discussion panels were also planned, with topics that included how to use the disciplinary knowledge and skills of a particular subject outside classroom settings, providing career services resources for faculty and helping faculty think about how the learning outcomes from their courses could be applied to the world outside. At the University of Maryland, a faculty resource directory was developed; this was a highly successful tool for identifying faculty willing to engage in a variety of out-of-class experiences. Programs were scheduled strategically around the demands of faculty, to increase participation. An academic achievement banquet was also held, to which students invited their faculty for a semi-formal evening program. At Indiana University, first-year residents hosted a faculty fellow for weekly formal and informal visits. Other academic–student affairs collaboration opportunities have included first-year seminars, learning communities, common intellectual experiences, community-based learning, undergraduate research and capstone experiences (to help students integrate various aspects of their

education and experiences, including culminating seminars, large synthesis papers and/or qualifying examinations).

2   *Resources and communications.* Student affairs and other support professionals can help develop materials to assist faculty in their role advising students on non-academic matters. Providing data on student activity to give faculty a fuller appreciation of their students' experiences is one possible example. Another would be to communicate directly with faculty through monthly faculty meeting notes. Hosting an orientation for new faculty, as well as all department assistants (who are often the key to reaching faculty!), might be another way to build a faculty alliance.

3   *Relationships.* On any campus, individual relationships with faculty are key, and many initiatives become successful because they are supported by these important relationships. Student affairs and other learner support professionals can invest much time personally cultivating these relationships, attending faculty meetings, writing personal notes recognizing faculty accomplishments, showing up at faculty events when possible, serving on committees/teams or even creating a faculty 'Facebook' website with links to identify their interests. Lastly, some personal relationships may be developed through other avenues and common interests (e.g. kids, dogs, hobbies, volunteer work, etc.).

Implementing a strategy

Once you have envisioned your ideal place on your campus, you must implement your strategy by connecting with priorities and provide evidence of success.

Connecting with priorities

Ensure that your program goals and your assessment strategy are aligned with your institution's strategic goals and assessment plan. Serve on key committees and other teams. Identify the key processes and functions in your area and create a plan for continuous improvement. Begin in earnest to develop relationships with others across the institution. Be prepared to potentially give up something and extend yourself and your area into endeavours that might not have otherwise been priorities (e.g. what is on the board of trustees' agenda?).

Example: develop a new program

At Saint Louis University, Student Development staff have developed a new social entrepreneurship program. The concept of this program became of interest as a means to support socially responsible student ventures, which help solve social problems and support non-profit organizations' interests. This program initiative developed quickly and gained the necessary resource support because it is so clearly university-mission-driven and strongly aligned with the priorities of two major University entities: the Student Development division and the School of Business, which has a prominent business entrepreneurship program. Often good ideas like this one go nowhere fast because they are not strongly attached to the institution's priorities.

Provide evidence of success

In this time of greater accountability, it is essential that we report facts and avoid making assumptions. It is important to promote the use of trend and comparative data, and to use this information to set 'stretch' goals. Moreover, it is a good idea to share important information from your area systematically with others on campus. Student affairs research must reflect the complexity of learning and be presented in ways that matter to key stakeholders (Brown et al., 1998). National surveys such as the National Survey of Student Engagement (NSSE) and those conducted through the Cooperative Institutional Research Program (CIRP) provide campus life data that are meaningful and potentially boundary-crossing. The Council for the Advancement of Standards (CAS) has created helpful frameworks for assessing learning development outcomes (CAS, 2006) as well, including a survey of existing qualitative and quantitative measures of learning outcomes. Lastly, Brown and Greene (2006) are developing the Wisdom Development Scale to measure integrative learning outcomes such as self-knowledge, emotional management, altruism, inspirational engagement, life skills, life knowledge, judgement and willingness to learn.

Example: impact analysis

The MHC career office tracks student traffic usage with a card swipe (which records day, time of day, class year, major and ethnicity), aggregates 'satisfaction' data about the career office obtained from larger institutional assessments and continually evaluates its workshops. Additionally, the office is in the process of assessing the career learning outcomes developed to provide the evidence that the institution values. These outcomes were derived after a thorough review of the organizational mission, which supported the institutional mission.

A summary of practical considerations

1 *Do not assume that things have to be done the way they have always been done.* Consider context and look at issues from the viewpoint of multiple frames – for example structural, political, human resources and symbolic (Bolman and Deal, 1991). Align your goals/objectives (including assessment strategy) and initiatives with those of the University and your division (National Institute for Standards and Technology: Baldrige National Quality Program, 2008). Emphasize what is most critical to accomplishing the goals of the university and your division. When you are developing an idea or proposal, remember that you are not the audience, others are! Identify key processes, functions or other areas in the university which may be directly or indirectly impacted by your goals and initiatives. Mitigate by working out potential solutions with those most affected in advance of submitting your proposal or recommendation. Ask yourself: can you help solve a problem for them? Make them allies, not foes. Consider using pilot phases as a way of working towards comprehensive implementation. Be prepared to back up your recommendations with facts and avoid making assumptions that you can't defend. Overgeneralizing data is a common error and one that may significantly impact your credibility as an objective professional.

2 *Articulate performance targets and outcomes from which to measure success.* Generic, non-specific measures and outcomes won't be very influential. Answer these questions: What would success look like? How will we conclude whether we've achieved success? Use trend and comparative data whenever possible to provide a context for determining the significance of your own data (National Institute for Standards and Technology: Baldrige National Quality Program, 2008). Provide specific action steps that describe implementation, including a timeline of milestones. Create a communication plan that indicates how and when you will systematically share information with others on campus about your important initiatives. Become more proficient at developing budget information for new initiatives. Use a standard business proforma template – don't invent your own. Make it straightforward and easy to understand in relation to the numbers you are presenting. Provide a clear explanation of your formula

for arriving at estimates/projections. Summarize the key points and figures that support your recommendation or the case you are making.

3 *Consider the Socratic method and principled negotiation methods as a means to engage and influence others (Dye, 1996; Samples, 1998).* Pose thoughtful questions as opposed to hard selling. Avoid hardwiring yourself to only one possible outcome or scenario. Negotiate interests rather than argue positions. Consider and pose scenarios to advance the dialogue. Present options for mutual gain (Fisher and Ury, 1991). Study real or imagined cases to test your hypotheses and discuss them openly with your colleagues, stakeholders and partners. Try to avoid having hidden agendas. Serve on committees and other teams (*de facto* campus internships) across campus as a means of extending your opportunities to influence and your overall knowledge and awareness of what is happening at the University.

4 *Stay the course and be persistent about what you believe in (Collins, 2001), but acknowledge that progress happens most often a little at a time (Weick, 1984).* Pick your battles and don't 'die on every hill'. It is possible to win a battle and lose the war. Focus on what matters most, which means you must know your priorities. Adopt a 'small wins' approach – a series of small but significant accomplishments may gain you more allies and allow you ultimately to achieve more than a single, large-scale endeavour (Hamrick, Evans and Schuh, 2002; Weick, 1984). Recognize that large-scale change all at one time is difficult to achieve. Break things down into achievable parts. Pursue a pattern of moderately scaled successes. Pursue a goal through a variety of activities as opposed to a single event. Pascarella and Terenzini (1991, 655) suggested: 'Rather than seeking single large levers to pull in order to promote change, it may well be more effective to pull more levers more often.' Also, the more integrated your efforts are with other institutional priorities, the better your chances of succeeding.

Influencing decisions and advancing initiatives requires a great many factors and skills that are all within the capabilities of student affairs or other learner support professionals. The ability and opportunity to influence involves, among other things: sound relationships; a sense of timing; an understanding of context, culture and politics; alignment with institutional priorities; institutional awareness; flexibility and adaptability; doing your homework (no shortcuts); good planning; a results orientation; persistence; and a healthy dose of humility.

Conclusion

This is an exciting time in higher education. Student affairs and learner support professionals can be hardwired into all aspects of undergraduate life from matriculation to graduation, with an opportunity to collaborate with nearly every campus constituency, including students, faculty, staff, parents and alumni. Consequently they can explicitly connect the classroom experience with the most practical and pressing needs of today, such as ethical leadership and responsible citizenship. They can also provide a direct interface between students' education and experience, helping students to translate and deepen the hallmarks of their classroom education into the skills and competences necessary to navigate and lead in a complex world. As professionals who support students and their development, we must continually strive to create powerful learning environments for our communities of diverse students, think systematically about our roles as educators, help students reflect on their aggregate college experiences, and work effectively with all members of the higher education community towards these goals.

References

American Association for Higher Education, American College Personnel Association and National Association of Student Personnel Administrators (1998) *Powerful Partnerships: a shared responsibility for learning*, NASPA.

Bolman, L. G. and Deal, T. E. (1991) *Reframing Organizations: artistry, choice and leadership*, Jossey-Bass.

Brown, S. C. (2002). A Model for Wisdom Development – and its Place in Career Services, *Journal of College and Employers*, **69** (2), 29–36.

Brown, S. C. (2004a) Placing your Lamp on the Peg: a call to the ACPA annual convention, *Developments*, **31** (3), www.myacpa.org/pub/pub_de.cfm.

Brown, S. C. (2004b) Learning Across Campus: how college facilitates the development of wisdom, *Journal of College Student Development*, **45** (2), 134–48.

Brown, S. C. (2006) Educator or Entrepreneur? Marketing and other strategies to increase career learning outcomes, National Association of Colleges and Employers, *NACE Journal*, **66** (2), 26–34.

Brown, S. C. and Greene, J. A. (2006) The Wisdom Development Scale (WDS): translating the conceptual to the concrete, *Journal of College Student Development*, **47** (1), 1–19.

Brown, S. C. and Roseborough, J. (2007) They're Just Not That Into You: working with disinterested faculty, National Association of Colleges and Employers, *NACE Journal*, **67** (2), 28–32.

Brown, S. C., Adler, J., Ashworth, C. and Chevry, G. S. (2007) What if Students Listened to Everything We Said? Developing a campuswide, comprehensive four year career curriculum, National Association of Colleges and Employers, *NACE Journal*, **68** (2), 28–34.

Brown, S. C., Stevens, R. A., Troiano, P. F. and Schneider, M. K. (1998) Exploring Complex Phenomena: grounded theory in student affairs research, *Journal of College Student Development*, **43** (2), 173–83.

Collins, J. (2001) *Good to Great: why some companies make the leap . . . and others don't*, HarperCollins.

Council on the Advancement of Standards (2006) *Frameworks for Assessing Student Learning Outcomes*, Council on the Advancement of Standards.

Dye, J. (1996) *Socratic Method and Scientific Method*, www.niu.edu/~jdye/method.html.

Fisher, R. and Ury, W. (1991) *Getting to Yes: negotiating agreement without giving in*, Penguin Books.

Hamrick, F. A., Evans, N. J. and Schuh, J. H. (2002) *Foundations of Student Affairs Practice*, Jossey-Bass.

Hollister, C. V. (2005) Bringing Information Literacy to Career Services, *Reference Services Review*, **33** (1), 104–11.

Janosik, S. M., Creamer, D. G., Hirt, J. B., Winston, R. B., Saunders, S. A. and Cooper, D. L. (2003) *Supervising New Professionals in Student Affairs*, Brunner-Routledge.

Keeling, R. P. (ed.) (2006) *Learning Reconsidered 2: implementing a campus-wide focus on the student experience*, 2nd edn, American College Personnel Association, Association of Colleges and University Housing Officers-International, Association of College Unions-International, National Academic Advising Association, National Association for Campus Activities, National Association of Student Personnel Administrators and National Intra-mural Recreational Sports Association.

National Institute for Standards and Technology: Baldrige National Quality Program (2008) *Education Criteria for Performance Excellence*, www.quality.nist.gov/Education_Criteria.htm.

National Leadership Council for Liberal Education and Americas' Promise (2007) *College Learning for the New Global Century*, Association of American Colleges and Universities, www.aacu.org/leap/documents/GlobalCentury-final.pdf.

Pascarella, E. T. and Terenzini, P. T. (1991) *How College Affects Students*, Jossey-Bass.

Saint Louis University (2008) *Strategic Plan*, www.slu.edu/provost/strategic/index.html.

Samples, K. (1998) *The Socratic Method*,
www.str.org/site/News2?page=NewsArticle&id=5631.
Weick, K. E. (1984) Small Wins: redefining the scale of social problems, *American Psychologist*, **39** (1), 40–9.

12

Transformation and integration through research and enquiry: a Centre for Excellence in Teaching and Learning perspective

PAT ATKINS

Introduction

This chapter will consider the role of research and enquiry in building transformative learning support from the perspective of the first two years of the existence of the UK Open University's PILS (Personalised Integrated Learning Support) CETL (Centre for Excellence in Teaching and Learning). It focuses on the Open University (OU) and addresses issues relevant to staff in many higher education (HE) institutions, particularly those whose curriculum is modular, those who employ part-time teaching-only staff and those who are embedding new technologies in their teaching and student support.

The 74 CETLs were set up in England in 2005 as a result of an institutional bidding process set in train by the Higher Education Funding Council for England (HEFCE). HEFCE wanted the CETLs to 'bestow recognition and distinction on their teachers, help to enthuse learners, provide high quality learning facilities, and stimulate development and change in teaching and learning' (HEFCE, 2004). Successful bidders received five years' funding. CETLs are therefore both a reflection of institutional priorities and a source of creativity and innovation due to their financial independence from their institution.

Murray Saunders, Director of the Centre for the Study of Education and Training at the University of Lancaster, in conversation with the PILS CETL, has suggested that he sees each CETL as a potential 'bridgehead to new embedded practices'. In order to become that bridgehead, institutions need good evidence that the new centre will deliver an improvement in the student experience. This view of the CETL as an agent of change suggests there is a central role for properly evaluated research and enquiry.

The PILS CETL's central philosophy of integration has led to the creation of a multidisciplinary team, bringing together staff and their various perspectives in search of a more holistic response to students' support needs. The current OU model is briefly described later in this chapter, in the section 'An integrated model of learning support?'. The PILS team includes:

- academics
- associate lecturers
- information professionals
- generalist information, advice and guidance staff
- careers advisers
- administrators/managers
- learning design technologists
- marketing staff.

Some members of the team work for the CETL full-time; others are partially bought-out from their substantive posts so have continuing dual responsibilities; associate lecturer members of the team are bought-in because their substantive posts, delivering direct teaching and learner support to students, normally involve about six hours per week maximum – see the later section 'A division of labour in teaching'. Other members of staff have a peripheral relationship with the CETL, attending team meetings to bring their expertise or seniority/authority to the work and taking the PILS philosophy back into their everyday work. This breadth gives the CETL wider access to expertise than the funding alone can purchase. In return it gives a broader group of staff direct input to the development of the CETL and expands the sense of ownership.

CETL staff believe that there are considerable benefits to this more holistic approach to both learning support and research into learning support. In particular, integrating perspectives from across the University ensures that research and enquiry is more likely to transform the practice of teaching, learning and student support within the University.

The Open University in context
The challenge of open entry

The UK Open University was created in 1969 to widen access to HE and deliver lifelong learning to adults at a time when less than 10% of the UK adult population had a degree. It has always sought to support a diverse group of students, many of whom (currently about 30% of new undergraduates) do not possess traditional HE entry qualifications.

This diversity has driven the need to do more than just deliver an HE curriculum in terms of content. The OU was one of the pioneers in the explicit development in students of the skills required to study at HE level. This was partly a reaction to open access, as many students needed greater clarity about what was required. It started with the embedding of study skills in entry-level courses, and has developed as the skills required have evolved. For example, the University is now working to ensure the development of skills to bridge the digital divide for students who are not yet IT literate, including information literacy skills.

The challenges of size and complexity

The OU is by UK standards an HE juggernaut, with roughly 200,000 students at any one time. In the international world of distance teaching, its size is not unusual. The students are mainly based in the UK but a substantial minority are spread across the globe. Most are taught directly by the OU but an increasing number are taught within partner institutions.

Like any other UK university, the OU has a complex curriculum, ranging from traditional academic disciplines through to professional and vocational programmes. It offers taught undergraduate and postgraduate programmes as well as doctoral studies. Its taught programmes are all modular, offering students high levels of flexibility and choice in their studies.

A division of labour in teaching

When the OU was created organizational structures were put into place to support the vision of a university for all rather than for an elite. Like any other mass-production system of its time it divided up the work into separate parcels. Academic roles are subdivided. Full-time academics carry out research, design curricula and work with other support staff to create distance teaching materials and assessment. However, they do not generally interact directly with students. On almost all course modules, students are supported by an associate lecturer (AL). Associate lecturers hold teaching-only contracts, to support students and facilitate their learning on one course module. So they work for the University in a part-time capacity, normally for not more than six hours per week. A wide range of other staff contribute to student support, currently in a semi-integrated fashion.

Integration

ALs' core work includes grading and providing extensive individual feedback on all summative assessment, delivered according to marking guidelines produced by the full-time academics to ensure a common experience for the student. These marking guidelines are just one of the re-integration mechanisms which the OU uses to overcome the problems created by the division of labour when aiming to deliver a consistent and coherent experience to a large number of students, spread across a wide geographical area, with no unifying campus.

Integration in course module production

One of the University's great strengths has always been recognized to be the quality of its distance teaching materials. It may be no coincidence that the production process has always been a multidisciplinary team effort, pulling together:

- academics
- resource researchers
- sound and vision specialists
- learning designers
- administrators
- editors
- material designers
- critical readers (associate lecturers and sometimes students).

This model worked well before technical developments (e.g. the internet) changed access to knowledge and ease of communication increased substantially and changed rapidly. The division between production of the content and teaching of the module is breaking down in the face of these developments. The need for academics to present relevant knowledge for the module is reducing, while students' ability to access up-to-date knowledge for themselves is increasing. At the same time, communication and learning through student activities, which can receive immediate feedback, is becoming realistic for numerous distant students. Holmberg (2004, 29) agrees that new technologies provide 'an excellent medium for interaction ... for students to search for information [and] ... for tutors to supplement preproduced learning materials'.

However, these changes also transform the mix of skills and of staff required in the academic process. For example, there is a greater need to develop students' ability to search and evaluate information, and to assess their much more personalized learning. These developments are leading the OU to ask whether the original division of labour might need redesigning in the face of such technological change, and how it could derive greater benefit for students from the expertise of the AL and other support staff.

An integrated model of learning support?

The traditional model of learning support in the OU includes mainly:

- multimedia course module material delivering both content and relevant skills development, once delivered by TV and radio but now delivered digitally (DVD, intranet, etc.) and also by post
- ALs working with a group of about 20 students to facilitate their learning through delivery of tutorials (originally face-to-face although now using a blend of delivery media), feedback on and marking of assignments and reactive remedial support when a student encounters problems
- end of course examinations/assessments marked independently
- access to very broad and increasingly important online library resource
- access to additional generic study skills resources, either on paper or online, including key skills such as IT skills and library skills
- access to careers service on request
- proactive additional support for students identified as at risk of drop-out, delivered either by the relevant AL or by a specialist
- access to an extensive information, advice and guidance service to support study planning and module selection.

The integration of learning support delivery services and systems has traditionally been less structured than the design and creation of curricula and individual modules, often relying on particular individuals to build a support network for students and course modules with specific needs. The PILS CETL is championing and researching a fully integrated approach to learning support to deliver a more flexible and more personalized experience for students.

The CETL has built on previous work in the area to take an inclusive view of learning support. Thomas (2006) considers a range of models of personal tutoring and concludes that the more integrated and proactive the support interventions are with the student's curriculum, the better it usually is for the student. In particular, students who are traditionally most at risk of drop-out 'are particularly likely to benefit from a proactive, integrated and structured approach that prioritises relationships' (Thomas, 2006, 31). This link with the curriculum is also found in Tait's (2000) three 'primary functions of student support' starting with 'Cognitive: supporting and developing learning' but also 'Affective' support through the creation of the right environment and 'Systemic' administrative processes. Tait makes a strong case for them being 'interrelated and interdependent' (2000, 289).

Recent changes in the UK HE environment, including an increasing emphasis on employability and skills from the government, the introduction of fees for traditional university students and a focus on widening participation and on lifelong learning, are making all UK HE institutions more diverse. The OU is no exception. This suggests a need to widen the student support focus to recognize the greater range of motivations which drive an increasingly diverse body of students.

The ARCS model of student support

The PILS CETL has therefore produced the ARCS model, integrating affective, reflective, cognitive and systemic support (see Figure 12.1). It aims to build on previous work, and also to take a student perspective and integrate these elements:

- Affective – How do I feel about studying? Am I confident, finding pleasure in it?
- Reflective – Why am I doing it? What are my motivations?

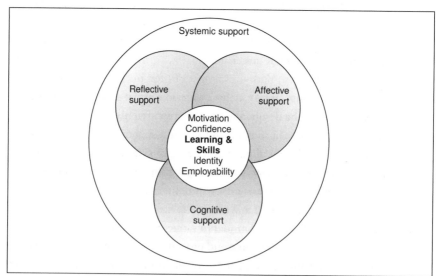

Figure 12.1 The ARCS model of learning support

- Cognitive – What am I learning and developing? Does it make sense?
- Systemic – Who and what is helping me with studying? Does it support me?

The ARCS model underpins much of the work of the CETL, including decisions about the type of developments to pilot and to research. As importantly, it provides an explicit recognition of the integrated nature of the support that students need and is one way of helping the OU understand why it now needs integrated delivery services and systems for students. It gives an academic rationale for change and for breaking down some of the old barriers between the academic process, the support process and the motivations of the student. It provides a theoretical basis for the integration the CETL is aiming for, mirroring that which has been achieved in course production through multidisciplinary teams.

The aim of this integration from the student perspective is to enable their development of:

- a stronger engagement with learning and with skills development through improved motivation
- improved employability, as they understand why they are being asked to develop certain skills and are better able to present their skills to employers
- a clearer sense of identity as a student of a particular subject and, where appropriate, as a developing member of a particular profession
- greater confidence as an independent learner who recognizes their growing abilities.

The Personalised Integrated Learning Support CETL
Building on excellence: modules, degrees and subjects

The PILS CETL was created to build on the OU's recognized excellence in supporting students, to develop a new and wider understanding of student need and to disseminate and embed that understanding. The case for excellence had been made based on many years of practice and research, but it was nicely reinforced when the OU came top in terms of overall satisfaction in the first National Student Survey in 2005, just as the CETLs were being established.

However, that still left the CETL with much work to do in addressing particular aspects of the student experience where learning support was known to be less well received by students, to deliver a more personalized experience of support for each student and to tighten the level of integration in a growing, diversifying organization.

The PILS CETL has a particular focus on improving support for students along their journey through a subject area. Current support systems focus heavily on support for students within individual modules, matching the highly modular curriculum. However, students are clear that they belong to the University whether or not they are currently studying. A more continuous perspective on support along their journey would provide an integrated system to complement the support offered on each module.

Associate lecturers and other teaching and support staff

One explicit aim of the CETL process was to recognize excellent teachers and to develop high quality teaching and learning. With OU teaching split between full-time academics creating teaching material, associate lecturers providing direct learning opportunities and wider support staff having direct input into the student experience, it was important to consider all the teaching and student support staff in the institution as potential sources of expertise for the CETL.

The real need was to engage the AL community, where so much excellent teaching takes place and where much of the practical expertise in student support resides. ALs have a contract which ensures continuity of employment for the duration of the life of the module: normally eight years. Many work for the University for many years, moving on from module to module. They therefore develop great expertise in student support even though they have part-time contracts. The CETL wanted both to recognize and to tap in to that expertise by bringing ALs in for practitioner enquiry projects alongside other staff.

Transforming learning support through developing evidence-based practice

The opportunity to pilot changes in teaching and learning practices is one of the most exciting aspects of a CETL. Research and the production of evidence is an essential aspect of what the PILS CETL does in order to produce transformations in learning support. However, the divided nature of the OU teaching process highlights the complexity of the situation which faces much of HE. The best teachers and supporters of students (including many wider support staff) are not necessarily the best or most prolific researchers in the traditional sense.

So, the CETL is aiming to strengthen a practice-based research tradition which will not only develop the staff involved in research but will also improve recognition of staff focused on teaching and learning support, irrespective of their employment terms and conditions. At the same time it will broaden the evidence base for transforming student support.

The CETL is building on earlier action research work conducted within the OU which suggested that the work could be 'very effective . . . as part of professional development and as a contribution to quality enhancement' (Coats and Stevenson, 2004). Of course the OU is not alone in this belief. Other institutions are seeking ways to 'improve University teaching through action research' (Gray, Chang and Radloff, 2007).

The aim of the CETL is to integrate practitioner interests with the interests of more senior members of staff. It is working to bring together two forms of research:

- practical pedagogic research, aimed at specifying real options for delivering changes in teaching and support processes at the most hands-on level
- institutionally driven research, aiming to elicit evidence on a larger scale to deliver change at a strategic level.

Practical pedagogic research

Alongside their expertise in student support, associate lecturers are also typically busy people, holding down a portfolio of both professional and personal responsibilities. Thus practitioner enquiry projects are normally expected to be relatively small pieces of work, no more than three weeks' work spread over six to nine months, although they can be scaled up or extended if appropriate.

Practitioner enquiry: some examples

ALs and other staff undertake a broad spectrum of projects. They can range from practical resource development and evaluation contributing directly to the work of other staff and projects within the University at one extreme, to something close to pure action research at the other. The explicit outputs may benefit students directly or they may support staff working with students or designing and developing future course modules.

These examples give a flavour of the types of practitioner enquiry being undertaken:

- extending critical thinking – the development and evaluation of exercises for ALs to use with students in an online forum/conference
- perceptions of plagiarism – an exploration of students' understanding of the term and the evaluation of a questionnaire for staff to use to improve materials on intellectual property, open up debate of the subject and improve student understanding of the issues
- credibility of published material – development and evaluation of a resource to help students develop their ability to assess the credibility of published materials
- mapping concepts and methodologies across modules within a subject area – creating a typology and map of a particular degree
- developing group work – action research into practice at tutorial sessions and what impact certain changes in practice bring about
- using new technologies in problem-solving – investigating the use of e-mail to support students' problem-solving skills
- building staff communities online – investigating the use of social networking tools to bring staff together at a distance.

Selection, induction and support of pedagogic research

Applications are invited for work within a limited number of themes or categories, currently:

- enabling progression – resources to aid bridging/revision of skills or content, to ease progression between modules
- tailored study skills – customized resources to support skills development such as information literacy
- subject-based teaching resources – non-module-specific resources which can be used by staff either online or face-to-face
- employability – personal development planning, skills recognition, support for employability processes and resource development
- programme mapping – mapping of skills development across a subject area to aid course module design and development
- blended learning – a pedagogic approach to use of staff and of mobile and other technologies to deliver a personalized experience to students
- AL identity and role development – community building for staff on very part-time contracts

- action research – development of individual staff members' understanding of the student perspective and how they engage with them in the learning process.

The CETL's use of themes and categories ensures that research work integrates practitioner interests with more strategic OU interests. For example, when a new course module is in production there may be specific pieces of work which would feed directly into that process. In another example, careers staff may be interested in supporting research into a particular use of e-portfolios to help them develop wider resources to support their use.

Defining themes and categories also provides a focus within each cohort of students, giving the opportunity for sharing ideas, peer support, challenge and debate, and working in pairs or larger groups to deliver more substantial projects. At the same time the CETL ensures that the work can be supported by the mix of expertise (e.g. careers and employability staff, information literacy staff and learning designers) available within the team.

For successful applicants, the CETL runs a weekend workshop with the dual aims of helping new researchers to develop the details of their research proposal and increasing their ability to deliver the research. In particular, they usually need induction into the research paradigms, methods and ethical issues involved in educational and human research. The workshop also gives an opportunity for the relationship between the researchers and the wider multidisciplinary PILS team to be cemented.

Stakeholder engagement and embedding new practice

Staff discuss proposals with relevant stakeholders around the University to gain a wider perspective before final research proposals are agreed. For example, a proposal to develop an online resource to map employability skills through a degree might require discussion with academics with a responsibility for that particular degree and with staff with an interest in careers and employability, information literacy and learning design. This early engagement of wider stakeholders is an essential aspect of bringing together practitioner and wider OU interests to deliver changes in practice.

At the end of their project, all researchers are expected to reflect on what they have learned and what impact the work will have on their teaching and support practice in future. Each project is then considered individually within the PILS team for potential impact, dissemination and further research.

Overall the process aims to match the huge ability and expertise of the staff in learning support with the needs and interests of the University, to produce relevant pedagogic research which will genuinely transform student support.

Institutional research

There are some research programmes which go beyond an exploration of personal practice. All CETLs are engaged in this type of institutional research, giving their universities a better understanding of how students learn in order to transform the support they can offer.

At this level, the PILS CETL has an interest in researching, piloting and evaluating structures and processes which might improve integration for the students and deliver a more personalized experience.

Modules and the pathways through them

A modular curriculum with open access to students offers them the great benefit of flexibility; it also offers the potential problem of complexity. This was one of the first areas of interest the PILS CETL explored as a team, using the expertise of marketing staff, Information, Advice and Guidance (IAG) staff, information professionals and website designers, as well as academics, to present more motivating and effective information for students on how to navigate the modules to achieve their goals.

The University has recognized the case for changing how it does this and has taken on and mainstreamed this work in new practices for information and advice for students.

Communities of students

The work on pathways through modules lead the CETL to a deeper interest in student identity within a subject area and how, in the face of decreasing attendance at face-to-face teaching and learning events, the University could do more to build a community of students online. The aim was to replicate the community which at its best might be found in a departmental common room, around a department's notice board or library resources, between formal teaching events as cohorts of students intermingle. It was informed by Wenger's (1998) concept of communities of practice as a basis for learning.

Again, a resource was created using the multidisciplinary expertise available through the team, and was piloted with a subset of students in two subject areas. While much of this work builds on work that is happening in many parts of the University, the holistic approach taken in the PILS CETL, driven by its integrated view of learning support, produced a unique online resource. It aims to:

- pull together online access to all aspects of study of a subject
- customize generic material to personalize it to the student
- set the student's study in the context of their life, their developing skills and their potential future employment.

The dynamic and interactive nature of the resource, with regularly changing notice board items related to the subject area students are interested in and online forums coming and going as topics come and go, means that students continually find items of interest to them and can also support each other.

Early student feedback through qualitative research suggested that this resource would be popular; the statistics for repeated student use of these resources are extremely good. Due to word of mouth around the staff in the University, the model was taken up in a number of areas before any formal dissemination took place. That some faculties have chosen to finance their own online communities testifies to how positively this model has been received.

Working across boundaries to transform learning support

The multidisciplinary nature of the PILS team is in itself a pilot for how cross-boundary teams can deliver a much better-informed type of support to students. Evaluation of the whole enterprise is built in through many levels. The team has considered ways in which knowledge sharing, which is at the heart of the team process, can be enhanced within the daily life of other staff in the University.

One initiative was the creation of a regular networking meeting to bring together those involved in the creation of replacement (and new) entry-level course modules, which are the first that most students encounter. There are a range of issues specific to these students, irrespective of subject area. The network meetings are designed around the practitioners; they are encouraged to set the agenda and have time at each meeting to discuss topics which are of concern to them. The course modules are all at different points in their development, so staff can share recent expertise in solving various problems, for example in relation to skills assessment. The involvement of the multidisciplinary PILS Team means that discipline experts are readily accessible and can offer advice and share experience to supplement peer support in what has become a developing community of practice (Wenger, 1998).

The evaluation of this initiative is informal but comes in the form of continuing voluntary attendance at these meetings by busy practitioners. The network provides a model for sharing knowledge at a time of rapidly changing technologies and student needs.

Conclusions: impact on learner support processes

In a complex institution, it is impossible to be precise about which aspects of the PILS CETL work have produced any particular impact on students. However, there are clearly some areas where the pedagogic and institutional research is benefitting students.

Course module design

Staff working on a number of courses, particularly new entry-level courses, with whom we have been collaborating most closely point to a number of elements of pedagogic and institutional research which have produced specific elements of course module design. For example, there have been changes in the way that information literacy is introduced in a number of courses, partly as a result of learning within the CETL.

Continuity

There is a greater emphasis on continuity of support for students, and on continuity of the look and feel of individual course modules along well-trodden pathways towards qualifications. For example, it was realized that the core courses in one popular qualification had slightly different referencing requirements, and this was impacting on students' behaviour and the likelihood of them plagiarizing due to confusion.

Communications

Students are beginning to benefit from more integrated communications as different parts of the University become more aware of what others are doing. However, importantly there is increased awareness of the potential to learn from students and for them to learn from each other. Online forums enable peer support and also enable feedback on course module materials and resources, so they can be improved.

Community

A major development is the renewed emphasis on bringing students into a community based around their own interests. This is facilitated by new technologies but also expressed in old technologies (e.g. paper-based prospectuses) and in educational relationships. It highlights the strength of the student voice and peer support, which can be challenging for institutions where students meet infrequently.

Customization

Generic student support resources such as study skills material, careers and employability advice and information literacy and IT skills development materials are being redesigned to enable easy customization. This will not only give a more personalized feel for the student but also will deliver efficiency and quality control in the production of such materials. The aim is to create an open source approach to these materials so that improvements made by one area can be made available to all areas.

Staff development

New approaches to developing staff are being taken, both through the engagement of a wider cohort of staff in pedagogic and institutional research and also in encouraging all such staff to disseminate their findings to their peers and engage them in the debates which have engaged the CETL. All staff must be allowed time to engage in debates if they are to adjust their frameworks for thinking about student support.

Student support staff roles

Recognizing the contribution of a wide group of support staff to the academic progress of students is an important step for the institution, and will inform the way that students are supported in future. Delivering a personalized experience of support does not mean that it will involve only one person – an academic – but that it needs to be informed by specialist knowledge and integrated. Supporting this development and ensuring its value is recognized in resourcing and promotion decisions is a further challenge.

Integrated teams to support the whole student

Multidisciplinary teams that genuinely seek to integrate the perspectives of all staff engaged with students offer a more holistic approach to learning support. As staff learn from each other and horizons broaden, there is an increase in excitement and energy, which feeds into transforming the student experience.

The PILS CETL experience suggests that if institutions can bring together their strategic vision with practitioners' multidisciplinary expertise in holistic environments that encourage enquiry and evaluation by staff integrated from across the institution, sustainable developments in practice will emerge and become the 'new embedded practice' – a real opportunity to create practices in learning support which can sustainably transform students' ability to succeed in HE.

References

Coats, M. and Stevenson, A. (2004) Practitioner Enquiry and Professional Development: 'action research' re-visited and re-viewed in the context of outcomes-based education. In *Conference Paper for the Association for the Study Evaluation Assessment in Education in Southern Africa (ASEASA), December 2003, Cape Town, South Africa*, http://oro.open.ac.uk/5555/.

Gray, K., Chang, R. and Radloff, A. (2007) Enhancing the Scholarship of Teaching and Learning: evaluation of a scheme to improve teaching and learning through action research, *International Journal of Teaching and Learning in Higher Education*, **19** (1), 21–32.

Higher Education for Funding Council for England (2004) *News Item*, Centres for Excellence in Teaching and Learning to be established, www.hefce.ac.uk/news/hefce/2004/cetl.asp.

Holmberg, B. (2004) *The Evolution, Principles and Practices of Distance Education*, Bibliotheks- und Informationssystem der Universität Oldenburg.

National Student Survey (2005) *Results by Institution*, Guardian Unlimited, http://education.guardian.co.uk/students/tables/0,,1574395,00.html.

Tait, A. (2000) Planning Student Support for Open and Distance Learning, *Open Learning*, **15** (3), 287–99.

Thomas, L. (2006) Widening Participation and the Increased Need for Personal Tutoring. In Thomas, L. and Hixenbaugh, P. (eds), *Personal Tutoring in Higher Education*, Trentham Books.

Wenger, E. (1998) *Communities of Practice*, Cambridge University Press.

13

Beyond artful doing: the role of practitioner research in developing holistic learning support practice

MARGARET WEAVER AND PHILIPPA LEVY

Introduction

This chapter will highlight the role and importance of multidisciplinary practitioner research in furthering our understanding of enhancing learning support practice. Taking a heuristic approach, some methods used by practitioners are presented, as are some tentative connections between relevant theory and practice across the professions. Current thinking about the value of 'storytelling' as a possible tool for professionals undertaking research is described, and storytelling is proposed as a way to enhance the evidence base and reveal researcher situatedness. The place of collaborative practitioner-led research in the evaluation of authentic learning support experiences and relationships is outlined, demonstrating the richness of research into the student experience and also its diffusion. A case study by Sheffield University contextualizes how one institution is facilitating practitioner inquiry-based learning approaches through the work of its Centre for Inquiry-based Learning in the Arts and Social Sciences (CILASS).

It will be helpful first to chart the development of practitioner research as a valid research tradition.

Practitioner talk

Schon (1973), in his seminal work on epistemological knowledge in practice, first coined the term 'reflective practice' to mean those thoughts and actions (or the lack of them) that practitioners performed in order to function and grow. He analysed the distinctive structure of reflection–in–action and its place in the construction of professional knowledge and meaning (Smith, 2001). His theories have been adopted widely across the professions as a way to develop individuals' power of critical thought through a continuous, intentional process. Usher and others confirmed that knowledge inherent in practice is to be understood as 'artful doing' (Usher,

Bryant and Johnston, 1997, 143). 'Artful knowing' takes this idea further; according to Usher, Bryant and Johnson, it arises when tasks and thinking become subconscious and are coalesced through 'vignettes in practice' and internalized, becoming 'knowing in action'. These conceptions follow an apprenticeship model of learning with information and knowledge transferring from novice to expert and back again in a cycle of critical review in and through practice.

Schon's work is widely respected for its contribution to the research-informed practice debate and appears on many student reading lists today. He is also credited with early thinking on learning organizations. For example, he correctly predicted that the loss of the 'stable state' (Schon, 1973) would lead to a greater emphasis on preparing for uncertainty as society, institutions and individuals would be in a constant state of change and transformation – an apt theme for this book. Learning was proposed as a way to mitigate this effect and social learning in particular (Bjorke, 2004; Smith, 2001). This is particularly important for multiprofessional working in higher education today, whereby a collaborative learning approach can work well not just for our students but for ourselves, as others in this book confirm. It has the potential to overcome structural boundaries and prior experience through enabling 'practitioner talk' (Usher, Bryant and Johnston, 1997).

Towards situated practice

Usher, Bryant and Johnston (1997) critique of Schon observes that reflection in action can be seen as critical practice, which is open to a question of its own situatedness. The socially located self in the research process is a central part of practitioner research and very relevant to a discussion of learning support in context, since it is generally acknowledged that researcher subjectivity can be a cause for concern affecting the internal and external validity of research. However, if we take as our starting point that our unique contribution as professionals is valid, we should perhaps immerse ourselves in our research as participant observers, more fully and more often, setting time aside to engage with our research subjects in the field.

We might also then wish to reconsider the place of our students in our future practitioner-based studies, which after all are concerned with understanding them and their learning, and deepen our investigatory relationships with students through participatory co-design, a method used successfully by libraries in the USA and South Africa (Somerville, 2007), and as illustrated by the case study in this chapter.

There is not space here to outline the diverse research perspectives that colleagues across our professions might utilize when undertaking research into learning support. Needless to say there is rich opportunity for further research, to understand the very nature of our thinking (our conceptions) about student learning (pedagogy), our professional identities and our practice.

A possible integrative framework

Dadds (2008) offers a fresh perspective on how to frame relevant practitioner research that integrates the elements of the cognitive (understanding) and the affective (feeling) within the researcher and his/her design, using what she calls 'empathetic validity'. She requires us to examine subjectivity in a new light, and critically so, focusing on the role of empathy and emotions in professional life to see oneself and others differently; this approach has parallels with the recent emotional intelligence perspectives of the workplace that place a stronger focus on connecting with people and their perceptions. She argues that a 'positive emotional transformation that enhances relationships can be a vital dimension of some, but not necessarily all, practitioner research'. A narrative-based approach might lend itself to at least exploring the 'emotional climate in which one situates a project' (Dadds, 2008, 287). To what extent this technique is being used in HE remains to be seen, but we do know that emotion plays a significant part in student learning (see Chapter 12 on the ARCS model).

Multiprofessional perspectives on practitioner research

There has been much debate about the existence of a gap between pure (theoretical) and applied (practitioner) research, and the relative position and value of the two types of research. In examining whether such a gap exists, it is useful to examine briefly how research is perceived in the various professional literatures through the eyes of learning technologists, librarians, educators and student affairs professionals.

Each profession has its own traditions and theoretical domains. Overall, it is clear that building theory is seen as valuable in terms of moving thinking on, but not for its own sake – only in the context of the developing enhancement of practice, and working towards artful knowing.

Learning technologists

Jones (2004) examines the relatively new field of learning technology and the theory/practice relationship as it applies to learning technologists (LT). He concludes that the LT practitioner takes his/her knowledge base from a variety of 'feeder strands' that have different discourses:

> The disciplinary backgrounds and theoretical traditions of learning technologists are diverse and it cannot be expected that any one learning technologist can have a grasp of all the available theories in use. This practical question is compounded by the process of professionalization that is taking place. There are active attempts to draw together the various strands of learning technology and the different groups of learning technologists into a single recognizable profession. This will involve some standardization and the setting out of a common canon of theory, even if there are different voices and a variety of positions that can be taken within that canon.
>
> (Jones, 2004)

Librarians

In the academic librarianship field, the body of knowledge is more developed. The rise of the evidence-based practice movement has gone some way towards connecting the theory/practice divide. This movement has its roots in the medical profession, where decisions about patient care became firmly rooted in the evidence base through a critical appraisal of formal research studies carried out by practitioners. The evidence-based practice approach is slowly transferring to other vocational groups such as educators and social workers.

Booth (2003, 16) demonstrates the lack of consensus about the existence of the research/practice gap, concluding that evidence-based information practice is merely one 'stimulant for reflection (as compensation for previous neglect)'. Other authors bemoan the lack of rigour in practitioner research. In the USA, Hildreth and Aytac (2007) have examined the methodologies used in selected library and information science literature, drawing attention to the dearth of appropriate qualitative methods.

Brophy's (2007) commentary on recent UK evidence-based library and information practice literature offers an insight into a possible way forward for practitioners to unite qualitative and quantitative methods. He highlights the potential of narrative-based practice to uncover meanings through storytelling. 'Educators need to include both the construction and the use of narrative alongside other research techniques, giving due prominence to issues such as what makes an effective narrative, how narratives should be selected and different ways of presenting them' (Brophy, 2007, 156). Further, he urges the librarianship profession to 'take much more seriously the role of narrative and find ways to capture narrative systematically as part of our evidence base' (ibid). Brophy believes this method to be transferable to other professions.

Examples of narrative methods applied to the support of learning are indeed emerging. One project, entitled *The Learner's Voice*, drew together five video case studies across the post-16 education sector to highlight the power of the student voice in determining future priorities for learning support. It records 'moments in learners' lives in their own words and gives a vivid insight into the experiences of learners as they use technology to support their learning' (Joint Information Systems Committee, 2007). Technology is therefore helping researchers and evaluators to utilize diverse methods to capture authentic verbal accounts of the experiences of students and staff when conducting research. However, whether these oral accounts will be accepted and subsumed within the largely written research tradition remains to be seen.

Educators

The debate continues as to whether qualitative methods used to research practice are sufficiently rigorous and reliable for 'proper' research studies in the professions, and as to the precise role of theory generation in this process. Clayton et al. (2008) studied the perceptions of teacher-practitioner-researchers in a collaborative school setting, and found that constraints existed in the minds of busy teachers as to why research could not be undertaken to a rigorous level: these were structural (government and institutional policies), cultural (not a strong tradition and fears about validity of non-numerical techniques) and temporal (lack of time). This could equally apply to higher education. Clayton et al. concluded that new methods were needed to capture professional judgements, such as:

- narrative-based approaches to assist meaningfulness and relevance
- peer-to-peer networks to facilitate discussion between researchers
- support to understand and apply knowledge.

Crucially, they identified a common drawback to conducting research in practice:

> The fact that so many professionals saw their action inquiry work as beyond their normal duties is telling. . . . It is viewed as something extra to normal duties and therefore as something that can be dropped when work pressures become too great. (Clayton et al., 2008, 79)

They also concluded that there was a need to demystify the meaning of 'research' for education professionals (80).

Some authors suggest that now is the time to 'put the controversies to rest regarding the value of qualitative evidence to support change in practice' (Given, 2006, 384) and accept that questionable research occurs in both qualitative and quantitative studies and in a variety of professional and academic areas. It appears there is no single measure of quality and that 'value perceptions' among researchers differ (Clyde, 2006).

Student affairs personnel

How is this debate rehearsed in the student development area? If the range of journals and articles is an indicator, there is certainly a more well developed body of knowledge in the USA than in the UK. Bloland, writing in the early 1990s, is critical of the application of student development theory to modern student affairs practice, saying that we need to deal with 'multiple realities and not one or even several theories working in concert will suffice' (Bloland, 1991, 8). He refers to work by Kuh, Whitt and Shed, who echo Schon and others by talking about the emergent paradigm or 'New Story, which is characterized by conditions of uncertainty, mutual shaping and ambiguity' (quoted in Bloland, 1991, 7).

As referred to in other chapters, the 'learning reconsidered' reforms in the USA are leading the thinking on the academic alignment of student affairs services with faculty and service priorities. This framework mentions the need to work differently and acquire new skills: 'We must be intentional learners and reflective practitioners, learning continuously about our campus and our students' (Borrego, Forrest and Fried, 2006, 59). Collaboration with other professionals is put forward as a central requirement.

Theory/practice divide?

In summary, there is a complex dialogical relationship between theory and practice and rightly so. A critical engagement with both is needed to understand holistic learning support perspectives. It follows that specific methodologies that facilitate in-depth possibly participatory, exploration of multiple perspectives will be required to embrace all actors and professional groups fully and deeply in a common dialogue: support practitioners, academics, researchers and students.

Rather than focus on the differences we should therefore focus on the common ground between the professions. Schenk and Eve outline areas of commonality between the research communities that might apply:

- the need for research leadership
- the need for joint working and funding
- the need for someone to make the first move (Schenk and Eve, 2007, 21).

One way these might come about is by the facilitation of new communities of practice across the professions.

Communities of practice

Lave and Wenger's model of communities of practice (CoPs) offers a lens through which to view collaboration and inquiry of relevance to learning support professionals and to learners when applied to education and learning in general (Bjorke, 2004). Wenger and Snyder (2000) transfer this concept to organizations outside education, indicating that CofPs will drive knowledge and business competitiveness, but warn they can't be managed in the conventional way because they are informal and dynamic yet need some systematization through the gathering of anecdotal evidence:

> The best way for an executive to assess the value of a community of practice is by listening to members' stories, which can clarify the complex relationships among activities, knowledge and performance.
>
> (Wenger and Snyder, 2000, 145)

Current research into practitioner-led approaches

There is little formal study of the scholarship of learning support; what does exist is centred on the tutor perspective. A recent longitudinal study in an Australian university reveals for the first time the relationship between the scholarship of teaching and students' experience of their course (Brew and Ginns, 2008). This link seems to confirm the importance of developing practitioner-led approaches in higher education, in order to enhance the experience of students. The work of the CETLs in the UK is a focus for influencing the learning, teaching and support practice of staff, allowing time and space for professionals to come together as a coherent, connected group to reflect in and on practice.

Centres of Excellence in Learning and Teaching

In the UK, the Higher Education Funding Council for England set up 81 CETLS in England and Northern Ireland with the aim of enhancing and promoting learning and teaching across the sector. The student experience is integral to the work of the CETLS, although a prime objective is to work with staff to influence best practice in educational research and dissemination of pedagogy. (Two of these are directly relevant to learning support and are covered in Chapter 10 and Chapter 12.) Some are funding the design of new learning spaces, to create conducive learning environments to support novel communities of practice that include a range of professional groups and, in some cases, learners. Most are also focusing directly on the diversity of pedagogic roles and their permeability, although not all directly include support professionals.

The following case study is a notable exception; it highlights the benefits of concentrating resource and strategic intent on active practitioner-informed approaches across an institutional change programme of learner development with students at the centre.

Case study: practitioner inquiry in learning development and support

Centre for Inquiry-based Learning in the Arts and Social Sciences (CILASS)

CILASS is a CETL at the University of Sheffield, which was awarded HEFCE funding in April 2005. Its five-year programme focuses on inquiry-based learning and encompasses strands focusing on:

- development and innovation
- reward and recognition
- evaluation and research
- enhancement of the University's physical estate for learning and teaching
- dissemination.

An academically led unit with a small core team of programme management staff, educational developers/researchers and administration staff, the CETL sits operationally in a space 'in between' the faculties and professional service departments with which it works in close partnership.

'Inquiry-based learning' is the term adopted by CILASS (and others) to refer to a broad spectrum of pedagogical approaches that are based on student-led inquiry or research, with all learning activities and resources designed to support students' inquiry processes. Students learn through guided exploration and investigation of the complex questions and problems of their discipline or professional practice in ways that mirror the scholarly and research processes of those disciplines and practices. The CILASS focus on student-led inquiry is set within the context of the University's commitment to research-led teaching, and its strategic aim of fostering strong links between learning, teaching, research and knowledge transfer. An important purpose of the CETL is to provide an opportunity for staff and students to explore the diversity of meaning and practical possibility represented by the concept of inquiry-based learning, including through cross-professional and multidisciplinary exchange, and the scholarship of teaching and learning.

CILASS has sought to develop a participatory and partnership-based approach to its working practices. Strong partnerships with professional service departments, and with academic departments, have been developed, and in this context a CILASS liaison librarian acts as a link with the library. Evaluation has indicated that this cross-professional model of working has helped to set a precedent in the University, leading to academic staff becoming more aware of the benefits of professional support staff participation in strategic discussions or project teams (see Levy et al., 2007). The theme of student partnership in educational development has also emerged strongly out of the CETL's style of activity and, specifically, out of the work of its student ambassador network.

Interim impact evaluation of the CETL has identified benefits in relation to impact on the student experience, and has indicated that it is perceived to be inspiring and enthusing staff at the University in relation to educational enhancement. Intrinsic personal rewards arising out of engagement with the CETL have been expressed in terms of personal validation and legitimization of effort spent on teaching, freedom to engage in open-ended exploration and the benefits of increased collaborative working in educational development and teaching. The CETL is also recognized as championing the scholarship of teaching and learning in the University. It is a leading contributor to an institution-wide change project entitled 'Building an Integrated Culture of Research, Learning and Teaching at the University', which is exploring the role, status and impact of practitioner-led pedagogic inquiry in the institution.

Practitioner inquiry

The premise that practitioner-led inquiry into practice is fundamental to educational enhancement is widely accepted within the field of education. This premise rests on a number of propositions about the nature of professional action and knowledge in teaching. Principal among these is the view that teaching is an intellectual and moral enterprise that calls on teachers to exercise professional judgements flexibly in contexts that are highly situated, constrained and dynamic, and that open up very real questions about how education should be thought about and approached. Inquiring teachers reflect critically and explore questions about educational content, processes and impact as a means of improving what they do. They are willing to look afresh at the assumptions and beliefs that provide the basis for their educational thinking in the light of alternative perspectives, and to engage explicitly with standards of judgement for the quality of their inquiries, and for their educational understandings and practices, from the wider field. Arguably, very similar premises can be applied to the adjacent professional domains of learning development and support.

'Inquiry' in its broadest sense underpins a wide range of forms of active, critical practitioner engagement, from reflection on practice to in-depth research. The idea of scholarship is central to CILASS's aim of building knowledge about inquiry-based learning collectively within our institutional context, and contributing to the knowledge base of the wider sector. A broad operational definition of the scholarship of teaching and learning is offered by the Carnegie Foundation for the Advancement of Teaching. Four core practices are identified – 'framing questions, gathering and exploring evidence, trying out and refining new insights in the classroom, and going public with what is learned in ways that others can build on' (Huber and Hutchings, 2006, 20). The latter authors advocate an inclusive definition of scholarship, from small-scale efforts to examine and document teaching and share what has been learned at one end of the spectrum, to large-scale studies using complex research designs at the other. Inquiry approaches used in the scholarship of teaching and learning include, but are not limited to, educational action research.

As mentioned earlier, the notion of scholarly, practitioner-led inquiry clearly challenges the distinction that is often made between those who produce educational theory (researchers) and those who apply it (practitioners). Practitioner knowledge is – and has to be – context-sensitive and evolving. It does not make claims to universality in the way that scientific knowledge does. However, this is not to suggest that practitioner inquiry does not have theoretical purposes or outcomes, but rather that the theory produced in this context might be thought of as a form of theory-in-process, as a dynamic, 'living' theory that is always open to refinement and elaboration through further iterations of purposeful inquiry carried out within the context of practice (Levy, 2007).

Alongside and closely linked with its development activities, CILASS aims to add to the existing opportunities within the University for practitioners in teaching, and in learning development and support, to explore questions arising from their practice. The aim is to provide a framework in which critically reflective and scholarly approaches to developing inquiry-based learning may flourish – affording opportunities for inquiring teachers, and development and support professionals, to develop the practice and living theory of inquiry-based learning from the inside out, by critically and reflexively exploring the educational questions that matter to them. The aim is provide a variety of ways to enable inquiry-based participation in the work of the CETL, and scope for different levels and forms of engagement over time.

A framework for inquiry-based practice

The framework for inquiry-based practice within the CETL is reflected in the roles of its staff as change facilitators, and in a variety of strategies designed to promote and support different inquiry activities for practitioners. Some of these are briefly highlighted below.

Blended development/inquiry facilitation

The model of pedagogical support that CILASS has developed is based on proactive and close partnership working between its learning development and research staff and academic staff who are working on development projects. CILASS learning development and research associates' (LDRA) roles are 'blended' in terms of development/research expertise and responsibility. LDRAs each have a specialist area of expertise within the broad frame of inquiry-based learning (including expertise in networked learning and information literacy). They play an important role in information exchange within and across disciplinary and professional boundaries, and are responsible for brokering liaison among academic staff and other support/development staff as appropriate. With detailed knowledge of an extensive portfolio of development projects, combined with personal research knowledge in inquiry-based learning and associated themes, they are well placed through their many interactions with professional services and academic colleagues to share information and foster new connections both within and across disciplinary and professional boundaries. LDRAs are encouraged to carry out scholarly activity relating to their educational development practice as part of their contribution to the wider CILASS research agenda, and in this context have developed personal action research associated with their roles.

CILASS LDRAs, along with the CETL's research associate, also support the evaluation of development initiatives and advise on other practitioner-led research activities associated with these. Academic and development/support staff are encouraged to explore the scope for pedagogical research arising out of their completed development projects. In some cases LDRAs are involved as full collaborators in research projects that are funded by the CETL and led by academic and professional services staff.

Inquiry-based evaluation

Impact evaluation is a central inquiry activity for the CETL, and from a communities of practice perspective plays a key role in the development of a shared repertoire and in the contribution of practitioners to collectively developing a body of knowledge. The CILASS approach aligns with an approach to evaluating learning and teaching development that has been applied more generally at the University since 2006 (Diercks-O'Brien and Powell, 2006). This is an adaptation of the 'theories of change' programme evaluation (Connell and Kubisch, 1996) combined with the use of enabling, process and outcome (EPO) performance indicators (Saunders, 2001). The approach is being applied both at the overall programme level and at the level of all CILASS-funded educational development and innovation initiatives. In this way, it offers a common framework for evaluation of diverse development projects, and for exploration of their relationship with each other and with overall CILASS programme-level activity and goals.

The CILASS theory of change approach works as follows. Through backward mapping, a causal narrative or 'theory' is established which identifies evaluation indicators and becomes the basis for an evaluation plan. For example, 'To achieve the desired impact on student learning experiences, the outcomes of the initiative need to be x, y and z; in order to achieve these outcomes, the processes or activities a, b and c need to happen; in order to carry out a, b and c, the enabling factors and resources d, e and f are required.' The narrative thus identifies three different types of evaluation indicator: enabling indicators concerned with structures and support, process indicators concerned with what needs to happen and outcome indicators concerned with the intermediate outcomes of an initiative and that are tied to broader and longer-term impact goals. The approach distributes weight between outcomes, processes and enabling factors and identifies them all as valid indicators of impact. Underlying the theory of change narrative are various assumptions, beliefs and values relating to the change initiative, its context, purposes and so on. Exploring these in the course of impact evaluation affords insight into why and how impact occurs.

At the level of the CETL's funded projects, the theory of change methodology offers potential to support reflective and scholarly approaches to evaluation, and provides a systematic framework that is amenable to meta-analysis and synthesis across datasets. At the level of the CILASS programme as a whole, it illuminates the over-arching change process and helps us to achieve greater understanding of the issues this entails.

Scholarship of teaching and learning initiatives

CILASS offers funding and support for Scholarship of Teaching and Learning (SoTL) projects through its inquiry-based learning grant scheme. One example of a SoTL project taken forward by learning development/support professionals is a study exploring the support needs of dyslexic students in relation to inquiry-based learning.

CILASS runs a fellowship scheme which is open to academic staff and learning development/support staff. The scheme provides part-time secondment to CILASS for staff to conduct development and research projects associated with inquiry-based learning.

A SoTL special interest group has been established to offer a focus for academic and learning support/development staff with interests in SoTL and inquiry-based learning to exchange ideas and feedback, and to develop collaborative research activity. It is co-ordinated by the CILASS research associate. The group has run a number of awareness workshops on the theme of SoTL within the University, and is developing a collaborative publication project.

Issues and challenges

This case study reflects a vision of learning and teaching enhancement situated within the context of critically reflexive practitioner inquiry, in which teaching enhancement, educational inquiry and theory-building go hand in hand. It is an integrated vision in terms of the engagement of learning development and support staff in scholarly approaches to practice, alongside and in collaboration with academic staff. It is an ambitious vision and there are very real challenges for its full realization. They include the following:

1   The status of practitioner-led educational inquiry in the University is ambiguous, and there are practical resource constraints. There are clear constraints on widespread engagement with the scholarship of teaching and learning among academic staff in both research-intensive and teaching-intensive institutions. Pressures on academic staff in terms of time and resource in all institutions are further exacerbated where the principal commitment is to the production of disciplinary (domain) knowledge. In UK higher education, discipline research is privileged over teaching and its scholarship; the UK's Research Assessment Exercise (RAE), whereby research output is assessed and funding is determined accordingly, historically, has accorded little recognition to pedagogical research in the disciplines. Learning development and support staff tend not to be subject to the same RAE pressures as academic staff. However, lack of reward and recognition for scholarly activity associated with learning development/support practice, and lack of time or resource for appropriate professional development and project work, means that there may be little incentive for engagement.

2   There is a practical need to achieve a workable balance, in the educational development context, between supporting development on the one hand and practitioner-led evaluation and scholarship on the other. The development and research strands of the CETL's activity, although closely interlinked, create different demands on staff capacity in the core team. The advantage, for CILASS, of the blended LDRA role is that its developers are fully engaged with the inquiry-based framework. However, it is easy for the more immediate demands of practical development work to take priority, on a day-to-day basis, over longer-term research-related work; time to support and carry out research has to be actively protected.

3   The fragility of sustainable impact when funding for enhancement combined with scholarly activity is short-term. The national CETL programme, which runs until March 2010, has provided the opportunity and encouragement to further the development of practitioner inquiry in teaching and in learning development/support in universities. However, to sustain activity beyond 2010 will require the embedding of practices, and associated commitment of resource, within broader institutional infrastructures. At a time of fierce competition for resources within institutions, this cannot be taken for granted.

Conclusions

The commentary and case study in this chapter highlight the transforming potential and outcomes that arise when embedded models of critical enquiry into learning and its support are employed and acted upon. Researching how this occurs, and how it impacts on student learning and support context and roles, is vital to our understanding of how students learn and will learn in the 21st century.

As CILASS illustrates, to be sustainable this research imperative requires ongoing strategic resourcing alongside inspirational leadership, staff incentives and expansive thinking, focusing on activities, knowledge and performance. This chapter confirms that research by practitioners leads to forms of extended practice (Clayton et al., 2008, 80) and should be supported and encouraged, not seen as a 'bolt on'. With notable exceptions such as CILASS, we do not yet have analytical accounts of this work. Iterative practice is developing quickly: theory isn't. Perhaps this is because learning support is so complex and relatively undefined in HE – related as it is to social, technological and personal development and to practitioner conceptions formed by exposure to all these elements.

Instead of focusing on differences, therefore, we need to focus on the similarities between the various professional groups and create ground for moving forward together that includes students in our communities of practice. The locus of control is changing; students are assuming a more influential role in research and inquiry-based practice (paralleled by developments in student-owned learning spaces).

Pedagogic evaluation is the collective concern of all working in higher education; the use of narrative techniques may encourage new dialogues and enable diverse insights to emerge between the various actors, yielding 'truths' and common understandings. How much richer will those stories be if they include a multiprofessional perspective? What new topics emerge when a paradigm of emotional validity is used?

We need to identify and evaluate learning support studies in this frame, beyond artful doing and towards artful knowing, with academics, students and professionals as true partners. Further research may be concerned with an even more holistic understanding of students, including their home and work cultures, and the conceptions of educators and support professionals will form a major part of such research. More urgently, learning from each other will be essential in order to provide a set of simple, engaging and evaluated services that students want to use.

References

Bjorke, S. A. (2004) The Concepts of Communities of Practice, Activity Theory and Implications for Distributed Learning, *Arendal*, 7 October, 1–12.

Bloland, P. A. (1991) *Student Development as a Reform Movement*. Paper presented at the annual meeting of the American College Personnel Association, Atlanta, GA, March 15–20.

Booth, A. (2003) Bridging the Research–Practice Gap? The role of evidence based librarianship, *The New Review of Information and Library Research*, 3–23.

Borrego, S., Forrest, C. and Fried, J. (2006) Enhancing Professional Development. In Keeling, R. P. (ed.), *Learning Reconsidered 2: a practical guide to implementing a campus-wide focus on the student experience*, Association of College and University Housing Officers – International, Association of College Unions International, National Academic Advising Association, National Association for Campus Activities, National Association of Student Personnel Administrators, and National Intramural–Recreational Sports Association, 59–63.

Brew, A. and Ginns, P. (2008) Relationship Between Engagement in the Scholarship of Teaching and Learning and Students' Course Experiences, *Assessment and Evaluation in Higher Education*, **33** (5), 535–45.

Brophy, P. (2007) Commentary: narrative based practice, *Evidence Based Library and Information Practice*, **2** (1), 149–58, http://ejournals.library.ualberta.ca/index.php/EBLIP/article/view/137/248.

Clayton, S., O'Brien, M., Burton, D., Campbell, A., Qualter, A. and Varga-Atkins, T. (2008) 'I Know it's Not Proper Research, But . . .': how professionals' understandings of research can frustrate its potential for CPD, *Educational Action Research*, **16** (1), 73–84.

Clyde, L. A. (2006) The Basis for Evidence-based Practice: evaluating the research evidence, *New Library World*, **107** (5–6), 180–92.

Connell, J. P. and Kubisch, A. C. (1996) *Applying a Theories of Change Approach to the Evaluation of Comprehensive Community Initiatives*, Aspen Institute.

Dadds, M. (2008) Empathetic Validity in Practitioner Research, *Educational Action Research*, **16** (2), 279–90.

Diercks-O'Brien, G. and Powell, A. (2006) *An Impact Evaluation Framework for Learning and Teaching Activity, Learning Development and Media Unit*, University of Sheffield [internal consultation paper].

Given, L. (2006) Qualitative Research in Evidence-based Practice: a valuable partnership, *Library Hi Tech*, **24** (3), 376–86.

Hildreth, C. R. and Aytec, S. (2007) Recent Library Practitioner Research: a methodological analysis and critique, *Journal of Education for Library and Information Science*, **48** (3), (Summer), 236–58.

Huber, M. T. and Hutchings, P. (2006) *The Advancement of Learning: Building the Teaching Commons: a Carnegie Foundation report on the scholarship of teaching and learning in higher education*, Jossey-Bass.

Joint Information Systems Committee (2007) *In Their Own Words: exploring the learners' perspective on e-learning*, www.jiscinfonet.ac.uk/publications/in-their-own-words/.

Jones, C. (2004) *Theory and the Practices of Learning Technology. Symposium 1 presented at the Networked Learning Conference, Lancaster University, England, UK, Monday 5th to Wednesday 7th April, 2004 at Lancaster University, UK*, www.networkedlearningconference.org.uk/past/nlc2004/proceedings/symposia/symposium1/jones.htm.

Levy, P. (2007) Exploring and Developing Excellence: towards a community of praxis. In Skelton, A. (ed.), *International Perspectives on Teaching Excellence in Higher Education: improving knowledge and practice*, Routledge.

Levy, P., Reilly, N., Oliver, M. and Hart, D. (2007) *CILASS Interim Evaluation Report*, University of Sheffield, www.shef.ac.uk/cilass.

Saunders, M. (2001) *Tools for Focusing Evaluations: LTSN evaluation*, University of Lancaster, www.lancs.ac.uk/fss/projects/edres/ltsn-eval/docs/tools.doc.

Schenk, N. and Eve, J. (2007) Breakout Session One: the view from current researchers, *Library and Information Research*, **31** (97), Special Edition 2007, 21.

Schon, D. A. (1973) *Beyond the Stable State*, Penguin.

Smith, M. K. (2001) Donald Schon: learning reflection and change. In *The Encyclopedia of Informal Education*, www.infed.org/thinkers/et-schon.htm.

Somerville, M. M. (2007) *Participatory Co-Design: a relationship building approach for co-creating libraries of the future*, World Library and Information Congress: 73rd IFLA General Conference and Council, 19–23 August 2007, Durban, South Africa, Programme and Proceedings, www.ifla.org/IV/ifla73/papers/122-Somerville-en.pdf.

Usher, R., Bryant, I. and Johnston, R. (1997) *Adult Education and the Postmodern Challenge: learning beyond the limits*, Routledge.

Wenger, E. C. and Snyder, W. M. (2000) Communities of Practice: the organizational frontier, *Harvard Business Review*, **78** (1), (Jan–Feb), 139–45.

Index